ALONE AT DAWN

ALSO BY DAN SCHILLING

The Battle of Mogadishu (co-edited with Matt Eversmann)

ALONE AT DAWN

Medal of Honor Recipient John Chapman
and the Untold Story of the World's Deadliest
Special Operations Force

DAN SCHILLING &
LORI CHAPMAN LONGFRITZ

GC

GRAND CENTRAL
PUBLISHING

NEW YORK   BOSTON

Grand Central Publishing
Hachette Book Group
1290 Avenue of the Americas, New York, NY 10104
grandcentralpublishing.com
twitter.com/grandcentralpub

First Edition: June 2019

Grand Central Publishing is a division of Hachette Book Group, Inc. The Grand Central Publishing name and logo is a trademark of Hachette Book Group, Inc.

The publisher is not responsible for websites (or their content) that are not owned by the publisher.

The Hachette Speakers Bureau provides a wide range of authors for speaking events. To find out more, go to www.hachettespeakersbureau.com or call (866) 376-6591.

Maps by Jeffrey L. Ward
Print book interior design by TexTech/Jouve and Thomas Louie.

Library of Congress Cataloging-in-Publication Data
Names: Schilling, Dan, author. | Longfritz, Lori Chapman, author.
Title: Alone at dawn : Medal of Honor Recipient John Chapman and the untold story of the world's deadliest special operations force / Dan Schilling & Lori Chapman Longfritz.
Other titles: Medal of Honor Recipient John Chapman and the untold story of the world's deadliest special operations force
Description: First edition. | New York : Grand Central Publishing, [2019] | Includes bibliographical references.
Identifiers: LCCN 2019000376 | ISBN 9781538729656 (hardcover) | ISBN 9781538729670 (ebook)
Subjects: LCSH: Chapman, John Allan, 1965–2002. | Afghan War, 2001—Aerial operations, American. | United States. Air Force—Combat controllers—Biography. | Takur Ghar, Battle of, Afghanistan, 2002. | Special forces (Military science)—United States—Biography. | United States Air Force—Commando troops—History. | Afghan War, 2003—Campaigns.
Classification: LCC DS371.412 .S35 2019 | DDC 958.104/742—dc23
LC record available at https://lccn.loc.gov/2019000376

ISBN: 978-1-5387-2965-6 (hardcover), 978-1-5387-2967-0 (ebook)

Printed in the United States of America

LSC-C

10   9   8   7   6   5   4   3   2   1

And you till trump of doomsday
On lands of morn may lie,
And make the hearts of comrades
Be heavy where you die.

—A. E. Housman, *A Shropshire Lad*

This book is dedicated to the seven U.S. servicemen who died at Takur Ghar:
SPC Marc Anderson, MSgt John Chapman, CPL Matthew Commons, SGT Bradley Crose, SrA Jason Cunningham, PO1 Neil Roberts, and SGT Philip Svitak

CONTENTS

—

INTRODUCTION

What follows is a select history of one of the deadliest and least-known forces in the history of human warfare. It begins, as many heroic combat tales do, with a crisis.

It's also the story of one man, John Chapman, who would earn the nation's highest honor for bravery when he saved the lives of twenty-three comrades at the willing cost of his own.

Finally, it is the history of John Chapman's fellow Combat Controllers during Operation Anaconda, America's first major operation in its ongoing Global War on Terror. How a handful of Combat Controllers managed to stave off disaster and destroy Al Qaeda and Taliban forces by the score using their unique expertise and wits has gone down in history, even as the doomed operation continues to reveal its secrets to this day.

The history of the men of the Combat Control Teams (known universally by the acronym CCT, whether applied collectively or to an-individual) laid down in these pages is by no measure comprehensive; rather it is representative, a distillation of commitment, capability, success, and loss. Delta Force officer Tom Greer, who led the hunt for Osama bin Laden, writes in his book *Kill Bin Laden* that Combat Controllers are "the best-rounded and uniquely trained operators on the planet. The initial training 'pipeline' for an Air Force special tactics squadron Combat Controller costs twice as much time and sweat as does the journey to become a Navy SEAL or Delta operator.... And that is just to get to a place where they can do the job for which they are really trained, calling those deadly airstrikes."

What's unique about the role of CCT is that wherever the need arises, they are there. In *Kill Bin Laden*, Greer notes that, "In the relatively finite black SOF world, assaulters and snipers are a dime a dozen. Yes, these men are trained in multiple deadly skill sets and the dark arts of counterterrorism. But...Just because you are the best of the best does not mean you are the best at everything. Any Delta operator can vouch for the capabilities of the Air Force Combat Controllers, and very rarely goes on a 'hit' without the men who wear the scarlet berets." CCT is not permanently assigned to the Special Forces (SF) teams or SEAL platoons they fight alongside but they are attached, to use military parlance (think integrated or embedded), when needed for combat operations. Consequently, in America's longest-running war, the men of Air Force Combat Control collect, in aggregate, more combat action than their special operations counterparts in the Navy and Army— making some of them the most experienced veterans in all of America's previous wars. During global humanitarian crises, they are often the first to arrive, unsupported, to deliver salvation where no other first responders can. Their motto: "First There."

Born of America's disastrous first attempts to insert airborne forces into battle during World War II, Combat Control predates their better-known SEAL and Special Forces counterparts, with whom they've served silently for decades in some of the most dramatic missions in US history. This is the story of one such mission.

PROLOGUE

—

The Night Stalker sliced the frigid Afghan darkness of the Shahi Khot Valley. Bristling with two 6,000-round-per-minute M134 miniguns on its sides and an M60 machine gun mounted on the tailgate, it was prepared for small-arms fire from Taliban fighters.

Chief Warrant Officer Alan Mack was on the stick of the MH-47E, America's special operations workhorse of a helicopter. This particular Night Stalker's call sign was Razor-03. In the rear were six SEALs from the most famous unit in Navy history, SEAL Team Six. Mack's only other passenger, the seventh member of a most elite package, was a US Air Force Combat Controller named John Chapman. All seven men were highly trained and themselves bristling with weapons and purpose. Their mission call sign was Mako-30. It was the early morning hours of 4 March 2002.

Mack had flown countless insertions in the early stages of America's newly ordained Global War on Terror in response to the treachery of 9/11. He'd been in Afghanistan for months and was comfortable with the hazards of the mountainous terrain and with the habits of the enemy. The team's insertion point that night on the summit of their objective, a mountain called Takur Ghar, was determined last-minute, and Mack wasn't sure he could pull it off, but he and the SEAL team leader agreed to attempt it. Even the helicopter he was flying was a last-minute change. He and his copilot, Chief Warrant Officer Talbot, had swapped their previous helicopter for this one when the other's number-two engine "ran away," accelerating uncontrollably, and had to be shut down, grounding the bird. The two pilots took on the new helo and, with it, the assigned enlisted crew comprising a flight engineer (who doubled as the right door gunner), a left door gunner, and two tail-ramp members, one of whom manned the tail gun. After a quick crew brief, Razor-03 took to the unwelcoming sky.

As the Night Stalker made its way through the night, frigid air poured into the cargo cabin from the two doors just behind the cockpit, where both gunners stood behind their M134 miniguns, projecting their primed six-barreled lethality through the openings. The heaters failed to keep pace.

On the tail ramp, Sergeant Padrazza surveyed their "customers" through night vision goggles (NVGs) from his position on the "stinger," a 7.62mm M60 strap-mounted machine gun. Unlike during training missions back in the States, that night the mood of the SEALs and Chapman was grim. The men were to be inserted by Razor-03 directly on top of the 10,469-foot mountain peak to establish an observation post. From their commanding position, Chapman, as the team's air expert, would call in airstrikes on Taliban positions throughout the valley. The somberness of the Mako-30 team was intensified by multiple last-minute changes to the mission, not the least of which was their commanders ordering Mako-30 to insert directly atop Takur Ghar mountain instead of offsetting the team, which would have allowed them to approach the summit clandestinely to determine possible enemy locations and capabilities.

From the cockpit, Mack could see another SEAL team's helicopter landing zone (HLZ) as they passed over it. That team, Mako-21, had been inserted by another Night Stalker. Approaching his own mountain from the north, he was roughly two hundred feet above the summit. As they began their long final approach, Talbot had control of the helicopter. Mack continued scanning the HLZ through his NVGs and identified a location where they could set the massive twin-rotor helicopter down; it was a relatively level spot adjacent to a grouping of trees just below the summit. As they closed the distance, Mack noticed footprints on the snow-covered slope. This wasn't alarming in and of itself—Afghans traversed severe and remote terrain in even the most adverse weather—but as the helicopter settled toward the ground, pushing a blizzard of snow in every direction, a figure ducked behind a knoll at their nine o'clock.

Mack keyed his intercom mike and told the SEAL team leader, Britt Slabinski, "You've got a guy at nine o'clock, stuck his head up and disappeared."

"Is he armed?" asked the SEAL.

"I don't know."

Poised to exit the helicopter and anxious to be on the ground, where the team would have more control, he responded, "Roger, we're taking the LZ."

From the front of the helo, Mack was looking through his goggles as the SEALs and Chapman prepared to be inserted, when he noticed a DShK Russian heavy machine gun at their one o'clock position, almost directly in front of them and only 150 feet on the horizon. The DShK is a lethal antiaircraft weapon, and the range of this DShK was point-blank. Before he could call "contact" to the gunners, reports of contacts from multiple locations poured in simultaneously—a donkey at three o'clock, a man ducking behind cover at their ten. The team leader reiterated they were still willing to take the HLZ. Nodding to himself, Mack asked his left gunner if he had the man at their ten o'clock. "Yes."

Mack was about to authorize the left gunner to "engage," when their world exploded. Two rocket-propelled grenades (RPGs) slammed into the helicopter's left side. The first warhead went through the left electrical compartment and then an ammo can before exploding, wounding the gunner and preventing him from shooting their assailant. He'd not been authorized to engage by Mack yet anyway, so the Taliban got in the first punch. And it was a knockout. The RPG killed all the AC electrical power to the stricken bird, and that in turn disabled the electrically powered miniguns. The gunner hit the floor. Before anyone in the helicopter could respond, a second RPG struck, knocking out their multimode radar system.

In the back, the SEAL team and Chapman kept their composure, readying to step off. Sergeant Dan Madden, in control of the ramp, put his arm out and blocked the team's exit just as their world caught fire. On the heels of this, he called to the pilots, "Ready rear, go go go, lift off!"

As the senior pilot, Mack took control of the damaged bird from Talbot as the helicopter's systems began failing, one after the other. First their multifunction displays failed, followed by the Nav system, then the automatic flight control system, and with it all the radios. The cockpit went black. One saving grace was the DC power, which remained, allowing the intercom to work so at least the crew could talk, even if they couldn't fight. The crew's NVGs, which were individually powered by helmet-mounted batteries, were also safe from the failing systems of the ravaged aircraft.

Mack rolled on more power through the collective stick and took off. But the added thrust for the high-altitude liftoff under extreme conditions caused a dangerous development: The rotors began to slow and droop. Though no instruments indicated this in the cockpit, years of experience told Mack he had a problem when he heard the pitch of the spinning rotors change. To compensate, he reduced power to regain desperately needed rotor RPM, causing the helicopter to jerk up and down above the now "very hot" LZ and mountain.

In the back, Petty Officer Neil Roberts, who'd not snapped his safety line to the aircraft, stood by the rear at the ramp's hinge, facing the blackness beyond, ready. The fact that he was not on the intercom wasn't a problem, since he wouldn't exit the helicopter until directed by the crew, and Madden had just blocked the ramp.

As the stricken helicopter struggled to lift, the situation worsened. A third RPG came screaming from the darkness and slammed into their right side, blowing out the right electrical box. Before they could gain any distance, yet another RPG hit the ramp where Roberts and Madden stood with Padrazza, the stinger gunner. The impact destroyed the flare dispenser, and the helo staggered under the impact. When it did, Roberts slid down the lowered ramp, with Padrazza on his heels, desperately trying to gain hold of the SEAL. Fully loaded with an eighty-pound ruck, combat gear, and an M249 SAW machine gun, Roberts weighed in excess of three hundred pounds. The two men managed to grab hold of each other as they tumbled toward the opening a few feet away.

Madden lunged for the two men. As they slid past, Roberts's legs flipped into the air. Still attached to the ramp by his gunner's harness, Madden grabbed on to the SEAL's ankle, only to be dragged along until he snapped to a violent stop at the end of his harness tether. Roberts slid past him, flailing as he approached the void. Madden and Padrazza briefly suspended the SEAL by the ankle above the snowy slope.

In an instant, he was gone.

Meanwhile, the helicopter picked up momentum as Mack battled to save all their lives, oblivious to what had just happened behind him. Madden watched helplessly as Roberts dropped ten feet to the snow, slamming onto his back, and receded into the night as the helicopter limped away.

Before Madden could call "lost man," the grim situation became even worse. One of the crew came on the intercom—they'd lost an engine. Mack, unaware they'd also lost the SEAL, knew they did not have single-engine capability, and he also had no way to determine which engine was out from his dead instrument control panel. The best he could do was to autorotate (land without power, essentially a controlled crash) somewhere in front of them and at the base of the hostile mountain. As Mack was working through the challenges of power, glide slope, a landing spot, and no instruments, Madden was pulling in Padrazza, who was dangling from the ramp and swinging wildly by his gunner's strap. On the intercom Madden shouted, "Both engines are running!" several times. He could hear them directly above his head at the aircraft's rear.

Mack wasted no time "pulling power" to determine the truth and was rewarded with level flight, which verified the intercom call. He now had options, but the helicopter soon began shaking and the controls fought the pilot, making them feel "heavy" in Mack's hands. He knew he needed to get the helo on the ground immediately.

He turned north, the direction from which they'd come, looking for a place to set down, when the call came from the rear that they'd lost a man and he was somewhere on the HLZ. Fuck. "Are you sure?" he asked. By this time Madden had dragged his crewmate into the helicopter, and both responded on the intercom simultaneously with "Yes!"

Mack was determined. "We're going back to get him," he announced over the intercom. Every crewman agreed with the decision, but the gunners reminded him they had no weapons. Mack asked for a test fire, but the guns were dead.

He began a right-hand turn anyway to come around and head back into the one-sided onslaught and firefight that surely awaited them. But as he did, the controls continued fighting back. Then the collective stick went dead and no amount of wrestling could move it. His helicopter, stricken and blind, was coming apart around him and falling from the sky. Returning to the HLZ was impossible. There was little hope for Roberts as the Night Stalker limped off the mountain and into the blackness beyond.

In the rear, Chapman held tight to his cargo net seat as it lurched and shook like the inside of a VW Beetle in a hurricane, powerless at that moment to affect Roberts's fate or his own. He had no idea what awaited Roberts alone on the mountain now seen receding into the night through the cargo ramp opening. Within minutes the HLZ was lost among the dozens of nondescript peaks surrounding the Shahi Khot Valley. It is impossible to say if Chapman understood his SEAL teammate's future at the hands of dozens of hardened Chechen and Uzbek fighters. He certainly had no inkling that in another two hours he and Roberts would face exactly the same situation, their destinies separated by a half dozen steps, each a lone man fighting against many.

If there was one among the seven-man team who could possibly survive alone in hostile territory against insurmountable enemy numbers, it would be Chapman, the lone Combat Controller—the only man with the overwhelming firepower of America's entire fleet of aircraft and death at his fingertips, and the expertise to wield them as either a precision strike on an individual or a crushing tsunami of tens of thousands of pounds of bombs over any mountain or massed force.

John did not know in that moment, in the rear of the darkened helicopter, that he was destined to soon save the lives of the remaining members of his SEAL team and another eighteen men who would ultimately commit their lives to rescuing John and the SEALs. How John came to be that man and hero on the frozen summit of Takur Ghar mountain is a remarkable and unique story about a force so unknown in American military history as to be invisible: US Air Force Combat Control. John would not be the only Combat Controller on Takur Ghar or the mountains surrounding it. Indeed, hidden in the folds of the US and allied special operations forces who were prosecuting Operation Anaconda, which was designed to push the Taliban to the brink of extinction and of which John's team was but a small part, were more than a dozen of these unknown warriors.

In the history of human warfare, no single individual warrior has ever possessed so much precision power over life and death. This is the story of John Chapman and his brothers, the deadliest fighters ever to have walked the fields of battle.

PART I

—

EVOLUTION

CHAPTER

1

—

July 1966

THE FLIGHT OF FOUR FIGHTERS SCREAMED OVER THE MOUNTAIN PEAKS toward their intended target, shadows streaking across the intervening valleys. One of the pilots, Lieutenant Ed Rasimus, knew troops were in trouble because his flight—call sign Whiplash Bravo—had been scrambled to provide close air support to a forward air control Combat Controller. From his cockpit, Ed could tell it was going to be a tough airstrike. Whiplash Bravo was flying deep into "Indian territory" and knew it. Below him, the local religion was not Islam but animism with a strong dose of the Buddha. It was the summer of 1966 and all Ed could see was the lush jungle of Laos in every direction, the oppressive heat and humidity creating their own clouds, clinging to the landscape like gray quilts and further masking terrain and potential enemy antiaircraft positions. It was not a good place to be.

One of Ed's wingmen tried the Controller (call sign Butterfly-44), a disembodied voice that would direct their airstrikes. Nothing. They were closing in fast, just forty miles from the contact point, when a weak and out-of-breath transmission floated across the airwaves: "Hello, Whiplash. This is Butterfly Forty-Four, do you copy?"

Finally. "Roger, Butterfly. We've got four nickels [F-105s] for you with twenty-four cans of nape and twenty mike-mike [20mm cannons]. We'll play for about twenty minutes and we're now about forty miles out."

Combat Controller Jim Stanford, Butterfly-44, wasn't airborne. The twenty-nine-year-old eleven-year Air Force veteran continued breathlessly, "Thanks, Whiplash, copy your numbers. I'm on the ground now refueling. I'm standing on the wing pumping gas in the airplane, but I should be airborne in about three more minutes. The target isn't very far away."

In his F-105 cockpit, Ed had to process this information. Butterfly-44 is *on the ground? Refueling his own airplane? In enemy territory?* While out of breath, the disembodied voice didn't sound overly concerned. The 105s established an orbit and awaited instructions.

"Whiplash, Butterfly Forty-Four's on the roll. Be with you in a minute. Are you ready for a briefing?" asked Stanford as his tiny unarmed and unarmored Pilatus Porter single-engine airplane took off from the dirt strip where he and his pilot had been forced to land alone and refuel their plane. It was a little after 1600 hours, and for Jim and his pilot, a CIA employee flying under the cover of Air America, landing on a short dirt space in the jungle was just another day in America's secret and illegal war in Laos, across the Mekong River from Thailand. And these were not even their first strikes of the day.

"Roger, Butterfly, go ahead." Ed, who had assumed the Controller would have come from Thailand like himself by sneaking across the border, assessed the man behind the voice. *If I'm stealing hubcaps by sneaking into Laos illegally*, he thought, *this guy is a full-fledged car thief.* It was going to be a difficult strike with the thick puffy clouds obscuring much of the ground.

"Okay, Whiplash. We've got a valley three miles north of my [location] with an estimated fifteen hundred Pathet Lao regulars

[Laotians fighting against South Vietnam and the US]. I've got about two hundred Royal Laotians on the hilltops to the south. I need you to put your napalm in the valley and we'll try and spread it around. Can you give me multiple passes dropping [in] pairs?"

"We'll be happy to do that, Butterfly." Ed revised his estimate of Butterfly-44. *He's not stealing cars or hubcaps. He's apparently running an entire mafia.*

"Whiplash, Butterfly Forty-Four has you in sight. If you check your ten o'clock low, you should be able to pick me up. I've got a white Pilatus Porter, and I'm level at six thousand feet in a left-hand orbit. Defenses in this area are small arms and automatic weapons with reported twenty-three and thirty-seven millimeter coming out of the valley earlier today. I'd like you to work the valley from east to west and come off south. The friendlies are on the hilltops to the south. Call visual on me."

"Okay, Butterfly. Whiplash lead has you in sight."

"Whiplash, I'm afraid I can't mark for you. The ROEs [rules of engagement] don't allow me to carry ordnance. But if you've got me in sight, I'll point out the target area with my left wingtip."

Ed Rasimus watched from 14,000 feet as the tiny white plane, so obvious and exposed against the green jungle, dipped its wingtip to indicate an area of trees.

The lead F-105 confirmed the target and called, "In from the east."

"Cleared hot, Whiplash. I'm holding off to the north."

Rasimus recalled the lead aircraft clearly. "I can see the shiny aluminum napalm cans leave his airplane. The fins keep them aerodynamically straight so they don't tumble and smear, but the fireball in the jungle is still impressive."

From his slow-moving, glaring target of an airplane, Stanford called, "Nice hit, lead. Two, put yours just west of lead's smoke. Three, step it further west, and four, finish off the end of the valley. Two's cleared hot."

The F-105s continued to napalm the Pathet Lao until they ran out of "nape," then requested permission to conduct gun runs with their 20mm cannons. When the fighters finally went "bingo"—out of fuel—and departed the little valley near the Plaine des Jarres, Stanford sent them off with gratitude. "Thanks a lot, guys. I'll forward some BDA [battle damage assessment] when our guys walk through there tomorrow, but right now all I can say is thank you. You've saved the fort again for another night."

As Rasimus headed for the border and safety of Thailand, he thought, *I can't imagine his situation. I can't conceive being in the jungle with a tiny airplane and a hugely outnumbered ground force. I can't believe that he lives there and controls an air war in which he isn't allowed to shoot back. As I cruise back to my safe airbase with my air-conditioned room, white sheets, hot shower, and a cold beer at the officers' club, I wonder what kind of man is this. I hope Butterfly-44 has a good night. I hope he has many good nights. He earns them.*

Stanford and his pilot also turned for home: the most secret airbase in the world, known as Lima Site 36 alternate. Referred to by them simply as "Alternate," it's a dirt airstrip built and operated by the CIA in the middle of the jungle. For Jim, most days ended around 1730 after a full day of airstrikes, rescue coordination, and other support to the Lao indigenous forces commanded by the legendary General Vang Pao. "When the sun went down, our day in the air was done. We would meet with General Vang Pao and then go up to the Air America porch, sit around and talk, have a few drinks, play with the dogs or the caged bears."

The talk usually focused on which Air America pilots would fly the Combat Controller the next day, a nightly decision with potentially grave consequences. Two CCT had already been shot down with their pilots and, though both men were designated as missing in action, were presumed dead. Never more than four in-country at a time, the CCT in Laos of 1965–67 ran the entire air war's targeting, and no one had ever even heard of them.

———

As Stanford enjoyed his well-deserved beer in Laos, on the far side of the globe in Windsor Locks, Connecticut, and a world away from America's latest war, Gene and Terry Chapman were busy rearing their third child, John Allan Chapman, born 14 July 1965. The town itself is something of a Norman Rockwell throwback, stereotypically New England. Mature hardwood trees—elm, oak, and maple—thrive along its narrow streets, offering shade on hot summer days and creating canopies bursting with the colors of fire when the brisk days of fall arrive. Windsor Locks was a community where you really did ask your neighbor for a cup of sugar, the neighborhood kids played outside together, and adults looked out for *all* kids, not just their own. John came from humble beginnings, and it was an ideal world for the newest family member.

As John explored Windsor Locks through the eyes of childhood and his youth, no one in the Chapman home could possibly imagine the direct line that would lead from America's secret war in Laos to their son becoming one of the most elite warriors in history.

———

Before Vietnam became a household word in the American lexicon, Combat Control Teams had existed for over a decade, and to fully understand them it's necessary to return to the global inferno of World War II, where they were originally formed to spearhead invasions on the heels of the disasters that marked the early attempts at airborne operations.

The first real use of American paratroopers was during Operation

Husky, the invasion of Sicily in July of 1943. The ill-planned and poorly executed operation saw some forces dropped as much as fifty miles from their objectives. Paranoid naval forces and conventional army troops landing on the beaches considered anything in the air to be hostile so, of the 144 transport planes slated to drop paratroopers, 23 were destroyed and 37 badly damaged by friendly fire. One pilot summed up the mission thusly: "Evidently, the safest place for us tonight while over Sicily would have been over enemy territory." Yet the major failure remained guiding Allied aircraft to the appropriate release point and marking them for drops.

For the D-Day invasion of June 1944, the US and the British had formed pathfinder teams to address those challenges, though they delivered limited success, as airborne troops were still scattered across the Norman countryside. Yet at least one unintended benefit resulted—numerous reports of such wide dispersal of Allied troops left the Germans unsure of where to rush their panzer divisions and reserve SS troops.

On 24 March 1945, the US and the British conducted Operation Varsity, an Allied assault across the Rhine and the last major airborne operation of the war. In a final attempt to stave off initial assault confusion, the plan included two "Troop Carrier Glider Combat Control Teams" equipped with the latest in navigational beacons. The operation's eight five-man teams were the first use of the term "Combat Controller." Each team was to insert by glider, mark the approach and departure end of landing zones (LZs), and then control air traffic over the two-day period of major force insertion. Although their equipment and tactics were only partially successful, this still represented a step forward. However, with the end of the war only months away, the capability and the requirement receded in priority, until, after the war, it was forgotten completely.

The creation of a separate Air Force (along with a newly minted and independently funded Central Intelligence Agency) by the

National Security Act of 1947 resurrected the necessity of drop-zone and landing-zone operations and spawned an interservice rivalry between the Army and USAF over whose mission it was. The Army argued that troops going into combat required Army control to ensure best placement. The Air Force, recalling the low priority afforded its pilots and aircraft during such operations as Husky, argued that control belonged with them until the Army forces were introduced into battle. By 1953, the Air Force had won the fight by refusing to drop *anything* for Army pathfinder teams without the presence of a Combat Control Team, the first of which had formed that very year.

Much of the Air Force's stance in establishing CCT, however, was its belief that navigational aids and capabilities would eventually eliminate Combat Control Teams entirely. The Air Force was a reluctant mission partner and didn't prioritize recruiting, equipping, and training its Controllers any more than the Army did, perhaps even less so. Given that attitude, the teams, all of them stuffed into Air Force aerial port squadrons (whose responsibilities were to marshal and move materials), were ill-equipped and often poorly led. The interservice competition and Air Force's low prioritization of the mission would have far-reaching consequences as America approached the end of the twentieth century.

Despite the neglect, in the years following the wars in Laos and Vietnam, Combat Control continued to transform. A series of operations and the creation of tailored organizations, better suited to fight America's new limited conflicts and counter the rise of modern terrorism, would shape the force. Five years after the conflict in Southeast Asia ended, the biggest change to hit CCT took place in an unlikely alliance between an overlooked Air Force major and a colorful Army colonel with a storied career in the recent war.

In the late summer of 1979, Combat Controller Mike Lampe and his Vietnamese wife, Thuy, were stationed in the Philippines, when chance introduced him to a twice-passed-over Air Force major named John Carney—known simply as "Coach" or sometimes "the Coach" from his time coaching the Air Force Academy's football program. He was looking for standout Combat Controllers for an initiative known as Project Requisition. The effort began in 1978, at the same time that Army colonel Charlie Beckwith was standing up what would eventually become the greatest counterterrorist unit in the world— Delta Force. Coach was building a bullpen of exceptionally talented and hard-core men to support Beckwith as he began conducting "Blue Light" operations, the precursor to Delta.

"Coach wanted to tighten his shot group," says Lampe of the time, "to put teams together to support Beckwith's nascent force." Lampe encountered Coach when he and a few other combat scuba-dive certified members of the Philippines team put Coach and a handful of his preselected men through scuba training in Key Largo, Florida.

The Coach was impressed by Lampe's professionalism and asked him to join the team, which at the time worked out of the back of a hangar at Charleston Air Force Base, South Carolina. Lampe, who'd survived multiple tours in Laos and Southeast Asia, had finally settled into a happy domestic and postwar work life and was preparing for another move with his young family. As he recalls, "I told the Coach thanks, but I've got orders for Rhein-Main Air Base in Germany to support the Seventh Special Forces Group. Maybe next time."

As fall approached, Mike, Thuy, and their young son were preparing for their move to Germany, a well-deserved and intriguing new adventure. They had already checked out of their quarters on Clark Air Base and were residing in temporary lodging. "We were literally getting ready for our flight when CBPO [the base personnel office] called me and said, 'You better come down here.'

"When I showed up and asked, 'What's up?' they said, 'Your orders have been changed.' To which I replied, 'That's not possible. I've got my orders to Germany right here.' 'Do you know a Major

Carney at Twenty-First Air Force? He's had your orders changed to the Four-Thirty-Seventh Military Airlift Wing in Charleston.'" The order left no doubt: Charleston was in and Germany was out.

Lampe's forced assignment to the 437th Military Airlift Wing was used as a cover by Coach to hide the team's activities as they supported the newly formed Delta Force. Lacking a formal name and hiding behind the 437th, the men called themselves (for lack of more imaginative alternatives) "Brand X." The existing CCT at the 437th had a legitimate mission to run airdrop and austere airfield training missions for the wing's cargo haulers. On paper, Coach was the officer in charge, responsible for the training mission, but in practice he completely neglected the conventional operations, focusing on Beckwith and Delta and leaving training to one of his noncommissioned officers (NCOs).

Mike Lampe reported to Charleston on 1 November 1979. On 4 November, the US Embassy in Tehran fell to the Iranian Revolution and fifty-two Americans were taken hostage—an event that sent relations between the two countries into a spiral from which they've never recovered. Lampe was trying to settle his pregnant wife and young son into a house in Charleston when the cataclysmic event unfolded, setting in motion the subsequent actions and tragedies that would create the world's largest special operations command. But neither Lampe nor Coach's Combat Controllers could possibly have predicted it at the time.

"I don't remember if I was home for Thanksgiving or not. It was all a blur. The handful of us, maybe six or seven guys at the time, were scattered to all points of the compass." There were four units involved in potential rescue planning by that time: Delta, as the lead; C Company, 1st Battalion of the 75th Ranger Regiment, who were tasked with supporting Delta with security and a rapid response of firepower; the 1st Special Operations Wing from the Air Force at Hurlburt Field, Florida, owners of the MC-130 "Combat

Talons," the only special operations insertion C-130s in the world; and finally, Coach Carney's handful of Controllers, who weren't even a real unit yet.

———

By 1979, and six states north, John Chapman had established himself as a young man possessed of an innate ability to tune into the feelings of others that transcended the attitudes of the times and ran counter to the instincts of most teenagers. Some of his unconventional friendships in high school weren't looked upon with approval by other members of John's "jock squad," the student athletes and cool kids. As a standout athlete, he blended easily with the "in" crowd; however, accepting those with disabilities was not part of their social program. Those with special needs were put into separate classes and shunned and harassed in the hallways, as often happens with teens.

Cara was one such girl who knew John because he always took the time to say hello and ask how she was doing. One day, kids jostling her in the hall gave her a particularly cruel hazing. She escaped around a corner as John was approaching from the other direction. When he saw her, he gave his usual jovial "Hi!" She was so rattled by the bullying that she lashed out, "Fuck you, Johnny Chapman! Fuck you!" and stormed down the corridor. In the hallway, kids laughed or looked away in embarrassment, but John pursued her, matching her almost-run. She tried to make him go away, but he wouldn't. Instead, he calmed and comforted the distraught girl, sitting with her till after the bell rang and her tormentors had gone.

John's high school friend Lynn Noyes has never forgotten his actions. "We didn't do such a good job of tolerating and promoting others who were different. I wasn't mean, but I wouldn't go out of my way to do something nice for someone everyone else shunned.

But that's the way John was. He was just so . . . out of a different time in the way he could rough it up on the soccer field but have the gentlest heart of anybody, not caring who saw." Lynn ended with, "I haven't been back to a reunion, because the only reason I would go back would be to see John and he's not going to be there, so . . ."

CHAPTER

2

—

Mid-April 1980

AS HAD BECOME HIS NORM, COACH WAS BACK EAST AT THE PENTAGON AND White House doing what Lampe calls "big-guy stuff and planning." He'd participated in only two training and scenario-development events. Also, he'd been gone for much of March to execute a clandestine insertion to survey a landing site in the remote Iranian desert. Accompanied only by his one-legged CIA pilot, Coach had spent the early morning hours of April Fools' Day walking and then burying covert, remotely controlled lights at a place called Dasht-e-Kavir for use as a staging point by Delta on its way farther into Iran. The site was designated Desert One.

In April of 1980, as John Chapman was nearing adulthood, and as the American hostage situation in Iran dragged on, Mike Lampe and Brand X were developing a potential infiltration method along with thirty members of Delta Force's B Squadron at Yuma Proving Ground, practicing desert overland driving movement using motorcycles and Mules, the four-wheeled Vietnam-era cargo-hauling buggies. They'd spent the entire night struggling with the vehicles in the sand and had discovered that the equipment of the day was not effective at moving men and materiel across adverse terrain, when they were recalled and flown back to North Carolina.

No one in Yuma knew what the recall meant exactly, but it was the first time they'd ever been pulled from training. They hustled back to base to find a lone C-141 waiting to take them home. When they arrived in Charleston they found Coach waiting for them. "It's a 'go.' Gear up, pack up, and get everything loaded on the C-141 we got outside."

With no time for additional consideration, Lampe and the other eight Combat Controllers who comprised Brand X loaded their lights, beacons, weapons, radios, and the motorcycle Delta had provided for use at Desert One, and left American soil without fanfare.

The first test of Brand X and Delta Force turned the nascent special operations force (SOF) on its head. In the remote darkness, problem after problem plagued the Americans. When the first plane landed, a busload of Iranians emerged unexpectedly from the night, leaving the Rangers no choice but to guard them. Then, the eight Marine RH-53 helicopters (not suited to the desert conditions) to be used in flying the assault force into Tehran suffered mechanical failure after failure during their insertion from their launch platform, the aircraft carrier USS *Nimitz*.

Lampe and the CCT were establishing the lakebed runways when the next crisis literally exploded. An illicit-fuel smuggler traveling the dirt road came upon the Rangers assigned to keep the airfield's perimeter secured. When the smuggler wouldn't stop, they fired a LAW anti-tank rocket and the truck's fuel load exploded, lighting up the night with a hundred-foot fireball.

Slowly Marine helicopters began to straggle in. "We're waiting on helicopters, when finally number six limps in and lands. On landing, the bird is inoperative; it's lost hydraulics. And we get word that it's the last bird. So we're on the deck, we still have the fuel smuggler's tanker burning on the horizon and fifty confused

Iranians at gunpoint, the conditions are complete brownout, and we only have five helicopters. Everyone knows our absolute minimum is six." Lampe paused a moment as he reflected on the significance. "Finally the decision comes. Pack it up. We're going home."

In order to evacuate the site, one of the MC-130s needed fuel from a tanker EC-130, forcing two helicopters to reposition. Lampe recalls what happened next: "I'm a hundred yards away when a helo picks up and the sandstorm returns, so I turn my face away from the sandblasting. Out of the corner of my eye I see it lose altitude and begin to drift. And then there was an explosion. There's still dust everywhere but I can see a huge fireball [as the helo hit the EC-130 refueler next to it]. The flight crew was cooked, done. It was already buttoned up with its fuel hoses, as well as Delta shooters. I recall people pouring out the right paratroop door."

In the midst of the catastrophe, Lampe and the others, along with Delta Force and aircrew members from the C-130s, managed to recover the victims and load everyone on the remaining MC-130s. As they flew to safety, Mike couldn't help but wonder, "Did we leave anyone behind? We left an aircrew behind for sure, our fellow warriors." It was an unfortunate end to America's first true counterterrorist mission, paid with the lives of eight Marines and airmen. For the men of Brand X, who'd overcome the challenges and successfully accomplished their airfield mission, it was a triumph over neglect by the Air Force, but a bittersweet milestone. Yet they were confident the unit's combat-demonstrated capabilities would allow it to continue to develop concurrently alongside their Delta counterparts.

———

Tom Allen was a soft-spoken and unassuming police officer in Windsor Locks when he volunteered to coach the Windsor Locks High School boys' diving team, starting with John's older brother

Kevin in 1977. John was in the eighth grade and watched as Kevin learned how to nail dive after dive on the one-meter springboard. Kevin was very aggressive and that caught John's attention. He decided he wanted to join the high school kids in their diving practices and asked Coach Allen, who approached John's father to see what he thought. "He's the best athlete in the whole crew," replied the father in reference to his third child, so Tom allowed John to practice too. Consequently, when John joined the team in his freshman year, he had an edge over divers from competing schools, even varsity-level athletes.

In John's first year he became fast friends with sophomore teammate Michael DuPont. Over the next two years, John and Michael pushed each other to reach for bigger and better dives as they traded placing first and second during meets. As with all great coaches, Tom realized his two best divers required little guidance, because their competitiveness and camaraderie pushed them harder than he ever could. What Michael remembers most about his friend was "his competitive drive and the inspiration he gave me while we were diving together. My favorite part about our friendship was during my senior year when we kept trading places on setting new diving records. He broke the record first, then I would beat his record, and back and forth. I believe he still holds the record for high score."

John's four years of high school diving were spent getting progressively better. In his freshman year he placed fifth in the State Championships, and the next year, third. By his junior and senior years, he reached number one, making him the top-ranked diver in Connecticut and the first number-one state diver in Windsor Locks High School history.

John graduated in June of 1983 and immediately enrolled at the University of Connecticut—UConn—his life seemingly planned out. He selected engineering as a major and joined the UConn Men's Diving Team, already ranked number one in their division for the one-meter board and number three on the three-meter board. He thought he would compete throughout college, complete his degree, find the right woman, followed by the right job, and his life would fall into place.

———

On 20 October 1983, as John was immersed in his first engineering classes and in UConn's pool, Coach Carney was enjoying a beer and Thursday night football on television at his home in Fayetteville, North Carolina. Florida State was mopping the floor with Louisville when the phone rang; it was the operations floor of the Joint Special Operations Command at nearby Fort Bragg. Major General Dick Scholtes, the JSOC commander, needed Carney to come in. Leaving Louisville, who were already going down in flames at 51 to 7, he arrived at JSOC's tightly secured compound at 2200 hours to find the general and his staff poring over maps and satellite imagery of an insignificant island called Grenada.

———

Three years earlier, in the summer of 1980, in the immediate aftermath of Desert One, the Coach had testified before the Holloway Commission, and the outcome was the formation of the new Joint Special Operations Command, incorporating the already validated but wounded Delta Force. The command began to take shape as SEAL Team Six (the newest SEAL team, created specifically for JSOC) materialized, Task Force 160 (the Army's premier helicopter unit) joined, and Coach's Brand X became Detachment 1 MACOS—short for Military Airlift Command Operations Staff, an innocuous name for the new and now most classified organization in the Air Force. "Det 1" was to be the Air Force's contribution to the new command. No one involved could have imagined that it would transform into the most dynamic and diverse special operations unit in the Air Force.

At the time, the boys in Det 1 were living like vagabonds out of the hangar in Charleston Air Force Base, South Carolina. "I've got good news and bad news," the Coach announced one day shortly after they'd returned to the air base from planning a second Iranian hostage crisis rescue attempt that fall. "The good news is we're gonna form our own standalone unit."

"What's the bad news?" queried Mike Lampe.

"It's going to be at Fort Bragg so we can be next to Delta. We're moving to Fayettenam," he said, invoking the alternative and derisive soldiers' name for the nearby town of Fayetteville, North Carolina.

When the team moved to Pope Air Force Base on Fort Bragg in 1981, the men lived out of a derelict mobile trailer until things improved. "We got a second mobile home," said Lampe flatly of their "improved" digs. By October of 1983, when Coach was called to JSOC, Det 1 had grown to twenty-four men and they were better trained (though lacking in facilities), having built on three years of exercises with the Rangers and Delta.

On 13 October 1983, as Coach's Combat Controllers were hitting their stride in the States, the latest in a series of coups had replaced the Grenadian Marxist leader, Maurice Bishop, after he'd made overtures to the US and was placed under house arrest. On the seventeenth, Bishop was freed by supporters but assassinated three days later, and the tiny nation descended into twenty-four-hour shoot-on-sight martial law. In addition to a heavy Cuban presence and the extension of Soviet influence into America's sphere, there were concerns in Washington about several hundred American medical students and tourists under potential threat on the island. The US plan was for the Rangers and CCT to seize Grenada's Point Salines International Airport as an airhead in order to introduce the 82nd

Airborne and other follow-on forces. Delta would rescue the medical students from their True Blue medical campus near Point Salines, while CCT established the airhead and then ran the international airport within thirty minutes of jumping onto the airfield, a metric that would become an advertised standard that remains to this day.

On the evening of 24 October, the mission was green-lighted. The Controllers had been working nonstop for days in the muggy Georgia climate alongside the men of the 1st Ranger Battalion, with very little rest. After they'd loaded the aircraft, despite the unknowns facing them, they gratefully took the opportunity to catch some desperately needed sleep.

In flight, the Rangers and Controllers began to don their parachutes for the five-hundred-foot paradrop when they were a few hours out. "Some guys put on reserves, others didn't." The drop was three hundred feet below the standard eight-hundred-foot combat altitude so as to fly under the antiaircraft guns positioned on hills ringing Point Salines. Because the guns could not depress their barrels below level, it was believed the invasion aircraft should be safe from the point-blank fire.

The entire force was invading with the dawn because the Marines had no nighttime capability and were seizing the island's other initial strategic object, Pearls Airport, at H-hour, as the start of the invasion was unimaginatively named. Failing to recognize (or possibly ignoring) the still painful lessons of Desert One, the Joint Staff pushed opportunities for each service to participate at the expense of operational applicability.

"I can see the coast and it looks *low*. Seems a lot lower than five hundred fucking feet, when we suddenly pop up. I remember seeing tracers from the triple A, but they're going over us. And then fuck, I don't have a reserve chute," recalls Lampe.

He said a little prayer for the rigger who packed his parachute and jumped out the left troop door. He exited the plane in the morning light, feeling completely naked as he waited for bullets to slam into his body and was yanked horizontally by the parachute's deployment as he dropped out the door.

On the airfield, with moments to spare, the CCT as air traffic control (ATC) cleared the first aircraft for landing and they were in business, as plane after plane was landed and guided to its designated parking spot. "The planes are dumping their cargo by doing combat offloads before making rapid departures. They'd drop the ramp, hit the throttle, and pallets of gear or gun jeeps would roll out the back." Combat Control ran the airfield for the duration of combat operations until civil control of the field could be returned to airport authorities, US forces had stabilized the island, containing Cuban forces, and the rescue of 233 American students at True Blue medical school was complete.

The CCT were spread among the Delta Force troops to take down other designated targets, their key job controlling airstrikes, particularly by the AC-130 gunships. Despite setbacks and interservice politics, the operation was a success for CCT as they ran the biggest contingency airport in US history and performed flawlessly with their Delta teammates. Grenada represented the maturation of Det 1 into the shape it would maintain for the next decade as it continued to grow alongside Delta and SEAL Team Six.

John Chapman watched the news of the invasion with the rest of America, mildly interested in the fact that it took place, but it didn't resonate with the freshman. He was too busy failing his classes. By the time the invasion was over and the semester ended, his grades were so poor he was ineligible to compete as a diver. He was certainly a smart young man, but as his sister Lori recalls John's own words, "Studying wasn't his 'thing'; *doing* was his thing."

Like most young men disinterested in college, John returned home and, as he mulled over the Air Force, took a job as a mechanic and tow truck driver. Then, in the third week of August 1985, John enlisted in the Air Force. He promised his mother he'd try something "safe," selecting information systems specialist as a job. To Lori, he was more to the point: "I need to do something more than stay in Windsor Locks my whole life. I want to see the world; I can't stay here."

While at Lackland AFB, Texas, John attended a CCT recruiting briefing given to all male basic trainees. Even though he was contracted with the Air Force to attend information systems technician training, Combat Control is authorized to recruit from among all eligible candidates, and if interested, any qualified trainee can relinquish their Air Force Specialty Code and try out. If they meet the standards of a Flying Class II physical examination and pass the CCT physical ability and stamina test (PAST), they're in.[1] Watching the video of Controllers jumping from planes, riding motorcycles, scuba diving, calling airstrikes, and conducting assault-zone landings hit John right where he desired most: challenge and excitement.

His promise to his mother remained steadfast, however, and he left the alternate Combat Control future unexplored. After completing basic and technical training at Keesler Air Force Base, Mississippi, John arrived for his first duty assignment at Lowry Air Force Base in Aurora, Colorado, in February 1986. He made the most of his new life and career, enjoying the Air Force, but soon the urge to

---

1   The PAST must be administered by a qualified CCT, Special Tactics Officer, or certified Air Force recruiter, in the following order: 500-meter surface swim (maximum time 15:00 minutes), chin-ups (minimum six), sit-ups (minimum fifty), push-ups (minimum forty-two), a 1.5-mile run (maximum time 11:30). If a volunteer stops, rests, or otherwise fails to continue until muscle failure during any of the calisthenics, the test is halted at that point and they are failed. Minimum numbers are frowned upon and typically indicate the volunteer is an unlikely graduate of the two-year training pipeline.

do something "more" returned. Unfortunately, he was obligated to his job for a minimum of three years—chained to a keyboard and monitor. By late 1988 he'd decided that he was going to try and cross-train into CCT.

He'd loosely followed Combat Control, reading about what little was known from Grenada as well as Desert One and the wars in Laos and Vietnam, vowing to learn everything possible and preparing for the PAST test relentlessly. Feeling that he'd kept his promise to his mom by trying something safer first, when three years had passed he submitted his cross-training paperwork. All he wanted was a shot—just one—to prove he could do something so difficult it would elevate him to the top 1 percent of military men.

His approval arrived in the spring of 1989 and John returned to Lackland Air Force Base that summer to attend the Combat Control Indoctrination Course—known informally as indoc—the toughest school in the pipeline and where the vast majority of volunteers wash out. He knew that 90 percent of the candidates who tried out for CCT failed to make it through training. He didn't know what exactly a 10 percent success rate translated into for those who couldn't or didn't have the heart to make it, but clearly there were many hazards and unknowns ahead. Yet it was merely the first of ten Army, Navy, and Air Force courses he needed to navigate to become a qualified Combat Controller. It would be a *long* year and a half.

———

Mike Lampe and Det 1 had changed much in the years between the Grenada invasion and the time of John Chapman's cross-training approval. By 1989, Lampe had been promoted to chief master sergeant and was the unit's senior enlisted manager (the most senior enlisted position in an Air Force squadron). The Coach had been promoted and had moved on, and the unit continued to go through a series of name changes to mask its identity and purpose.[2] He and the new commander, Major Craig Brotchie, had also implemented a formal selection process that mirrored Delta Force's famous assessment, which culminates in "the long walk," but with one distinct difference: Delta Force was open to any member of the Army regardless of background, whereas the (now) 1724th Special Tactics Squadron—referred to obliquely as "the Hill" for its location on the JSOC compound above Pope Air Force Base—only considered volunteers who were current combat-deployable Combat Controllers with two years of operational experience and a recommendation from the individual's commander.

As Chapman arrived at "indoc" in the summer of 1989, another crisis developed. Manuel Noriega, the Panamanian dictator, had ignored the country's presidential election results, choosing to remain in power while also managing his lucrative cocaine shipping empire. By 15 December, Noriega, possibly under the influence of his own product, declared a state of war existed between his country and the US. The next day, Panamanian Defense Forces killed a US Marine and then accosted a Navy lieutenant and his wife, physically abusing the couple. On 17 December, President George H. W. Bush obliged the dictator's call for war by green-lighting "Operation Just Cause," the invasion of Panama.

Mike Lampe was home on 16 December when his beeper went off. His boys, seeing the news on television, attempted to keep their father from leaving, but he promised he'd be back in time to drive the family on its planned Christmas vacation to New Hampshire.

At the unit, he learned the operation they'd rehearsed seven times had the green light. Again, JSOC would be leading America's latest

---

2   The unit's actual naming conventions were Brand X, 1977–June 1981; Det 1 MACOS, June 1981–June 1983; Det 4 NAFCOS, July 1983–April 1987; 1724th Combat Control Squadron, May 1987–September 1987; 1724th Special Tactics Squadron, October 1987–March 1992; 24th Special Tactics Squadron (informally known as "the 24"—pronounced "the two-four"), March 1992–present.

major overseas intervention (the nation had eschewed a declaration of war, something it hadn't done since World War II, preferring to conduct "named operations")—this one, the largest airborne invasion since the Second World War—and as was becoming tradition, CCT would enter the theater ahead of their JSOC counterparts.

On 20 December, just after midnight, the invasion arrived in thirty C-130s over Rio Hato and Omar Torrijos (Tocumen) airports. The CCT "bike chasers," the nickname given to the men who followed motorcycles dropped for use in clearing the runways of obstacles, were the first parachutists to jump from the lead aircraft, seizing the international airports, literally making them "First There," CCT's motto. Before any of the forces jumped, however, three CCT quietly infiltrated the Omar Torrijos airfield to establish and assess the airport and then to control the air invasion.

It was the largest employment of Combat Controllers in history at the time, and the CCT manpower requirements were so extreme that the 1724th was forced to augment its missions with men from the 1723rd Special Tactics Squadron at Hurlburt Field, Florida.

As advertised, within thirty minutes of jumping into the darkness, the Controllers were running both airfields, and the number of aircraft under their control for landing, moving to take down multiple targets throughout the country, and close airstrikes was staggering— 171 different special operations airplanes and a near-equal number of helicopters were moving in the nighttime airspace over the tiny Central American country. Almost all of them were under the direction or guidance of CCT. The twenty-by-twenty-mile airspace was roughly equivalent to the area inside the Washington, DC, beltway. Despite no radar usage or prepublished air plans, every single flight maintained safe separation. Not only were there no air-to-air mishaps, there wasn't a single ground incident or a near miss. The only aircraft lost during the invasion either crashed or were shot down.

As for Mike Lampe, he'd managed to join a Ranger platoon as they raided Noriega's beachfront hideaway near Rio Hato the day after the invasion began. During the search for potential intelligence as to Noriega's whereabouts, the Rangers rifled through the dictator's office. They'd missed him by a mere fifteen minutes but didn't come away empty-handed. In Noriega's desk were hundreds of 14-karat gold paper clips. A Ranger gave one to Lampe who, upon returning home long after Christmas was over, gave it to his wife as a Christmas present. Her gift to him was a beautifully wrapped shoebox stuffed with civilian "Help Wanted" employment advertisements.

CHAPTER

3

—

July 1989

SIX MONTHS BEFORE THE PANAMA INVASION, SERGEANT JOHN CHAPMAN
returned to Lackland Air Force Base, only this time his purpose had
crystallized. He was starting a journey of self-discipline and performance like nothing before. High school diving was based on one's
own competitive desire to win. For all who dared, the CCT pipeline
was a standard by which they measured themselves, yet it was far
beyond anything John had ever experienced. If he could make it
through the next year plus, his life would be forever differentiated
from the masses, *he knew that*, but what was it that crushed hardy
men and drove scores of them to quit in the first weeks of training?
Whatever it was, he thought, as he emerged from the taxi in front
of his first home on this new journey, he'd see for himself soon
enough.

Operating Location-H—OL-H for short—occupied a pair of
Vietnam-era two-story barracks in the "low-rent district" of Lackland
AFB. The buildings were tired: Even the bland tan and dark brown
trim advertised neglect. Referred to by the young men there to test
themselves as "the oh-el" or "indoc," it stood as the gatekeeper for
each man's ticket to ride the remainder of the pipe. In front of the

building was a symbol of a bygone era, an H-model Huey helicopter mounted on a pole, appearing to swoop toward those who walked the sidewalk as if it were setting up a gun run on the unsuspecting. Across the concrete pad in front of the building, John was greeted by a fifty-by-twenty-foot wood-bordered dirt patch, home to a set of dip bars and pull-up bars, and two thirty-foot ropes that hung from a wooden arch. Between the ropes, hanging from the crossbeam at the top, was a shiny brass bell. At the door was a sign: OL-H MACOS, with the motto QUALITY NOT QUANTITY stenciled across the center. On each side were two military flashes, modern versions of European coats of arms. One displayed an angel, wings spread above her head, two arms stretched around a globe as if embracing it, and the motto THAT OTHERS MAY LIVE below the name USAF Pararescue. The second was bordered by a wreath, leaves pointing to the top, the center a globe with latitude and longitude lines. A yellow lightning bolt stretched diagonally from upper right to lower left; below the bolt in the lower-right corner was an eight-pointed compass rose, and opposite was a parachute. Across the bottom was written "U.S.A.F. Combat Control." Between the tips of the wreath at the top, a motto: FIRST THERE.

More than 120 men were set to start John's class in a few weeks. OL-H, as the sign in front announced, was for Pararescue (PJ) trainees and potential Combat Controllers alike. The Air Force's undisputed toughest jobs had much in common, including sharing two-thirds of the pipeline training, so they started together. Most of the initial 120 men trying out were there to become PJs, the better advertised and better known of the two careers. Roughly fifty of the men were there to become CCT.

Arriving around the same time as Chapman, Joe Maynor was the absolute embodiment of a Tennessee country boy. His hometown of Athens was little more than a village sixty miles north of the "big city," Chattanooga. At basic he'd attended the recruiting brief and thought, *Let's see where this takes us*. He survived the PAST test and flight physical examination and, upon graduation from basic, was met by another indoc candidate to be taken to the OL-H. Candidates were not allowed to walk anywhere, they ran . . . to lunch, to training, to the base exchange, to check-in. And so, along with a few other hardy (or foolhardy) souls, Joe double-timed it to his new destination wondering if perhaps he'd made a mistake, dragging his duffel bag and all his worldly possessions as he ran through the Texas summer heat, dripping sweat before he'd even checked in.

Joe and John were processed along with many other nameless men. Arriving candidates were treated with disdain or indifference, largely because many of them would not survive the waiting period to even start class. The first thing they learned was they were in "casual status," meaning not formally in training or on orders for an assignment, and were referred to as such. "Hey, casual" was a common summons to those unworthy of a name; instructors didn't bother learning names until candidates were well into the class. The second thing they learned was that casual status was anything *but* casual. Each morning was spent in calisthenics sessions, runs, and pool training to prepare them for the upcoming seven-week trial. During this period, the young men faced the reality of their choice—CCT training was not about parachutes, exotic locations, and motorcycles. It was about pain and never being fast enough, strong enough, or aquatic enough. Those who realized their mistake early suffered less. To quit, one merely had to utter the words. Instructors—seasoned PJs and Controllers, specially selected for the assignment—were notorious for spotting weak moments or individuals and singling them out for attention. Sometimes, to cull the herd, they tortured the entire batch of casuals with sessions in the mud pit until someone quit.

By the first day of class in early September, the instructor cadre had whittled the number of candidates down to a manageable seventy, Joe and John among them.

The OL-H course spanned seven weeks of physical conditioning and testing, coupled with basic academics in such subjects as scuba diving physics, which mostly served to occupy the candidates for an hour or two each day and allow for physical recovery. Each week got progressively harder, faster, longer.

Grueling calisthenics sessions ruled each morning, followed by a run, usually between three and six miles, or sprints on the nearby track. But the worst was pool training. Each day after lunch, the men learned firsthand the value of oxygen to the human body. Pool sessions consisted of a series of different events, all designed to strengthen the mind and the body—and to separate the very strongest from all others. There is no more compelling drive in the human body than the need for oxygen; it overcomes all thought, instinctive in an absolute sense. To push oneself past the physiological need to breathe is to master oneself. And the OL-H had devised surefire ways to test the hypothesis.

The first oxygen debt exercises they were exposed to were "underwaters"—swimming the length of the Olympic-size training pool submerged, then touching the far wall and sprinting back across the surface using freestyle stroke. This was repeated eight times, with decreasing intervals to resupply oxygen to the body and never long enough to completely replenish. Breaking the surface even once during any iteration was failure—and immediate removal from the course. Another instructor favorite was drownproofing, where the student's hands are tied behind his back before he is pushed into the pool. He must use the bottom of the twelve-foot deep end to push off, undulate to the surface, and catch a single breath, repeating for five minutes—more art than science. Struggling to stay afloat without use of the hands and arms is impossible, and those attempting to flounder at the surface are failed in any case.

Then there were the crossovers. The word instills gut fear in everyone who's ever done them. They start during the third week, after students have been conditioned to oxygen deprivation through various other exercises. Of all the brutal water tortures, crossovers were undeniably the worst and were a requirement to pass for graduation. Each student donned a set of twin eighty-cubic-foot galvanized-steel scuba diving tanks. The tanks had no regulators for breathing; indeed, they weren't for that purpose at all. Each student would also don mask and fins. Finally, each fastened a sixteen-pound weight belt around his waist.

They would drop into the deep end of the pool along the long side, wedged together with one arm holding them to the security of the wall, lined "nut to butt." They were then given the preparatory command, "Prepare to cross over." That was the signal to take one final huge lungful of air. "Cross over!" would come a moment later. All the students would sink straight to the bottom and, upon reaching it, fin as hard as they could to the other side as a similar group from the far side also finned simultaneously. The groups met in the middle, one designated to go "high," that is crawl over the "low" group, both then continuing on their way to the other wall. Only when they reached the far wall were they allowed to push off the bottom and rise for the precious and distant air that awaited them.

Gasping men, crawling past each other, clawing for air, sputtered to the surface on each side. This would be repeated eight times, with reduced intervals from forty-five to thirty seconds between crossovers. To add to the excitement, instructors were in the pool with them, for safety in the event of a near drowning but also to harass the students, sometimes pulling masks from their faces to induce panic. Other times, they would stand on a particular student's back, holding on to the tank's manifold, and "surf" the student for a few feet, creating an incredible amount of extra drag, forcing the student to crawl for his life.

As the next batch of students stood freezing in the cold water at the shallow end, waiting their turn, instructors offered words of "encouragement" to the men gasping for air. "Come on, you know you want to quit." "It's all over, and there's a great Air Force job waiting for you. Just quit." Occasionally, when they sensed someone was close to the edge, or was particularly whiny, they'd converge as a pack on the frightened student: "Say the words! Say it!"

"I quit."

At these words, sometimes uttered meekly, other times shouted back in a form of final defiance, the instructor's face would change. Gone was the fierce anger, the challenge to the individual; in its place, a calm and reasonable human would appear, with a simple instruction: "Move to the shallow end of the pool. Take off your gear and report to admin."

John, as student leader, watched as other young men, almost all of them younger than he, would skip lunch. Burning through thousands of calories a day, they needed every carb they could get, but "the pool" held them in its liquid grip. Others, trying to take in needed nourishment, would instead vomit from anxiety in the barracks before the pool session. Occasionally, some would get out of the pool to vomit or just vomit over the side.

In the pool, some men pushed themselves past the point of no return, blacking out in the water and having to be pulled to the surface by instructors and resuscitated. When they came around, they would be given a choice: "Get back in the pool or go to the lockers." After the daily pool sessions, which included underwater knot tying (a series of knots to be completed on one breath) and buddy breathing (students shared a single snorkel, passed back and forth for air, while instructors harassed them to prevent them from breathing and tried to pull them apart, which meant failure if they could), the pool day was concluded with a swim, either freestyle or with fins, of between 1,500 and 4,000 meters.

On land, things were little better. Mud-pit torture sessions, thousands of extra push-ups and pull-ups, or "motivation" runs were common. No-notice room inspections, where instructors would turn out the entire class for any infraction or contraband, always loomed. During all of these, John and the other NCOs were expected not only to perform to standard but to demonstrate leadership and selflessness. Joe recalls the first time he and John bonded. "We got in trouble for nothing"—a typical student observation. One of the fiercest instructors, Sergeant Rodman, called them all onto the front concrete pad and had the men, now down to less than thirty, mount the dip bars. These were four feet off the ground and ran in parallel. Gripping them like gymnasts, the men would support themselves with straight arms and then dip down till their shoulders were level with the bars, before thrusting up again. This constituted one dip.

"Rodman had us do a set of fifty," he remembers. "But in between each dip we had to hold ourselves up for a minute." Those who reached muscle failure were relegated to the mud pit, where two other instructors were inflicting even worse torture. "John and I were the only ones to make it all the way to the end."

The young Tennessean was about to comprehend what they all were doing there. As their reward for completion, both John and Joe were excused from further torture; they could shower, get something to eat, and relax (as much as anyone could at the OL). Joe, realizing reprieve was upon him, started for the barracks door. But John ran, not walked, to the pit. "Where do you think you're going, Chapman?" shouted Rodman.

"The pit, Sergeant, to join my team."

"You're off. Get out of here."

Chapman didn't move. One of the guys in the class threw mud at him, hitting him in the head. Rodman, not needing much incentive to encourage teamwork, stated, "Well, you're muddy now, you might as well join your team."

Joe had watched the entire exchange and, seeing his desperately needed decompression evaporate, jumped into the pit with his team leader. "John and I bonded over that moment. I'll never forget it. It was the first time I realized what we were doing was about more than just me. It was the team."

———

Of the 120 men who signed up for OL-H class number 89-005, scheduled to begin on 18 September (the Air Force's birthday), and the seventy men who survived to start the class, only seven would graduate—five PJs and just two CCT, John Chapman and Joe Maynor. The two men, representing 4 percent of the Combat Control candidates, had their pipeline tickets to ride. The next gut check came immediately: the US Army Special Forces combat diver qualification school in Key West, Florida.

Arguably one of the toughest Army schools, SF CDQ, as it is known, fails between 25 and 35 percent of all who attend. However, for Joe and John, it was the course they'd spent months and months of pain and preparation for. Forty men started the class in mid-November; fewer than thirty graduated. Dive after dive, nighttime, infiltration, LAR-V Draeger rebreathers (a system that uses 100 percent oxygen and recycles breath so as not to leave an air-bubble trail), and of course, PT: long runs and cal sessions. For the Army soldiers, the pool sessions with their crossovers and harassment were the worst. To the OL grads, it was just another week.

After Key West, the relentless pace continued. More water work awaited them at the Air Force water survival school in Homestead, Florida, south of Miami, in the form of a three-day course in how to survive a crash and recovery at sea. In contrast to the first two schools, it was an "easy" and mostly academic course.

As 1990 arrived, the two potential Combat Controllers found

themselves at their second Army course, Airborne School at Fort Benning, Georgia, universally known among CCT as "Air Force appreciation." For John, jumping was exciting and something he took a liking to. He talked to Joe about taking skydiving lessons while they were still in the pipeline and before they attended HALO school, the military high-altitude/low-opening freefall course.

After making the five jumps required to graduate, they hopped on a plane to the next stop, Air Force aircrew survival school on Fairchild Air Force Base, Washington. The two-week course was designed to expose Air Force members to survival in the woods, covering such things as basic land navigation, hiding and evading, and procuring food. In addition, it provided resistance training for interrogations in the event of capture.

By then the two men were inseparable and well on their way. In February they arrived at Keesler Air Force Base to attend air traffic control (ATC) school, one of the most academically demanding courses in the Air Force. Many who couldn't hack the pressures were reassigned to other jobs, and potential Combat Controllers were no different. If you couldn't control air traffic, you couldn't be CCT.

John had flown home from survival school to retrieve his car, a piss-gold-colored four-door Ford LTD yacht, from his dad. "It had worn vacuum hoses," recalls Joe. "So the headlights would dim until you hit the gas, then as the pressure built, the headlights would brighten. At stop signs, they'd go dead. It was a real piece of shit." Still, the car equaled freedom, and they used it to explore the Gulf Coast and release the pressures of ATC training.

There remained one last hurdle to becoming Controllers—Combat Control School at Pope Air Force Base, North Carolina. The base was encompassed by Fort Bragg, home of the 82nd Airborne, Delta Force, and the 24 STS.

Combat Control School incorporated everything the men had learned to that point on their journey, and then built on that foundation to give them the basics of being a Controller. It was the last school before they earned their berets, but by no means was it the final school; they still had to complete HALO and achieve their joint terminal attack controller certifications, among many others. For John and Joe, "We thought we'd made it already and didn't realize that's not how the instructors saw us till we started class."

Morning PT sessions were grueling (again) and were followed by a daily in-ranks inspection to check each student's ability to pay attention to detail. Infractions for a string on the uniform, a poor shave, or scuffed boots incurred push-up penalties. Then it was on to the classroom to learn radio and navigational equipment capabilities, how to establish assault zones, advanced land navigation, and small-unit tactics (patrolling, ambushes, and assaults), in addition to advanced weapons training, including grenades and demolitions. The academics of the classroom were complemented by field training, the euphemism for being in the woods of Fort Bragg under the watchful eye of the CCT instructors. Unlike at previous schools, mistakes "in the field" were rewarded not just with calisthenics but with CS (chemical smoke), the military term for tear gas. Instructors used it to induce stress, since shooting at students was not something one could do to simulate combat conditions. The sweating men would don their gas masks to protect their eyes and lungs, but there was no escape from the burning, particularly in their crotches and armpits, where the searing doubled when coupled with raw moist skin.

The students frequently parachuted into training to acclimate them to jumping. Joe recalls the nighttime jump the team made into one of Fort Bragg's drop zones named Normandy. They were to land at Normandy and navigate to their next target, Sicily DZ, to establish a C-130 dirt assault strip, and then control and land an actual plane. In the plane waiting to jump into the dark, John was next in the stick to jump behind Joe and leaned forward to shout in his ear over the roar of the plane's engines and the wind rushing past the open jump door. "I'm going to piggyback you. I'll be right on your ass!" Joe, no fan of jumping, merely nodded, *Yeah, right*.

When Joe cleared the door and the round chute fully inflated above his head, he looked up to see imprints of feet sinking into the billowed fabric and making their way across to the edge of the canopy. The next thing he knew, John's body dropped into sight next to him. John had jumped so close to his friend their parachutes opened atop one another and John had to walk across Joe's. When he got to the side, Joe's canopy had stolen his air, dropping the older student down to his level. "We were level, side by side. And John was giggling with adrenaline." The boy from Tennessee, however, was far from elated.

As the weeks turned into months, the team prepared for their final field training exercise, FTX, held at nearby Camp Mackall. There the men were tested on their ability to insert into a hostile country, patrol to various targets, conduct assault-zone and other operations, and suffer. Food and water were never withheld, but sleep was a luxury. And of course, to help keep them motivated, there was the dreaded CS gas.

The last event of the FTX was for the men to hump their rucks and weapons the fifteen miles back to the Combat Control School (CCS) building. Like everything else the students did, it was a timed and competitive event. Tired, but driven by the knowledge a mere fifteen miles separated them from their goal, every member of their seven-man CCS class finished. On a sweltering July night in 1990, John and Joe, the only two survivors from OL-H class 89-005, walked across the stage of the Pope NCO club, donned their red berets, and bloused their black leather paratrooper jump boots for the first time.

The Air Force's newest Combat Controllers, now more brothers than friends, both received orders to the 21st Special Tactics Squadron, a move that took them directly across the street from the Combat Control School. Whatever challenges and adventures were to come, they planned to face them together.

CHAPTER

4

—

July 1990

JOHN HAD FINALLY ACHIEVED HIS DREAM OF BEING "SOMETHING MORE," something only a select few had ever accomplished, only to discover along his pipeline journey that qualifying as a Combat Controller was only half the measurement of success in his new world. The other, greater, metric could be realized only in actual combat. He couldn't have known it, but in late July 1990, his first opportunity was only weeks away.

One of John's other local buddies was Joe Puricelli, an Army 82nd Airborne paratrooper he'd met at Airborne School. On 2 August, a Thursday, Joe invited John to travel back to his hometown of Windber, Pennsylvania, to hang out for the weekend. John thought, *Sure, why not?*

The same day, half a world away, another man executed some travel plans. Saddam Hussein invaded Kuwait at midnight on 2 August, bombing the capital and the tiny emirate's paper military, seizing key facilities using helicopter-borne commandos. Within twelve hours it was all but over; Kuwait's military was either wiped out or had fled, along with the royal family.

The news made a global splash as the US mulled what to do

about this realignment of 65 percent of the world's oil sourcing, yet it was barely a blip on John Chapman's radar. John and Joe stopped at a gas station as they rolled into the rural borough and ran into Valerie Novak, one of Joe's best friends from high school, who was completing her last year of nursing school. Valerie had long brown, wavy hair, blue eyes that shone with a mischievous twinkle, and a raucous laugh. Her tiny five-foot-four-inch frame belied her vivacious personality, which she enthusiastically demonstrated when she gave Joe a big hug and said, "Hey! You're home! Let's go out tonight!" Joe smiled and said, "Well, I have a friend here with me," and introduced her to John. Valerie responded with a hearty, "Cool!" and they were off, spending the night hanging out at one of Windber's bars. During the evening, and long into the night, as Valerie remembers, "We went dancing and drinking...We drank *lots* of tequila." For John, the weekend passed way too quickly, and immediately after he returned to Pope AFB, John and Val started calling each other and writing letters and cards. As often as he could, he drove the eight-hour stretch to Windber so he could spend time with Valerie. Almost as often, she would come off a twelve-hour shift, jump in her car, and drive the eight hours to see him at the condo he'd purchased in Fayetteville. Somehow, they made the long-distance relationship work, and by fall the two were inseparable.

While John was falling for the petite brunette, the US and Kuwait had called an emergency UN Security Council meeting, which dutifully passed Resolution 660 condemning the invasion and demanding Iraq's immediate withdrawal. For the next few months, Iraqi overtures and negotiations were met with repeated rejections by President Bush and a militant British prime minister, Margaret Thatcher.

In November, while the Iraqi situation deteriorated, John and Val joined his father for Thanksgiving in northern Michigan. During a horseback ride, John was thrown and landed hard and in an awkward position, but he got up, "rubbed some dirt on it," and continued riding.

In the wee hours of the morning, John woke Valerie, telling her he was in incredible pain. Valerie remembers, "I checked him, and his stomach was enlarged. I immediately knew we needed to get him to the hospital." When the ER doctor examined John, he shook his head and said, "You're one lucky dude. If you had waited *any* longer, you'd be dead." John had ruptured his spleen. Though surgery wasn't necessary, he was ordered sidelined for six months.

Relegated to nonphysical duties, such as working drop-zone and assault-zone training across Fort Bragg, he watched as the rest of his squadron trained up for war and deployed. Christmas was depressing for the new and untried Combat Controller. His only solace was the time spent with Valerie, who'd traveled down so they could spend Christmas together. By January, his squadron, the 21st STS, was a skeleton crew of nondeployable and stay-behind airmen.

———

For CCT, the war proved to be a watershed moment. Across Iraq and Saudi Arabia, Controllers from different squadrons established and ran airports and airfields, conducted beacon bombing (using beacons to determine known points for accuracy) missions with US and coalition aircraft, and liberated allied embassies with British Special Air Service (SAS) and Special Boat Service (SBS) troops. Hunting Scud missile launchers in the western deserts of Iraq with Delta Force to keep Israel on the sidelines and hold George Bush's coalition together was the 24's sole purpose. Overall, their efforts dropped Scud launches into Israel to virtually nil. One CCT, Bruce Barry, supported by a Delta troop, managed to destroy an estimated twenty-seven missile launchers alone. When the war ended, General

Norman Schwarzkopf, the US commander, flew to Delta and the 24's operations base in Arar, Saudi Arabia, near the Iraqi border, to congratulate them.

"So this is the guy who kept Israel out of the war," said the hero of America's Desert Storm campaign as he regarded Bruce Barry, the other, unknown, hero of the coalition when they were introduced. It was a proud moment in the 24's continued transformation into the most distinctive and versatile unit in special operations.

———

In North Carolina in the spring of 1991, as the troops were coming home from Desert Storm, John Chapman watched as his brother Combat Controllers returned to a hero's welcome, offered by a nation taking pride in a victory that scrubbed away the stains of the national protest and social divisions that marked the Vietnam conflict. He'd missed the entire war due to his injury and subsequent sidelining, and now, it seemed, there'd be no opportunity for another in a stable new world order led by the sole remaining superpower, America.

With his work life stable, if a bit unexciting, John picked a June weekend nearly a year after his chance meeting with Valerie to drive to Windber and propose. She knew what John's job entailed, and she knew she would have to move from her hometown to destinations unknown. His one solace at missing the entire war with his brothers was the other piece he'd been missing in his life; and here she was, in the form of a vivacious swirl of energy who'd agreed to be his wife.

In November of 1992, they packed their belongings and shipped out to Japan for John's next assignment with the 320th Special Tactics Squadron. Overseas military assignments tend to bring service members and their families closer to their fellow Americans, and

John and Valerie were no exception. While she worked at the hospital, John and the other Controllers trained: more dive operations; HALO parachuting; small-boat, drop-zone, and assault-zone operations. Conducting NEOs, or noncombatant evacuation operations, was a prime focus of the unit. Because of the 320th's central location in the Pacific theater, theirs was the go-to unit when disaster struck. Evacuating embassies, airlifting out American citizens or disaster victims... These were important missions to rehearse, and the unit had a proud humanitarian legacy that seemed, in a peaceful world, like it might be John's best chance at using the skills he'd been developing for years.

———

While John toiled in the Pacific, the 24 added to its legacy and mystique on the remote coast of Africa in another country most Americans had never heard of: Somalia. In an operation that came to be known as Black Hawk Down, one Combat Controller, Jeff Bray, kept the besieged force of Delta operators, Rangers, and fellow CCT and PJs alive during the fiercest portion of the historic eighteen-hour gun battle, using his unequalled airstrike expertise. The operation and, more specifically, the firefight that took place on 3 October 1993, shaped special operations and US foreign policy for the next eight years, until an Arab scion would declare war on Western civilization, and America in particular, and change the course of international history.

———

John learned of the Somalia operation in the same fashion as the rest of the world, through media reporting and grisly images from the streets of Mogadishu. But within the Combat Control community, word slowly spread of the heroics of the CCT involved. By then, John was well into the second year of a three-year tour in the Far East, gaining valuable experience and enjoying training missions in exotic countries like Thailand and Korea. But they were just that, training missions. As 1995 approached, he realized he wasn't satisfied, not completely. Something was missing, exacerbated by his having missed the First Gulf War.

There was only one place to gain combat experience, or at least execute highly dynamic operations with national implications. If he was to attain the experiences he desired and validate the years of training under his belt, he needed to go to this place. But to do so, he would need to be more physically fit, more proficient in his skills, and more mentally committed than he had ever been in his life, because the destination he had in mind took only the absolute best of an already elite group of men. That place was the 24th Special Tactics Squadron.

———

Assessment and selection for the 24 is singular, yet simultaneously similar to the process at the other most elite military units in the world, SEAL Team Six and Delta Force.[3] Within Combat Control it is unique because, among all the operational Special Tactics squadrons, it is the only one that requires the individual to voluntarily submit a package and request assignment.

From Scud hunting in Iraq to man hunting in Mogadishu and every significant American counterterrorist operation from Desert One forward, the 24 has played a key role. No other "black" SOF unit

---

3   Delta selection is open to any soldier regardless of background, whereas SEAL Team Six, like the 24, only takes volunteers from within the ranks of its "white" SOF teams. For CCT, that was every other Special Tactics squadron.

(defined as a unit operating with restricted congressional oversight) has been involved in as many nationally prioritized and high-risk special operations. The 24 doubled in size from the time of Grenada to the First Gulf War, and then doubled again, occupying increasingly greater space within the JSOC compound at Fort Bragg.

In the spring of 1995, John Chapman looked to add his name to the best of the best in the world. It would be daunting. He was applying to one of the most demanding units in the history of America's armed forces. Of the men in Combat Control who applied, only half would succeed in the two-week selection and six-month Green Team training process. John knew little about the unit, mostly snippets from the few former members who circulated among the other Special Tactics squadrons (24 members rarely reentered the "white" SOF system). Yet if that's where the truly best of CCT went to demonstrate their excellence, then he'd go there too. And there was another calculus for the now ten-year veteran: He wanted the chance to prove himself in combat or combat-like operations and, at age thirty, he was rapidly approaching "old guy" status. Once in the unit, he could conceivably stay for the rest of his career—but getting in was the trick.

As with everything else John did since Val came into his life, his approach to this new opportunity incorporated her.

"I want to do this, but if you say no, I won't," he'd told her in early 1995. Two decades later, Valerie remains convinced that had she said no, the matter would have been dropped without resentment. "But I didn't want to look back at age eighty and realize I'd kept him from something he wanted so badly." And he did want it badly. He knew that wanting it was part of what it took to make it, just like the pipeline, only this time he was being measured against the other best of the best, with a metric only the 24 selection committee knew.

John attended selection in the summer of 1995 and successfully assessed for assignment. Much of what is known regarding Delta and SEAL Team Six selection is based on previously released books by former unit members. The 24 selection process, while similar in many ways to its Army and Navy counterparts, remains a closely guarded trial of the human spirit. He came home and announced the great news to Val, who was thrilled to return to North Carolina, where they still had friends at the 21st STS and would be closer to family. Then she added news of her own...They would be bringing home a small piece of Japan when they returned. She was pregnant.

By October, the expectant couple was back in Fayetteville, happy for the overseas experience so many service members enjoy, and even happier to be home again. They bought a house and settled in for what they believed would be the rest of John's career. Valerie even returned to her previous job as an in-home nursing care provider as she awaited the birth of their first child.

Two new adventures lay ahead for them: their first child and John's assignment as he waited for Green Team to begin. For John, the first six months would be a return to the grind of passing another pipeline, only this one had higher stakes and risks but also offered compensation by virtue of the unequalled caliber of the men he was training with on Green Team.

Green Team was set to start in late January, and the couple spent the holidays reconnecting with old friends and making new acquaintances. For John, one particular CCT stood out: Pat Elko. Thin and athletic, the six-foot-two-inch first-term enlistee had little by way of experience but put in a strong showing at selection and was accepted into the unit. John took an immediate older-brother liking to Pat.

The early morning hours of 18 January 1996 were frigid in North Carolina, in a bone-chilling way that only the humid weather of the South can produce. John and Val were snuggled tightly in bed when John's newly issued beeper went off on the nightstand at 0516 with coded instructions to report to the unit immediately. When the newest members of the 24 arrived, they learned Green Team started *NOW*.

What followed was every kid's dream of what the military is supposed to be but in reality was reserved for a very select few who rose to the top of their professions in special operations. They seized airfields with Rangers in Louisiana and Georgia. They trained day and night on cross-country motorcycles, with NVGs and full combat loads. They had their first orientations to Delta and SEAL Team Six, the latter involving exposure and operations on the Navy's HSAC (high-speed assault craft), the offshore racing boats the SEALs used for attacking targets in the ocean and for launching operations on land. These kidney-damaging/brain-pounding boats were a source of either excitement or misery, depending on how well one handled the seasickness and physiological impact of boat operations. For Chapman, a water natural, the boats were exhilarating.

Advanced shooting instruction was provided by the Green Team instructors (seasoned CCT and PJs from the 24, including Jeff Bray, one of the unit's heroes from Somalia), augmented by contract civilians at the legendary Thunder Ranch and Y.O. Ranch in Texas (where John's team managed to drink the facility out of beer in the first two days of training). When they weren't on the road, the team spent time utilizing others' facilities, such as Delta's obstacle courses, located conveniently down the road from the 24.

As their training progressed, the men began the process of gelling as a team, meeting each other's wives, kids, girlfriends, or dogs, as the case may be, sharing beers and meals, and of course coming to rely on one another completely. Early on, Pat was adopted by John and Val. Pat, now an FBI agent in Dallas, recalls, "I can only guess the number of nights I spent there. John and Val were kind of like my parents away from parents, except we drank a lot of Miller Lite."

The team's next stop was HALO and HAHO (high-altitude/low-opening and /high-opening) training. Parachuting is a critical skill, and much time was spent in the air at a classified facility in the western US, as well as on the drop zones of Fort Bragg, and included day and night jumps from as high as 25,000 feet. The parachute training culminated in what one of John's Green Team instructors refers to as "a full-benefit, night, oxygen, ruck, and weapons HAHO jump." The men, looking to push the boundaries, "plotted the GPS and drop calculations to the maximum" over the desert, covering twelve miles under canopy to land within seventy-five yards of one another, taking their place as members of the military's best combat parachutists.

Amid the demands and the steep learning curve of an intense training regimen, on 13 May 1996, John and Valerie welcomed their first child, Madison Elizabeth Chapman. Valerie recalls the moment the three became a family. "The first time he held Madison, the spark in his eye was like nothing I'd seen before. It was like a kid in a candy store, he was so excited." While sharing the moment with his wife and receiving hearty congratulations from his new teammates, there was little time to revel in or reflect upon the profound change Madison's arrival would produce on the Combat Controller. Training and missions went on despite the other facets of life, and nothing could replace the absoluteness of contingency preparation and execution at the 24, so after a week off, John returned to training and his team.

In Fort Walton Beach, Florida, the team practiced scuba and low-signature rebreather diving insertions through the ocean surf, navigating with compass boards in the dark and honing skills necessary to work alongside their SEAL counterparts. There, they also practiced air-dropping rescue RAMZ (rigging alternate method Zodiac) boats into the ocean. These approximately three-foot cubed packages contained a rolled-up raiding-craft boat and motor, including fuel, and rucksacks with weapons, all in a single container. In the water, the boat would be inflated with compressed gas, getting the team underway toward a target or water crash site in less than five minutes.

For the CCT, no training was more important than close air support. They traveled to Fort Campbell to work with the 160th's helicopter gunships, F-16s and F-15s in Gila Bend in Arizona, and A-10s at Fort Leonard Wood in Missouri. Finally, on 29 July 1996, the men stood together and were welcomed into the most prestigious Air Force special operations unit as full-fledged brothers. Together, John and Pat went to Red Team (one of three colors, the others being Blue and Silver) to begin their new lives. In addition to their own specific training requirements—airstrikes, surveys of critical facilities and airfields—Red Team alternated training with Delta and SEAL Team Six.

Madison grew, and the family shared time when John was home. They settled into a rhythm revolving around his demanding job and travel schedule between exercises and training with the Army and Navy. By summer of 1997, Valerie was pregnant again. Nearly two years to the day after Madison was born, her younger sister arrived. Brianna Lynn Chapman was born 5 May 1998, completing the small family.

By the time Brianna turned one, John had turned another corner. The girls had come to be his life, and the allure of Delta Force and SEAL Team Six waned in the face of his new and true purpose. Recalls Val, "When he was home, he was home." He preferred bathing the girls and brushing their blond hair to beers and wrenching in the garage. "He could have killed five thousand people at work, and when he walked in the door, you'd never have known," reflects Valerie on how complete John's transformation was after the girls' arrival.

However, as he was psychologically moving in the opposite direction, John's first opportunity to execute a real mission appeared on the horizon of another frigid East Coast winter day in 1998 while working with SEAL Team Six. The Navy unit was deploying a force to the NATO-led stabilization force in Bosnia to hunt Yugoslavian war criminals, the latest incarnation of Delta's man hunting in Somalia five years earlier. Delta was also in the region, but this time the SEALs were getting their own shot at leading and executing a similar operation. John's SEAL element target was Goran Jelisić, a Bosnian Serb wanted for genocide and crimes against humanity. John's job was handling tactical communications for his entire team as it pursued its man on cobblestone streets in the small villages surrounding Tuzla, where Goran was believed to be housed. The SEALs and the Combat Controller arrived in the conflict-ravaged region in January, and while much of the detail of their operations remains classified, they captured the fugitive who'd vowed never to be taken alive and delivered him to the International Criminal Tribunal for the Former Yugoslavia. There, at his trial, he was acquitted of genocide charges but not of crimes against humanity. He was sentenced to forty years in prison and remanded to the Italians to serve out his term. There were other hunts and captures, and by April, John and the SEALs redeployed. In keeping with the sensitive nature of the operations, John never told Val where he'd been or what he'd done.

When John returned home to his family, he'd arrived at a decision. The window for getting on operations and gaining combat experience was closing. It was time to spend more time at home with his girls. He didn't want to hold out for another opportunity to get into combat; the only missions on the horizon appeared to be more of the same and, while exciting at times, they were more of a letdown than a validation. He left Red Team behind and joined the 24's survey team. Survey, as it was simply known, focused on comprehensive surveys of locations the 24's "customers" (Delta and other units or organizations) valued around the world. In Survey, John built on the basic airfield and drop-zone survey skills common to all Combat Controllers, adding AutoCAD computer drafting to his expertise. John found he liked the work as much as he appreciated the more predictable schedule for his blossoming family. Though not high-octane like being on Red Team, the survey team had its share of intense situations, placing men, often working alone, in precarious situations around the globe.

Meanwhile, Madison was growing fast, Brianna hot on her heels, as the family entered the new millennium. John, now well settled into the drafting and computer skills of his survey job, came home in the evenings to little ones awaiting his nightly entry. Inside, and much to Val's dismay, he often grabbed the girls up, bundled inside a blanket, and would toss them into the air, brushing the ceiling, to catch them again, then toss them, tiny arms flailing, onto the couch.

By September of 2001, the couple had devised a plan. While John's new computer and survey skills sharpened, his core counterterrorist skills and proficiency dulled as he made peace with the fact that there'd be no war to validate his military career. He contemplated the future after Combat Control.

John and Val had agreed he was only going to do twenty years, then use his drafting and survey skills to increase his salary in preparation for the girls' later schooling. They were already attending a costly private academy, supported by the income from Val's in-home nursing career, and the proud parents intended to continue providing the best academic preparation. Secretly, though, John harbored a dream of opening his own custom auto shop where he could create and wrench vehicles like the Cobra kit car he was building in his spare time. On the night of 10 September, he stood in his garage with a beer, looking at the project and wondering when he might finally get the time to finish the vehicle, still barely a frame, with an engine, drivetrain, and various parts scattered across his workbench and garage. The world was peaceful, his relationship with Val was strong, his girls were growing, and he accepted a future that didn't involve proving himself in combat as he'd once hoped. As things stood, John was just fine with that.

CHAPTER

5

—

11 September 2001

THE 23RD STS[4] SITS ON THE FAR SIDE OF HURLBURT FIELD'S RUNWAY, across from Headquarters Air Force Special Operations Command (AFSOC). The base, itself home of the majority of AFSOC's forces, is actually an auxiliary field of the giant Eglin Air Force Base and test range, thereby reducing Hurlburt's status from "base" to "field." Older maps identify it as Auxiliary Field #9 and show only a smattering of buildings, not the sprawling amoeba of compounds it is today. At the time of the founding of the original Air Commandos for use in Laos and Vietnam, it was the perfect location, tucked anonymously away in the swamps of the Florida Panhandle, hidden from prying eyes. The famous 1970 Son Tay POW rescue attempt was planned and rehearsed there for that very reason.

On the morning of 11 September 2001, the 23rd was planning to hold a squadron-wide "monster mash" physical endurance training event consisting of a series of unusual physical challenges in which teams competed against one another. Pedaling his bike from home to

---

4   The same unit that augmented the 24 for the Panama invasion.

the monster mash that clear summer morning was Calvin Markham, a sixteen-year master sergeant and CCT. Despite putting himself at an energy deficit disadvantage (monster mashes could go on as long as half a day, leaving participants depleted for several days, depending on which group of Combat Controllers planned them), he regularly rode in to work, regardless of the day's schedule.

A giant of a man with round features and a burly but friendly personality to match, Calvin kept a closely cropped haircut to de-emphasize a high hairline. Parking his bike near the entrance to the unit's team rooms, he walked in to jarring images blaring from the television in the corner. The first twin tower of the World Trade Center in New York City was heavily damaged, smoke billowing out in waves from the initial plane strike. By the time the second plane struck, the men of the 23rd were already packing: precision micro-wave airfield landing systems, combat search and rescue gear, radios, laser markers, and weapons. They knew what was coming.

Three weeks later, Calvin and a fellow CCT, along with a Special Tactics officer, were running an airfield called Karshi-Khanabad—known to all as K2—in Uzbekistan, where the US would begin staging in preparation for its first operations in Afghanistan. The three men were literally "First There" in establishing and operating the airbase for the US.

By the first week of October, the 5th Special Forces Group had planned to insert two Operational Detachment Alphas (ODAs or A-teams) as the first teams to link up with the allies' newest partners, the loosely organized and fractious Northern Alliance (in actuality several groups of differing tribes and leaders, some of whom would rather fight each other for local dominance than the Taliban). The two ODAs, each made up of between ten and twelve Green Berets with different specialties—such as weapons, communications, or medicine—were numbered 595 and 555, the latter known by the moniker "Triple Nickel." The first would strike out for Mazar-e Sharif, the other for Bagram Airfield, the abandoned Soviet airbase just north of the capital, Kabul, in the hope that it could be secured and readied for when US operations moved within Afghanistan's borders.

Each ODA was commanded by an Army captain and seconded by a chief warrant officer. Their missions were to establish contact with the Northern Alliance, determine the battlefield dynamics, and crucially, employ airpower to destroy the Taliban and Al Qaeda forces in northern Afghanistan. The two ODAs were responsible for separate locations and took radically different approaches in their planning and execution, which would have significant consequences in the coming weeks. Both ODAs were offered CCT to coordinate and apply airpower. ODA 595 rebuffed the offer. In the words of Combat Controller Bart Decker, "They didn't want anything to do with CCT." ODA 595's decision to exclude CCT would provide the definitive case study showcasing the difference between forces that had a Controller and those that did not.[5]

ODA 555, familiar with the expertise of Combat Control, recognized not only the value of a Controller but its necessity if they

---

5   The first two ODAs to enter Afghanistan went in the same night, but their initial effects through airpower could not have been more divergent. ODA 555, with Calvin Markham, put bombs on target beginning with his first strike, as outlined in this chapter. ODA 595 (the team featured in the Hollywood movie *12 Strong*), electing to go without a CCT, was so unsuccessful in airstrikes that the 5th Special Forces Group commander, Colonel John Mulholland, directed a CCT, Matt Lienhard, along with a Tactical Air Control Party (TACP), to be attached to them even though they were already in the field. According to Bart Decker, one of the "Horse Soldiers" in Doug Stanton's book of the same name and the man in the most circulated photo of their exploits, "They were 'yard-saleing' bombs all over the place." From his location with their field commander, Major Mark Mitchell, he helped coordinate Lienhard's insertion, recognizing that 595 needed the Controller if they were to succeed and not kill friendlies. "Major Mitchell was a smart commander and a great guy," recalls Decker. On 22 October the two airpower experts joined ODA 595. It was not an easy assignment. "Toughest job in the world is to try and integrate into an ODA that doesn't want you," adds Decker. But Lienhard and the TACP performed flawlessly, dividing themselves into separate 595 elements and calling numerous "danger close" airstrikes with surgical precision.

were to be successful in their third mission tasking. Green Berets are experts in aligning with, training, and fighting alongside indigenous forces, with a proud legacy founded in Southeast Asia. And while authorized to call in airstrikes, as indeed any soldier or sailor on the battlefield can, they were by no means experts, or even proficient.

ODA 555 was provided a list of available CCT and discussed the names internally. One name stood out—Calvin Markham. Calvin and one of the sergeants, Greg McCormick, had gone through the Special Forces combat diver course together as swim buddies and had remained in contact over the years. McCormick identified the Controller as "the guy," and the matter was settled. By the end of the first week of October, Calvin had moved into isolation with the team and began his own planning. ODA 555 was commanded by a captain, although the one actually in charge was the chief warrant officer, the most senior and experienced man on the team, David Diaz. Calvin had great respect for Diaz, stating, "He'd been in Afghanistan in the eighties, and he knew how the people thought. He was a great leader and was respected by all the guys."

Calvin's air plan, however, was hardly solid, which was a source of concern for the Controller. In the early days of the war, there were no Air Force air operations strike-planning cells. Instead, a few Controllers from the 23rd, the first Special Tactics squadron to arrive in-country, along with a handful of pilots and air planners, built the strike plan from scratch. Bart Decker and the others did their best to coordinate for the unknowns. Decker described it as merely "CAS [close air support] on call. There were no procedures. No one knew what was going to happen."

On 19 October, Calvin and ODA 555 were about to find out. After two attempts at clearing the 20,000-foot peaks of the Hindu Kush range in the midst of severe weather, the joint team finally skimmed the snow-covered terrain and passed into Afghanistan. His immediate boss, Special Tactics Officer Kurt Buller, had walked Calvin to the helicopter, telling him, "You're the first," adding, "I don't know if I envy you or I'm sending you to your death. This could very well be a suicide mission." Buller stayed on the helicopter as it taxied, to ensure there were no problems with the helo's movement, climbing off just before takeoff. The two men shook hands as Buller wished him happy hunting.

Because of the altitude, the men were piled into two separate special operations MH-47s that had been stripped of all armor and flew with the minimum fuel required to insert the team across the border. At their designated HLZs, both helos were offloaded without incident or enemy contact, then they left the men behind to pursue their perilous missions.

Calvin's team was met by a group from the Northern Alliance shortly thereafter and began the critical task of establishing mutual trust over tea and raisins offered by the Afghans. The entire group of several dozen mounted a convoy of old trucks and SUVs and headed into the Panjshir Valley. Even though the Taliban often attacked local villages, Calvin and the team made no enemy contact for the first two days. Instead, they focused their efforts on winning over the Northern Alliance leader, General Mohammad Qasim Fahim, a man whose distrust of the Americans and their reasons for being in his country ran deep. But there was one foolproof way they could demonstrate their commitment and value: airpower. Calvin recalls, "They were pretty skeptical of us. They'd been promised air before." The Afghan leaders had yet to see any of this mysteriously magical war-changing promise.

Calvin's chance to represent the entire might and commitment of the US came on 21 October, a bright and cold morning, when Chief Diaz sent a reconnaissance (recce) team to find the Northern Alliance front line. It was believed to be near the airfield at Bagram and under the command of an Afghan leader named Babajon, whose girth led to the natural Americanization of "General Papa John." The men clambered aboard a few trucks and drove south.

As the small recce team moved onto the north end of Bagram Airfield, the front turned out to be the airfield itself. They dismounted the vehicles and proceeded on foot. The Northern Alliance owned the former Soviet airbase only from midfield north; the Taliban held everything to the south. This World War I–style stalemate had existed for years despite fierce attempts by each party to dislodge the other. If Calvin could deliver airstrikes on the entrenched Taliban positions, he could single-handedly change the course of the stalemate, perhaps the war. As they moved cautiously across the flat terrain, dotted with leafless trees preparing for the coming winter, Diaz told Calvin, "Get where you can establish a good OP [observation post]. Hide in plain sight."

They crept close to the Taliban, and Calvin's observation post materialized before his eyes, the air traffic control tower. Who would expect the Americans to climb into the most obvious building on the airfield? Perfect! The men cautiously approached the structure and then cleared its rooms to ensure no Al Qaeda forces were waiting inside. By then it was late morning, the warmth of the sun a welcome respite from the cold. As Calvin and the team surveyed the airfield through binoculars and a spotting scope, he set about preparing the tools of the Combat Control trade. First were the SOFLAM laser target designator and rangefinder. Then he erected his SATCOM antenna and checked his communications link with the nascent Joint Special Operations Air Component. The JSOAC would be his source for air when he needed it. After he'd checked in, the Controller next began identifying targets he might be able to strike. With enemy lines blurred and only a few hundred meters from his location, the potential for fratricide was significant. The one thing he couldn't do: kill men from his own side. And apart from the few Green Berets with him (and their CIA interpreter, the only member of 555 who could communicate with the locals), he didn't know any of the friendlies or how to tell them apart from the Taliban. Everyone looked the same through binoculars or the spotting scope.

A short time later, the JSOAC called Calvin. "You've been approved for aircraft. Your first flight will arrive on station at noon." He checked his watch—less than an hour. Shit! Calvin hadn't even requested air yet, and now two F/A-18s launched from the USS *Theodore Roosevelt* were already inbound. Sprinting the seven hundred miles from the aircraft carrier's location in the North Arabian Sea, they were flown by two pilots anxious to get close-range kills directed by someone on the ground.

Calvin set one Green Beret on the SOFLAM to designate targets, while another manned his SATCOM radio. Calvin got on his primary strike radio. He carried two and, as usual, his CCT ruck weighed more than anyone else's on the mission. He was ready. The tension in the air traffic control tower was building, everyone sensed something big was about to happen...except Papa John. Recalls Calvin, "He was pretty skeptical. Thought we were just there for show. Then the first aircraft arrived."

Diaz had the target in the crosshairs of their spotting scope and asked Calvin, "Is that the target?"

Taking the handset from his ear and looking through the scope, he confirmed, "That's it." Then he cleared the aircraft "hot." "Thirty seconds," he told everyone in the tower.

The heavyset general bent forward and looked through the offered scope, but not before giving everyone in the room a final doubtful look. Seconds after he put his eye to the scope, the bunker Calvin had ID'd for his first target disappeared in a direct hit from two 500-pound bombs. The tower shook and General Papa John stood upright to look out the windows, which had long since been shot out of the tower cab, as if the spotting scope was playing tricks on him. Before him, the former Taliban headquarters bunker was a blackened smoking heap of earth and rubble, the smoke of the bombs still rising in the air.

Calvin had no time to enjoy the view. His next planes, F-14s also from the *Roosevelt*, were already checking in. Behind them, the first Air Force hunters, F-15 Strike Eagles and F-16 Falcons, were chomping at the bit, no doubt wishing their Navy brothers would clear out of the airspace.

The men in the tower watched the battle tone change across the airfield. Taliban positions were frantic. The CIA interpreter, now on the Taliban's frequency, passed himself off as one of their own, asking about damage. The response was immediate and alarmed: Their frontline leader had been killed. In the very first airstrike in the struggle for the Afghan capital, Calvin Markham, with the help of his team, had just killed the most important man in the battle. Papa John was elated at the prospect of so many dead Taliban and the ease with which it had happened.

Calvin "cleared hot" each plane in order, striking Taliban positions to within three hundred meters of their location, causing the men in the tower to take cover behind the flimsy walls of Soviet-quality construction as shrapnel and shock waves rocked the top floor. Not a single friendly fighter was injured during Calvin's first strikes of the war.

In a handful of strikes, these few Americans, led by the skill of one unique individual, broke a three-year Taliban stranglehold on the airfield. Papa John and the other leaders of the Northern Alliance were no longer skeptics. Calvin recalls, "The CIA guys couldn't get the CAS on target. When I got bombs on that first day, hitting C2 [command and control] and rocket sites, our credibility was immediate." And Calvin and the Triple Nickel were just warming up.

Their next mission was an eighteen-by-thirty-seven-mile target area in the Panjshir Valley, but a handful of fighter aircraft diverted at the last minute were not going to be enough to displace thousands of well-armed and armored Taliban. Calvin needed more air, and lots of it. To strike an entire valley, he needed bombers, but he'd also have to be close enough to differentiate friend from foe and adjust fire. Calvin and the Triple Nickel needed to be among the Northern Alliance fighters.

After pleading with the JSOAC for more air for a week, he finally got his wish. ODA 555 established three observation posts in the valley, and on 28 October, nine days after arriving in Afghanistan, Calvin received multiple B-1s and B-52s, fully laden with hundreds of 1,000- and 2,000-pound bombs.[6] Throughout the first week of November, "We broke the back of the Taliban," recalls Calvin. So many bombing runs took place nonstop that he began coordinating them to hit while he slept. He knew the valley better than any training range he'd called air onto back in the States and began to share the "cleared hot" burden with his teammates, who by then were becoming proficient in the art themselves.

By this time, the men of 555 and the Northern Alliance shared a strong bond, sleeping in the same locations, sharing both the MRE rations of the Americans and the local Afghan food, including slaughtered goats and sheep. Calvin would call in resupply drops, normally delivered by C-130s, to keep the team in ammunition, food, and other necessities, the most critical being batteries for his radios and targeting equipment. Unfortunately, it didn't always work out well for Calvin and 555. "This dumbshit colonel in Germany who was in charge of rigging our resupply didn't want to use her precious (and expensive) chutes." Instead she sent disposable high-speed versions, which blew up on opening at the high altitudes. "They burned in, sometimes costing us our entire resupply." The men in America's first major conflict since the Gulf War, it seemed, were not immune to the vagaries of the military's logisticians and bean counters.

---

6   A B-52 can carry as many as fifty-one 500-pound bombs and thirty 1,000-pounders distributed inside its cavernous bomb bay and slung from its wings. A B-1's payload (all of it internal) is 5,000 pounds more than the venerable 1950s-era B-52's, but it enjoys a sleeker design and a reputation for speed of delivery.

With no showers for more than two weeks, they'd begun to take on a most Northern Alliance ambience as well, but that didn't make them Afghans. The white Americans, using Northern Alliance vehicles to move about the country, were now being targeted by a reeling Taliban. To combat the possibility of assassination or ambush, Diaz began masking their intentions by coordinating vehicles for a certain destination and then changing it through their interpreter once they were rolling. But it would be only a matter of time before the Taliban countered the tactic and struck the men at one of their various camps.

The potential problem was solved by the Northern Alliance leaders, who were gaining confidence with each successful airstrike and were pushing to take Kabul. On 11 November, 555 was told the Afghan force was moving on the capital. The Triple Nickel wasn't prepared for, nor tasked with, such an audacious mission, but in the end there could be only one course of action. If the Afghans moved, they would too. "Higher [HQ] was so worried about us going into Kabul, but we really didn't have a choice. We were in [Northern Alliance] trucks, so where they went, we went," recalls Markham.

They weren't, in fact, the first Americans to approach Kabul. The CIA's Jawbreaker team, its first on the ground, was already on the edge of the capital and also armed with a 24 CCT. But the Triple Nickel *was* the first to bring airpower. Calvin realized his requirements were going to be immense, and his faith in a sluggish JSOAC request system, never strong, was diminishing. "It was a bit comical; someone thousands of miles away with no idea of the situation [on the ground] was deciding how much air I needed or would get." As with the Northern Alliance's push, he had little choice but to request "everything they had, especially bombers," in the hope the JSOAC would grasp the gravity of a full-on assault on the Taliban and give him what he needed.

An all-out battle was at hand, two sides facing off with all available men and weapons. "It was like *Braveheart*, with both sides lined up" as the battle formed, recalls Calvin. The two armies, no more than five hundred meters apart, prepped weapons, passed orders or encouragement for their men, and waited. Going into deliberate battle for the first time, 555 discarded their CIA-provided Afghan clothing and donned uniforms. They would not go into battle as anything but Americans. Calvin and a couple of 555 soldiers occupied a two-story building, repeating their Bagram strategy, and readied the Controller's equipment. Nearby, in another building, Diaz established a sniper's hide to provide protection for his men and the Combat Controller, enabling them to focus on turning the battle.

The Taliban, with no idea the ODA was there, were completely oblivious to the amount of destructive power inbound against them. At 0800 the morning after 555's arrival in Kabul, the Taliban opened fire on the Northern Alliance. In the hope of routing them, the Taliban fired everything they had prepped. "The exchange of fire was stunning. I'd never seen fire anything like it in my life," remembers the Combat Controller. The exchange went on for hours. Meanwhile, Calvin and his teammates were already calling in strikes as fast as they could. The aircraft arrived in droves, forcing the Controller to start stacking them in air traffic holding patterns at different altitudes, just as Bruce Barry had done a decade earlier in the remote desert of Iraq. Only this time, there was an entire battlefield surrounding the CCT, and the fates of thousands of men—friend and enemy alike—were in his hands.

At an insane pace, he scribbled call signs, payloads, and play times (the time a particular aircraft was available to remain on station). Bombers, fighters, Navy, Air Force, coalition—they kept coming as word of the significance of the battle spread. This forced the Combat Controller to employ innovative sequencing and use of aircraft. "I was putting B-52s in timed strike patterns. When they rolled in, my fighters were out and they could drop their bombs from thirty thousand feet. Once those bombs hit, my fighters were rolling in and putting bombs right on. It was like the B-52 was marking the target for them," he recalled in an interview.

After two hours of the most intense airstrikes of Calvin's life, the battle was still not turning in the Northern Alliance's favor. The Taliban, with superior numbers of men and equipment, now rolled on the friendlies with Soviet tanks and heavy antiaircraft weapons, aimed like rifles at allied positions, including the fire control building occupied by the Controller and his team. To protect the most valuable man on the battlefield, Northern Alliance troops were instructed to defend the American position. The battle was raging with hand-to-hand fighting at the base of the building, and Diaz's overwatch was insufficient to hold the enemy at bay.

"By the time of the [airfield] battle, whenever we were under threat, their mission was to keep us alive at all costs," Calvin recalls of their Afghan security force. While he continued focusing all his attention on receiving targets from his Green Beret spotters and laying down bomb strikes, below him, Northern Alliance soldiers were laying down their lives to protect his. Eighteen years after the battle, these nameless men remain close to his heart, their sacrifice not forgotten by the man whose job it was to liberate their comrades. "There's no greater respect in the world than someone who's willing to lay down their life for you in combat." Of the men who died for him he states simply, "They weren't the best equipped or trained. But they were men. I'll never forget them or the honorable way they died."

Despite the Afghan protection that allowed him to continue bringing airpower to bear, the tide was turning against the Northern Alliance. Thousands were already dead on both sides, but the Taliban's superior numbers were proving decisive. The Northern Alliance, including 555, for whom there would be no retreat without their selfless Afghan brothers-in-arms, was in danger of being overrun. Calvin could still see two thousand Taliban troops, supported by armored personnel carriers in addition to the tanks, staged for a final and massive push. Behind them, a second wave waited. He needed to take a game-changing gamble.

Overhead, he had another B-52 poised to strike, but this one was different. It was loaded with twenty-seven 2,000-pound bombs, which he intended to place within five hundred meters of his own position—from 30,000 feet. Unfortunately, none of the bombs were precision guided, but were merely "dumb" bombs, subject to winds and atmospheric disruptions through six miles of airspace without correction. Such a mission at home on the training ranges of Nellis AFB, Nevada, required a five-mile safety standoff distance.

With such a massive single delivery, if he was off with any of his multiple calculations (the coordinates, his position, the friendly locations—all derived from an inadequate and antiquated Soviet map), not only would the Northern Alliance lose the battle for Kabul but he and the rest of his team would be vaporized by his own hand.

The Combat Controller looked to his teammates. They looked back, poised behind their weapons and the targeting equipment, as a battle for survival was being waged one floor below them and across the fields to their front. Men were fighting and dying. The Americans stared for what felt like an hour but in reality was merely seconds, while everyone weighed the consequences. He asked his team, "Are you guys good with this? Are we going to do this?" To a man, all agreed.

He rechecked that his SST-181 radar beacon (the only device he had to mark their position for the bomber) was working, checked the strike coordinates a final time, and called in the airstrike.

After inputting the data at 30,000 feet, his aircraft traveling at nearly 500 mph toward the men's fate below, the pilot asked the Controller to confirm he wanted the strike placed immediately adjacent to their own position.

"I told him that if we didn't, we were going to be dead anyway."

Despite the desperation on the ground, the Controller waved the pilot off his first pass and sent the bomber around again, using the time to reconfirm every decimal.

When the plane reported inbound the second time, Calvin, gazing out upon the surreal scene before him, almost Hollywood in its drama, took another breath, keyed his black plastic handset, and stated clearly and calmly, "Cleared hot."

Seconds later came the pilot's reply: "Bombs away."

Bombs released at 30,000 feet take roughly one minute to fall to earth. Outside the strike building, thousands of warriors, committed to their opposing causes, continued to fight, oblivious to the gravity-delivered destruction headed their way. Through the Alliance lines, 555 sent the word, "Get down!"

Committed to a destiny of his own devising, Calvin looked up at the clear blue sky, so deceptively serene, and at the B-52 high overhead as it left four contrails from its eight turbofan jet engines, and thought of his family back home. He took a deep breath and hugged himself to the floor.

The strike was perfect: 54,000 pounds of explosive death detonated parallel to the remnants of the friendly line directly in front of them. Black smoke blossoms of dirt and fire, stretched out over a mile-long line, exploded into the air. Then the sound hit, concussion after concussion rocking everyone on the battlefield, stealing the breath from their lungs. Calvin's building buckled but stood. In slow motion, heavy pieces of armored carriers and tanks tumbled through the air, their landings silent as they were drowned out by the deafening roar of 2,000-pound bombs releasing their energy at an atomic 25,000 feet per second in every direction.

In the immediate silence that followed, itself strangely deafening, the line of huge craters, bordered by pieces of men and rifles and the hulks of armored equipment, revealed themselves to the stunned

Taliban and Northern Alliance witnesses. Beyond the destruction, the Taliban's second wave could be seen racing south in retreat.

The road to central Kabul was suddenly open, and within an hour of his battle-ending airstrike, Calvin and 555 were again in the back of Northern Alliance vehicles, riding into the city in a scene reminiscent of a liberated French town from the Second World War. Pockets of resistance remained, but the capital fell, and Calvin Markham arrived in the city at 0800 on 13 November. It was his twenty-sixth day of combat. What Pentagon planners believed would take more than six months was accomplished in less than a month by the commitment of a sometimes-fractious Northern Alliance and one Special Forces ODA with a lone Combat Controller. During the handful of days immediately following the insertion of ODA 555 and the other A-teams with CCT, the Northern Alliance's control of the country went from less than 15 percent to 50 percent.

In his Silver Star citation, Calvin Markham, the first Combat Controller to direct airstrikes in America's response to 9/11, is credited with directing dozens of airstrikes "involving over 175 sorties of both strategic [heavy bombers] and attack aircraft resulting in the elimination of approximately 450 enemy vehicles and over 3,500 enemy troops. [This] led to the eventual surrender of hundreds of Al Qaeda and Taliban ground forces" during his first mission, lasting forty-two dangerous and often desperate days. They would not be his last days of danger.

After the big battle, among the rubble of the formerly besieged Afghan capital, two friends met, CCT from different squadrons. They were dirty and disheveled, both having gone nearly a month without bathing. Their clothes were stiff with crusted sweat and dried mud, and their beards and hair were grungy as they hugged each other in brotherly fashion. Calvin was wrapping up his first mission. The other, a man named Joe O'Keefe, was a 24 operator and member of its Advance Force Operations team. Joe was the CIA's Jawbreaker

Combat Controller. Like Calvin, he'd snuck into the country weeks before, but with a four-man Agency team.

Calvin, having just delivered victory in the first major battle of the war but with severe frustrations over the way commanders and planners in the rear delivered everything from batteries to bombs, shared his experiences. "We brainstormed. How can we do this better?" says the burly CCT. As much as they were fighting the enemy, they were also fighting an Air Force bureaucracy, coordinating its air support through a rigid process stretching back to the 1970s of Laos and Vietnam. "There was no procedure for what we were doing. We were writing the books," he recalls.

———

Stateside, John Chapman wasn't writing the book on new airstrike procedures. He was trapped in the survey shop writing survey assessments and generating products for others to use in contingencies or war. And as in the Gulf War, he found himself sidelined. Only this time it was by choice; he'd chosen to move to surveys, and now the newest war, striking the United States from a clear blue sky two months before, had the entire focus of the US military, except himself it seemed.

———

In Bagram, Joe O'Keefe and Calvin Markham went their separate ways, knowing they were at the beginning of a long war with a bureaucracy both antiquated and constipated and an enemy well established and fanatical. Calvin headed to a well-deserved R & R. Joe was about to embark on another Combat Control first, this one in a place neither friend knew existed—a mountain cave complex a hundred miles east of Kabul on the Pakistan border. A place called Tora Bora.

CHAPTER

6

——

11 September 2001

COMBAT CONTROLLER JOE O'KEEFE WAS ON HIS MORNING SIX-MILE run around the flight line of Pope Air Force Base when a 24-STS four-wheeled Mule cargo buggy pulled up beside him. The driver shouted, "You better come back to the squadron. Now!" He hopped in and returned to the 24 inside the JSOC compound to find the first World Trade Center tower smoking on television, and he knew he was going—where, was difficult to say. Joe, an eighteen-year veteran CCT, was part of a pilot team of Controllers working with Delta Force on advanced force operations (known as AFO), in essence troops who would arrive before anyone else in sensitive or hostile areas. So wherever he was headed, Joe was guaranteed to be at the farthest edge of America's response.

A short time later, he was on his way to Uzbekistan with a fellow AFO team member by the name of Mario. The two men were to be CCT's forwardmost element, chopped to the CIA's Jawbreaker team (responsible for the Agency's response to 9/11 in Afghanistan). At a stopover in Germany, they and their Delta counterparts split into separate teams: The first, with Mario, went to Pakistan; Joe and his Delta teammate, a sergeant major named Dan, were joined by a CIA case officer and paramilitary contractor and deployed to Afghanistan as a four-man team, designated Jawbreaker Team Juliet.

From Uzbekistan the men, all wearing indigenous civilian clothing provided by the CIA, caught a flight to Tajikistan, where Joe was introduced to Gary Berntsen, the CIA's lead case officer for Afghanistan and its hunt for Osama bin Laden. The next stop was Kabul, where Calvin Markham and the Triple Nickel were already targeting and destroying Taliban forces. The team flew in a dilapidated Soviet-era Northern Alliance Mi-8 helicopter, skimming just over the Hindu Kush mountains already flush with snow on their 20,000-foot peaks. Below him, Joe watched the ghosts and relics of the Soviet invasion slip past the windows: rusted tank hulks and armored personnel carriers—here and there, artillery pieces and small villages. The steep lunar landscape and abandoned equipment shared an eerie resemblance to the secret test ranges on which he'd trained north of Nellis Air Force Base, Nevada.

When they landed at Kabul, which had yet to fall to Calvin Markham and the Green Berets, they staged for their first mission: the rescue of eight Shelter Now International aid workers, two of whom were American. But at the last minute, the rescue was passed to another group. The situation in the capital was fluid and dangerous. As the only CCT attached to the CIA in Kabul, Joe was tasked with landing the first coalition plane at the former Soviet airbase, Bagram Airfield, in support of the Agency, even though it was still a no-man's-land. He drew on his eighteen years of experience to bring in aircraft. "Then I got orders to land an Iranian plane." The Iranian government wanted their embassy up and running as soon as possible to counter the American influence but refused to participate in multinational actions or assist the Afghans. As he worked his first days at the airfield, much was in motion but little was known. "There were a lot of things passing in the night," he recalls. At

Bagram, Berntsen approached Joe one day and asked, "Can you help me out?" The CIA case officer, and now station chief for the newest CIA base, had two-foot aviator kit bags stuffed with cash and wanted Joe to manage them—millions of dollars that the Controller dutifully lugged around for weeks, doling out and recording hundreds of thousands of dollars in transactions. "Berntsen was great," he recalls of the legendary case officer. "He had complete faith in us, and we were fully included in all planning and intel, including cable traffic [the CIA's classified communiqués]."

By mid-November, the early gains in Kabul by Markham and the follow-on forces were coming apart as factions and nations staked out turf and foreign policy by force. Joe and Delta Dan helped to establish the CIA's base of operations in a Kabul hotel, where the Agency was holding its first captured Arab Al Qaeda fighters. Under interrogation, they revealed bin Laden was at Tora Bora. Joe recalls, "We're trying to figure it out. What's a Tora Bora?" No one had heard of it. Berntsen told Joe's team, "We're pushing forward to the Panjshir Valley," north of Kabul.

Before they departed the hotel, Joe met up with Markham. "It was invaluable. Calvin gave me the lay of the land, pointed out details of the Tora Bora region and Jalalabad." A CIA safe house at the latter was their next stop and became the staging base for operations to find bin Laden in Tora Bora. There, Joe met George, the CIA's forward station chief. Also working in the vicinity was a 5th Group ODA with a CCT friend of Joe's, Bill White. The CIA wanted the Special Forces with Bill to move into Tora Bora and conduct airstrikes to kill or flush out the Al Qaeda leader.

At Bagram, Berntsen spoke with 5th Group commander Colonel Mulholland and requested that he send the ODA and White forward. Mulholland asked if the CIA had detailed information on the situation in Jalalabad.

"It's bad," admitted the CIA agent. "Nobody's really in control, and large groups of armed Taliban and [Al Qaeda] fighters are still creating havoc."

"Do you have a fixed location where you're going to set up?"

"No, I don't," he said, adding, "I'm not prepared to wait for security to improve. I'm going now." Berntsen, knowing any lock on bin Laden would be fleeting, was not going to miss perhaps his only opportunity to kill the terrorist.

Mulholland, an experienced Special Forces soldier, was aware how fast things could change; his first two ODAs with Markham and another CCT named Matt Lienhard were lucky to be alive. Gambling another entire team on the CIA's assessment of an uncontrolled battlefield was not a solid bet in what was shaping up to be a long war, and he declined to commit the ODA.

With Mulholland's refusal to commit, the CIA was stuck. Upon receiving the news at the safe house in Jalalabad, George turned to Joe and Delta Dan. "Don't you guys do this?" he asked. When Joe answered that yes, he could coordinate and call in airstrikes from anywhere, George stated, "Okay. Be prepared to move out as soon as it gets dark."

Joe and Dan exchanged looks, knowing their decision, while fully within their capabilities to execute, had committed them to a mission they knew little about. Joe quickly drew up a fire support plan. "I forwarded it up the food chain, and just like that, we were in. We four Americans were the first to arrive at Tora Bora." The date was 3 December.

But getting in wasn't just half the challenge, it was almost the fatal half. The four Americans were placed in the back of a covered truck and had cargo stacked on top of them to facilitate being smuggled into enemy territory. Bouncing through the night, they felt the truck stop at a checkpoint. Beyond their claustrophobic confines, an argument broke out between the ten or so Afghans ferrying them and the unknown checkpoint guards. It occurred to Joe at that moment that their lives were in the hands of CIA-purchased Afghans belonging to a warlord named Babrak. "We had AKs [AK-47s] and Afghan garb and hats, but we're, you know, *white*." If they were discovered, there'd be no doubt the four men were Americans. Luck, however, was on their side, as the situation calmed, and the team felt the truck finally lurch forward and continue on its way, eventually stopping where they unloaded. From there, they proceeded on foot alongside mules packed by their Afghan guides.

After walking several miles in the dark, they were introduced to a village chieftain, who was their next link forward but who was concerned the Americans would bring more of the bombs that had already decimated other villages. "I assured him we were there to ensure *no* bombs hit villages," states Joe.

The team told him they needed to move farther, but the chieftain was under orders not to let anything happen to the Americans, not so much for *their* well-being but because, as the Afghan currently responsible for their security and moving them forward, Babrak feared that if he lost "his" Americans, the CIA cash he was receiving would stop. So he refused to take them deeper into the White Mountains, where the locals knew bin Laden and hundreds of Al Qaeda had established a redoubt. The Americans insisted, however, and continued higher and deeper into the snow-covered slopes. They were deep inside Al Qaeda's lines, topping 11,000 feet in elevation but with no idea exactly where the concentrations of enemy forces were, or of bin Laden's location.

Joe recalls, "We're underequipped, not prepared to engage anyone. I've got an AK with three magazines. My gear space is taken up with my SOFLAM, laser rangefinder, and batteries." Though they were all overloaded, like virtually every CCT, Joe was carrying more weight than anyone else on his team.

After more punishing miles and some understandable paranoia, they arrived at a suitable observation point, facing the highest mountain peaks, and got their first good look at the enemy and what they were up against. Joe set up the SOFLAM and put Dan and one of the CIA agents in charge of turning it on and lasing the targets he'd call in. The other CIA agent, a former Delta Force member, surveyed the enemy positions in front of them and determined their first target while Joe set out his radios and laser rangefinder, checked the equipment, reviewed his procedures, and made his first call to an AWACS, an airborne battlefield platform expressly designed to coordinate complex air situations. The AWACS aircraft circled above the battle space as Joe told them where he was and that he needed strike aircraft. There was no higher headquarters or clearance for the small team; they'd been empowered, not by the military but the Central Intelligence Agency, to execute their mission at their own discretion. It may have been a CIA mission, but Joe was now in charge.

The AWACS sent his first aircraft, a two-ship formation of F-14s with GBU-10s (laser-guided 2,000-pound bombs). "My heart was pounding. I can see the AQ [Al Qaeda] guys right out in front of us." Joe waited for the planes to arrive, and because the F-14s can self-lase, there was no need for the team to turn on the SOFLAM on the first strike. When the Navy fighters reported in, "I cleared them hot and the bomb dropped right in the position."

As two thousand pounds of mixed TNT and aluminum powder (a heat impulse enhancer) tritonal explosive obliterated an unaware enemy bunker, and the roiling smoke and telltale mushroom of the explosion and its shock wave reverberated throughout the confined valley in front of them, the four men looked at each other and nodded. Joe O'Keefe had just opened the personal war on Osama bin Laden (within the military he was known by the acronym UBL). He reattacked immediately with additional AWACS-provided fighters, and the team, working together with Dan on the SOFLAM, cleared the immediate vicinity surrounding their first target, creating a one-kilometer clear free-fire zone from which they could operate.

Their CIA lead agent called back to George, who was working from a location between the team and their safe house in Jalalabad, and reported their intent to bound forward into the airpower-cleared space.

George, himself former military, was elated and told the men, "Great news. Listen, this is being briefed at the White House and they're really interested in this. I want you to keep moving forward."

However, not only were the men and their Afghan guides not armed for a gunfight, they weren't equipped to operate unsupported in the frozen mountains. Of their supplies, Joe recalls, "I had a one-quart Nalgene water bottle, one MRE, and only a couple spare batteries. We were only supposed to be out for one night. But okay, we're doing it." The men continued their 11,000-foot march through the frigid mountains, aware that each ridgeline they crossed could hold dozens, if not hundreds, of Al Qaeda. Each step was one snowy footfall from death.

At their next OP, as they set up their position, Joe had the other men sketch targets and work up the data to support airstrikes while he drew up a terrain map of the mountains and enemy in front of them. They'd managed to take the high ground and were looking down on a hornet's nest of activity. When one of the Agency guys passed him a sketch and coordinates to their own location, Joe was confronted with a reality about his situation as the lone CCT. "I realized I couldn't go to bed. I couldn't leave them alone to call strikes unsupervised." It was his responsibility to ensure no friendly-fire incidents occurred and that their own position was safe. Should he fail in this single task, the burden of failure wouldn't rest on any other man's conscience. Joe stayed awake for the next forty-five hours, without break, calling every airstrike while the team around him fed him coordinates and battlefield information.

Joe and the team didn't know that the first fratricide of the war had just taken place, and an immediate halt to precision JDAM

(Joint Direct Attack Munition, the ubiquitous laser-guided bomb) employment had been directed, with one exception: call sign VB2, Joe O'Keefe. As a result, every aircraft loaded with weapons in Afghanistan or on its way was now being pushed to the Combat Controller.

It is in this type of situation that a Combat Controller and all others certified to call airstrikes diverge. Joe explains: "I had so many aircraft thrown at me, I started stacking them in two-thousand-foot increments using standard non-radar air traffic control procedures. All of them dissimilar. I had B-1s, B-52s, F-16s, F-15s, F/A-18 Hornets. It was endless, really." The planes would check in with the AWACS, who forwarded all of them to Joe. As it had with Calvin Markham, and as it would over and over again throughout the new war, it was the expertise of a Combat Controller that drove the mission's success.

The situation was incredibly complex—he had his headset on, listening to the AWACS in one ear and controlling airstrikes and managing an international coalition airport above his head in the other, keying the mikes on his two radios, one after the other. His map border and notepads filled up with call signs, aircraft types, and bomb loads. He became the most popular man with every pilot in-country. As each plane checked in with the AWACS, Joe could hear them requesting, "I want to go to Victor Bravo Two," because they knew they'd get to strike right at the heart of Al Qaeda, even if they weren't aware that Joe was trying to kill bin Laden himself.

That's when things really got exciting and exhausting for the Controller. He began a nonstop, around-the-clock bombing campaign that went on for days. Without sleep, through the below-freezing nights, without food, Joe bombed Al Qaeda. Two days into the onslaught, his Agency team leader called back to Berntsen and stated, "We're going to shut down now and catch some sleep."

The relentless CIA officer, who viewed himself as the long arm of American retribution, was incredulous. "What? What the hell do you want to sleep for? You're killing the enemy!"

"Chief, I'm sorry. But we've been doing this for fifty-six hours straight. Before that, we had to hump up here. We're wiped out." The men had bounded forward four times, deeper into Al Qaeda–held territory than any American force. Yet they were still only four men.

From the comfort of CIA station Kabul, Berntsen realized he couldn't appreciate the pressures or conditions the men were facing. "I'm sorry. Get some rest. Help's on the way. We'll have an SF [Special Forces] team there in less than forty-eight hours."

"That's great news. We'll be back up on the air in six hours. Juliet Forward out." The team was so played out they were unaware of the approach of the village chieftain they'd met days earlier. Their security, provided by Babrak, had quit two days prior, leaving the Americans entirely alone. The chieftain, clad in sandals and Afghan "man jammies" (the ubiquitous outfit worn by Afghan and Arab males that to Westerners resembles a calf-length dress), walked up on their position in the snow without warning. His purpose? Having watched the utter destruction of the mountainous valley during a continuous inferno of smoke and earth-shaking explosions, one after another, he had traveled to thank the Americans for killing the Arabs. "If he'd been Al Qaeda, we'd all have been dead," recalls Joe, adding, "If [Al Qaeda] had even sent out patrols to find out how the Americans were targeting them, we'd have been wiped out." But Al Qaeda never caught on to how the new game was being played.

The other team was the ODA provided by Colonel Mulholland, with CCT Bill White attached, now in position on a ridge on the opposite side of the valley from Joe. After a single six-hour break, Joe and the team stayed up sixty-five of the next seventy-two hours, moving ever closer toward the most hardened Al Qaeda fighters and their leader. When Bill showed up with the Green Berets and occupied a location across the valley from Joe, the two Controllers began coordinating from their different OPs, dividing the terrain and aircraft to keep the pressure on. Because Al Qaeda was communicating on open radio frequencies, CIA SIGINT collectors were getting real-time intelligence on the impact the airstrikes were having. "We're getting B-52s dropping forty-five Mk-82 [500-pound unguided] bombs in a single pass. All this within a couple kilometer square. It was unbelievable."

From 3 to 8 December, Joe O'Keefe, a single CCT, controlled and cleared 688,000 pounds of bombs in the Milawa Valley of the White Mountains, a record that still stands for tonnage dropped by a single CCT, or anyone else, during an engagement in the history of airborne warfare. The exhausted men, out of food, out of batteries, were exfilled by the CIA on the eighth and returned to the Jalalabad safe house, knowing they'd killed hundreds of hardened fighters, but not having destroyed bin Laden. The CIA had pinpointed the Al Qaeda leader's transmitter only 1.8 kilometers in front of VB2, but that was as close as the ill-equipped team got. "I was spent. No food, no water. But it was adrenaline city," recalled the first CCT to directly target UBL. He would not be the last.

More help was at hand. Delta Force had been forwarded by JSOC commander Dell Dailey to enter the fight and kill bin Laden. Forty Delta operators, led by a young officer by the name of Tom Greer and accompanied by Mike Stockdale, a 24 CCT and teammate of O'Keefe's, arrived as the Jawbreaker team pulled out.[7]

---

7   Stockdale is known as "the Admiral" inside Delta Force for his name's resemblance to the Vietnam naval Medal of Honor recipient's. All Delta Force operators use a personalized call sign to identify themselves. Tom Greer, the team leader, was Redfly and would go on to write the story of Delta's and Stockdale's Tora Bora mission in the book *Kill Bin Laden* under the pseudonym Dalton Fury. The Delta A Squadron sergeant major also there to lead the mission was a man whose inexhaustible courage, resilience, and leadership on the Tora Bora mission remain legend in Delta. His Delta call sign: Ironhead. The names are bestowed by group consensus and not chosen by the individual.

Mike Stockdale was relatively junior at the 24 in the fall of 2001. A Denver native, he'd graduated from the 24's Green Team in 1998. Unlike O'Keefe, he'd been in Hungary on a JSOC exercise at the time of 9/11. After returning home with the majority of the command's staff and operational units, he'd quick-turned and found himself on strip alert as part of a CSAR (combat search and rescue) package in Turkey, where nothing exciting happened. He got his break when Delta's A Squadron needed another CCT and he found himself on an MC-130 Talon to Bagram, where he met up with A Squadron's sergeant major, Ironhead, and his new immediate commander, Tom Greer, known by all as Redfly.

Tall, thin, with weathered eyes, brown hair, and an easy disposition, Mike already had a reputation as unflappable inside Delta, but this was his first opportunity to go to war with them. He was met by another CCT, Sean Gleffe, who outranked him, but when Greer pushed farther north to Jalalabad with his forty-man contingent, and from there to George's forward-staged Jawbreaker position, Gleffe gave the mission to Stockdale, telling him, "We got Al Qaeda and UBL up there. Get airpower on it."

As Stockdale arrived in the vicinity of Tora Bora, he watched the drop of a BLU-82 15,000-pound bomb, affectionately called the Daisy Cutter. The size of a VW van and of similar shape, the bomb was dropped by an MC-130 Talon, extracted by a parachute that gently delivers it to its target. The resulting mushroom cloud resembled an atomic bomb's. Along with the Delta operators, friendly "muhj" forces (the term Delta used for friendly Afghan forces), and Al Qaeda fighters in Tora Bora, he was stopped—stunned—by the immense, singular display of firepower. The bomb was a parting gift to bin Laden from Joe O'Keefe.

George, still running the overall battle for the American side, was pushing local warlord General Hazrat Ali to get his forces into the fight and planned to use Delta as the catalyst. Redfly and Ironhead had prepped their shooters and CCT as the sun set and the temperature dropped. They were to move out for a mission, planned to last several days, beginning in the wee hours of the coming morning.

With a hundred-pound rucksack full of radios and batteries, his SOFLAM and laser rangefinder prepped for the mission, Stockdale finally lay down, hoping to get a few hours' sleep before they departed, ready for what was to come: his first battle. He'd just nodded off when a Delta operator shook him awake. "They need you." He found his immediate boss, a Delta sniper and recce team leader called Hopper, who told him, "The muhj are saying they've got momentum to break through the AQ lines, but they're stalled out on the mountainside. They need air support."

Stockdale nodded. "Got it."

"We're gonna go fast, go light, and go now."

"Got it," repeated the Combat Controller. In his corner of the CIA's forwardmost safe house, an abandoned schoolhouse, he stripped his "go" ruck (a mini backpack) from his hundred-pound recce ruck. He stuffed in a radio, a few batteries, his IZLID IR pointer, and some water. They were only going to be out for a short time. He rolled up his SOFLAM, too big for the "go" ruck, inside a threadbare wool blanket and carried it by hand. Their team would be Hopper, Stockdale, an Afghan driver for the Toyota Hilux pickup, and Khan, one of George's CIA men, a former Afghan national and Marine who had been forwarded to Berntsen and George by another government agency.

Stockdale's instructions were simple: (1) Make sense of the battlefield, and (2) support the assault to break through enemy lines with air support.

The four men climbed into one of the beat-up-looking Hiluxes. (Appearances were deceptive; in actuality, they were specially engineered trucks equipped with beefy suspensions and winches and were tuned for high altitude. They were intentionally made to look beat-up to avoid attention.) As they drove up into the mountains, it quickly became clear that the front lines were close. On the ridgelines above them, they saw muhj recoilless-rifle positions. As they wound their way up the single-track road toward the Milawa Valley, they started to receive sporadic Al Qaeda mortar fire, which didn't seem too bad until they rounded a corner and were confronted by a stuck Russian truck with a twin-barreled 27mm antiaircraft cannon mounted in the rear. In front of it was an ancient faded Soviet T-55 tank, attempting to pull it out. Hopper, the most experienced operator in the vehicle, immediately recognized the peril and wasted no time. "Let's get out of this truck and into some defilade. Now!" he shouted as the men scrambled into an adjacent deep-channeled ravine.

No sooner had they dropped behind some rocks than an 82mm mortar round landed right beside the Hilux, sending shrapnel shrieking over their heads and peppering the pickup. A group of muhj was squatting nearby when another round dropped among them, center mass, killing them all. When the Russian truck was pulled clear, "We jumped back in and were on our way, rounds still coming in, targeting us as we drove," recalls Stockdale.

At the next intersection, half a kilometer upslope, they found another disabled T-55, this one with two muhj cowering underneath. They skirted the tank and drove to where the road petered out. Their driver, motioning up a ridgeline, stayed in the cab. Clearly it would be by foot from this point. For Stockdale, it turned into a bit of a circus as they scrambled up a rock scree field in the dark, NVGs their only advantage, allowing them to make the climb. Above them, "We'd encounter one group of muhj, then be passed to another, all of them sort of taking possession of us. It was major confusion."

When they finally arrived at the military crest of a ridgeline—the name for the terrain just below summit, which allows for travel without fear of being silhouetted against the sky—and found some vantage over the fighting, he was stunned. The mountainsides and valley in front of him were strewn with the detritus of battle, uprooted trees, splintered and mangled. Joe O'Keefe had done his work well.

From their position, Stockdale could see three separate Al Qaeda DShK pits chewing up the muhj fighters. He and Hopper prepped his gear so he could get airstrikes onto the closest DShK. Within minutes, "the Admiral" had a pair of F-18s inbound from the USS *Carl Vinson*. With steep terrain and no ability to put a laser right on the DShK, it was going to have to be an old-school talk-on to the target, Laos style—the art of Combat Control. It was also Stockdale's first in combat. With the impossibly steep terrain and well-masked positions, any miscommunication or misinterpretation would result in a potentially catastrophic miss. Meanwhile, the evil green arc of DShK tracers continued to track and destroy the Afghan forces. Hopper watched Stockdale at work as he calmly talked the planes on and destroyed the first DShK position. "When the first DShK went down, it completely changed the dynamic, because it was really chewing up the forces."

The three men and their newest muhj "handlers" used the destruction to move farther forward onto the battlefield, against the desires of the Afghans, as Stockdale continued to call strikes. Into the day the battle raged. Stockdale recalls, "Those first planes are the only ones I remember," as strike after strike blurred together. Finally, night began to fall and he received great news: "I'm getting an AC-130. Now it's going to be 'game on.'" They were now among the muhj fighting positions, and the Afghans were launching RPGs wildly. "It was ringing the shit out of your bell. [Hopper] was doing his team leader thing, keeping down the chaos and the muhj under control so I could do my job." He had his SOFLAM set up and his IZLID pointer ready for the AC-130.

"It was the perfect situation," he recalls. "The gunship is going to be rolling in, Saxon [a British AWACS] is vectoring more air my way." His next set of strike aircraft were B-1s. But before they or the lumbering four-engine angel of death could establish themselves overhead, clouds descended rapidly in the high mountains, rolling down the mountainsides like avalanches. A storm was coming. "The pressure changes were so extreme my ears were popping," he remembers. With the storm inbound, gunship and B-1s were lost, and the men were forced to sit out the freezing weather.

The next day broke with new promise and renewed effort. Planes began pouring in and Stockdale was ready, calling strike after strike in the confined few kilometers of the most contested space in Afghanistan. The battle hit fever pitch. To the Delta operators, "The Admiral is one smooth talker on the radio," stated Greer in his book *Kill Bin Laden*. "Most important in this business was his willingness to risk everything for his fellow man, an unhealthy but common trait among Air Force Combat Controllers."

By that time, Stockdale, Hopper, and Khan had moved into the middle of the battle space, stunning the muhj fighters, protecting themselves as best they could behind the wall and destroyed structure of a shepherd's hut.

At George's schoolhouse, he received an eight-digit grid coordinate on bin Laden's location, putting the terrorist within a ten-meter spot on the earth, the first real fix on the world's most wanted man since the late 1990s, and he gave the information to Redfly (Greer). It was the opportunity all had been waiting for. Across the battlefield, as the other Delta forces tried to maneuver, they "listened to the Admiral steadily bringing in the bombers while the distinct sound of gunfire muffled some of his calls. Just listening raised goose bumps on Jester's [another Delta team leader] arms," reported Greer.

The Admiral had just emptied nine F-18s and a B-1. "He had no idea that he was likely the primary reason that bin Laden, the most wanted man in the world, was on the run." His own position was under extreme enemy counterfire, forcing him to make his calls with his head pressed into the battle-mulched earth. An intercept from the enemy confirmed that "Father [bin Laden] is trying to break through the siege line." Listening in with Ironhead, Greer knew the three-man team was in a perilous position.

Hopper told Stockdale and Khan they'd done all they could and needed to move back. The enemy had a bead on the exposed American team, and the three battle-formed friends suddenly realized their muhj handlers were missing. They'd abandoned Stockdale, Hopper, and Khan. Only three muhj had remained, and the six of them were trapped, pinned down. In their exposed and lone position in front of the friendly lines, Hopper knew their situation was untenable. They couldn't fight on their own, and to stay would be to wait for death. In the fluid dynamics of a pitched battle, they were no longer forward of the friendly lines, but deep inside Al Qaeda territory. They were going to have to escape and evade (E&E) death, or even worse, capture. Stockdale, wrapping his SOFLAM back into his hobo blanket, ever the calm voice, made the radio call announcing friendlies were on the run for their lives. "Warpath. Warpath. Warpath."

As the three began winding their way through no-man's-land, friendly fire stretching out over their heads at Al Qaeda positions, and the enemy returning it, the bombs stopped while Stockdale was off the radio. There was still another CCT, Bill White, in the mountains with the Special Forces, but since no one knew where the three men were, restarting airstrikes was out of the question. Greer and Ironhead were left with a choice: Continue to pound a fleeing bin Laden or throw every man they had at recovering the E&Eing men. Greer's orders had been clear: "Kill bin Laden" and bring back proof. If the risks and costs of such a task were low, it wouldn't be a Delta mission, but the choice was not made lightly. As Greer pondered his options, Ironhead stated, "Your call, sir, but whatever we do, I don't think we should leave here until we have our boys back."

Greer certainly agreed they must eventually recover the men, but

UBL just might be killed within the next few hours. He pondered an eternity of a minute before saying, "We need to concentrate on recovering our boys first. If things change between now and then, we'll go for bin Laden too." He would recall that the decision was simultaneously the hardest and easiest of his career.

The full force of all available Delta operators, along with Controller Sean Gleffe, tried to wind its way through the mortars of Al Qaeda. There was a very real chance that Al Qaeda, with hundreds of well-armed and mortar- and rocket-supported men, could mount a serious counterattack, especially given that their leader was still somewhere in the caves and cliffs of Tora Bora.

Stockdale, Hopper, and Khan, crawling and evading across bomb-cratered earth, managed to make it through two kilometers of enemy-held territory over the next two hours, gratefully arriving at the abandoned friendly T-55 tank...only to find it was no longer quite so friendly. The muhj of General Ali they'd been supporting and risking their lives for, some of the very men who'd abandoned them, were now managing it as a checkpoint and wanted payment for the Americans to pass through. A furious Khan held back his anger and promised Ali would pay them later. The tribal custom of bribery was common, but a pissed-off Khan neglected to tell Ali that any money was owed. While Khan was negotiating their "safe" passage, Stockdale took the opportunity to get on the radio and contact Greer, who was elated to learn he hadn't lost any men in the battle, yet.

Safely back at the schoolhouse, Stockdale and Hopper rearmed and refitted. This time, Delta was going out in force. Augmented by British SBS troopers, the new plan was Delta on each flank, with their CCT on the high ground for airstrikes, and SBS up the middle. But a cease-fire was under negotiation between Ali and the other warlords and Al Qaeda, bringing offensive operations to a temporary halt. Greer was under strict orders not to spearhead any assaults on bin Laden's position, only to facilitate muhj advances and remain close behind. The lone exception was airstrikes. Combat Control would remain Delta's only direct shot at killing the terrorist.

When operations were resumed, a wily bin Laden had already safely escaped. Airstrikes and Delta patrols went on for days, with both Stockdale and Gleffe on the radio, but UBL was gone. Of Stockdale's performance, Ironhead would recall, "During the Battle of Tora Bora he proved his mettle. He and [Hopper] were separated from the rest of the squadron behind enemy lines. Stockdale took the entire episode in stride and got right back in the fight."

Ironhead's sentiments are representative of the strong relationship between CCT and the other best units within black SOF, particularly Delta and SEAL Team Six. To men like Greer and Ironhead (who would go on to become the sergeant major of the entire Ranger Regiment before retirement), their Combat Controllers weren't some "attachment," some "other," but respected members of the Unit (as members refer to Delta) with expert skill sets of their own. In *Kill Bin Laden*, both Stockdale and Gleffe are simply listed as part of "The Boys of Delta" in the book's list of key characters.

Stockdale's view of the events was summarized humbly as, "I basically jumped out of the back of a truck, running from Afghan to Afghan, trying to figure out where the war was." But he discovered that the war went where he did, and wherever that was, he had the power to change the course of history through the handset of his radio.

CHAPTER

7

—

October 2001

FOR THE 24 STS, 9/11 CREATED A SHARED SENSE OF PURPOSE AND DESTINY unlike any in the unit's history. The Combat Controllers knew there were going to be opportunities to kill terrorists, some they'd been tracking for years and others, the perpetrators of the assault on their homeland, no doubt unknowns, who were in the offing for the first time. The unit was the sharpest point of the special operations blade, and anticipation of what was to come coursed through the hallways of the building like surges of adrenaline.

For John Chapman, the weeks immediately following the attacks were the antithesis of adrenaline fueled. Being on the survey team was interesting and intellectually stimulating, but it came at an opportunity cost. John was no longer trained and poised for no-notice contingency operations with the most elite Army and Navy units in the military. The trade-off had been worth it—more predictable travel schedules, time with Val and the girls—until now. He watched from his computer station as his teammates packed, planned, and then left with the first waves. Some snuck into country even before ODAs 555 and 595. Others, into Pakistan to conduct the first combat

HALO parachute infiltration since the Vietnam War. And there he sat, on the sidelines. Again.

He was torn between the plans he and Val had for their family's postmilitary future and his primal urge to avenge the thousands of deaths on American soil. The decision came to him. The unit had largely emptied out with the first wave, and due to needing to keep a portion of the unit on alert in the event of a crisis elsewhere in the world, those not assigned to Delta or SEAL Team Six were at least getting their chance to be on deck. Still, it wasn't the war.

By October, John was in Virginia Beach and attached to SEAL Team Six's Red Team sniper element, a team he liked, having worked with them before as part of the alert force. The element was led by a humble and wiry SEAL named Britt Slabinski, known as Slab. He was topped by a thatch of sandy brown hair and had a quiet competence that belied a fierce drive to prosecute his mission. John quickly re-integrated into the team and settled into the alert routine—PT in the mornings, afternoons on the rifle range, or executing more complex scenarios at night—yet it was still mostly a Monday-through-Friday affair, punctuated by reports filtering back from the front lines as the war unfolded.

Tora Bora held everyone's attention, and the SEALs were envious that Delta might get UBL until word came back he'd slipped away. Perhaps Six would finally get their chance at the terrorist leader later and possibly dispel a bit of the second-class-citizen legacy that haunted the unit when compared to Delta Force. Then came word—John, along with Slab's team, would be deploying to Afghanistan in January. What he'd suffered and trained for was at hand, yet it still gave him pause. He wanted so much for his girls—to prepare for life after the military, only a few years away—but he also hadn't lost his desire to join his brothers and finally validate himself in the crucible of combat. In the end, the choice wasn't his; the 24 needed him to go, and he was going. Christmas came and went as John enjoyed what time he could with the girls, who'd come to stay with him in his temporary rented Virginia Beach apartment. Their time together was all too short.

Then, with the New Year came news that John's paternal grandmother had passed away suddenly on 4 January. John was faced with another choice: Deploy, or travel to Michigan to support his family, particularly his dad, Gene. It wasn't a difficult choice; family came first, and if you could help, that's what you did. It would put the 24 in a bind—someone would have to replace him at the Beach, and they were stretched to the breaking point already—but he told his team leader he needed to go back to Bragg. They'd have to send another Controller north.

Combat Controller Mike Lamonica was dispatched to deliver John's replacement and his gear to Virginia Beach and bring John back to Bragg so he could process emergency leave paperwork before catching a flight to Grand Rapids, the closest city to Gene's home. He recalls the drive back, just the two of them, friends but not close, as if it were yesterday. It was a clear but cold and windy four-hour drive, and John did most of the talking, centered on the one thing foremost on his mind... not his grandmother, not even the war, but his own family. For Lamonica it was an intimate and largely one-sided conversation.

"He had a lot on his mind, and I mostly listened," as "Chappy" (his nickname from high school and throughout CCT) recalled his time with Val at Kadena Air Base, where they lived on a quiet cul-de-sac, sitting with other parents, watching their children play. He spoke of how he and Val approached raising the girls as a team. John contrasted his approach with that of many other Combat Controllers, who viewed family as something that came second to missions or career, and how it wasn't until Madison and Brianna were born that he recognized the error of that approach.

"My job now is to serve my country, but there's a greater thing than that. When this war is over, I'm going to dedicate myself to my family," John declared.

"You could see the profoundness of the words he was sharing," Lamonica remembers. "It was intensely personal to him, and it was clear that he and Val loved each other deeply and had discussed those plans as partners."

When asked his opinion on John, Lamonica adds, "He was rebellious against authority, but that doesn't make him unique in CCT. What really stood out was his humanity and the way he approached family." He paused in thought. "It was the last time I ever saw him."

After his grandmother's funeral, John returned to Fort Bragg and the 24, and learned that Slab's team hadn't deployed after all—not yet—but the Combat Control position now rightfully belonged to his replacement. John felt like history was repeating itself, and his opportunity to get into the war was somehow slipping away.

There was one man who could return John to Slab's team so he could join the war. Lieutenant Colonel Ken Rodriguez was the commander of the 24 and had deployed with the first waves in October, spending the next three months in theater with his forces. Recalling the early days of the war, he said, "It was groundbreaking and historic for all . . . but especially the Special Tactics community: airfield seizures, multiple static-line and HALO missions, daring assaults. [But] back home, the guys were fit to be tied and itching to join the fray."

In January of 2002 he was back at the unit and plowing through the backlog of never-ending paperwork that awaited every commander who dared leave the office, when John knocked on his door. They knew each other from their assignments to the 21st STS together, and

Rodriguez, happy for the excuse to break from performance reports, ushered him in.

As John sat in the chair opposite Rodriguez, he leveled a look at his boss and cut right to the chase. "Colonel, I need to know how soon I can deploy."

Rodriguez leaned back in his chair, considering the NCO and the situation. He knew the war wouldn't end anytime soon but could see the agitation on John's face. Attempting to placate, he replied, "Don't worry, you'll get your opportunity. This is not going to be a short war." John only became more frustrated. "For John, if you knew him, that was a flushed face and a certain intensity in the eyes," recalls Rodriguez. It wasn't the answer the Combat Controller wanted.

"RZ," he led off strongly, using Rodriguez's operating initials, "with all due respect, I should have gone last September. It's now been more than three months since this war began, and I'm still here with my thumb up my ass. I need to get over there *now*."

Rodriguez had never seen the normally calm and reserved Controller like this. "I don't think we were about to throw down," recalls Rodriguez, but the urgency and strain in Chapman were obvious. As he left Rodriguez's office, his determination was clear; the Controller was going back to the Beach, and to the war.

———

At the same time, halfway around the world, one of John's 24 teammates was having no problems getting into the war. Combat Controller Andy Martin was in Oman, the staging base for most of the operations going into Afghanistan. A native of San Diego, he was stocky, with a slight swarthiness to his complexion, rapidly receding dark hair, and a direct personality that was sometimes off-putting to those unfamiliar with him. He'd started his military career in a reserve Special Forces unit but joined the Air Force in 1988 expressly to become a Combat Controller, eventually finding his way to the 24. By December, Andy had already racked up two combat jumps: one with the 24 as they inserted by HALO to survey and run a night-time desert landing strip (the first since the Iranian rescue attempt at Desert One decades earlier), and another with SEAL Team Six. He had two more missions planned with other units when one of the 24 squadron operations officers informed him, "You're going to come back and link up with the [SEAL Team Six] Red Team snipers."

To Andy Martin, a man who wanted to hunt down and kill terrorists, "it's what I'd waited my entire life for, because I knew the Red Team snipers really well, and those guys were going to get it on." His early missions in the war were good, but he'd yet to kill a terrorist. The First Gulf War was fun, but there was no killing, and to Andy Martin, that was one thing he wanted to do before he died, and he knew the SEALs would see it the same way. Little did he know how apropos the axiom "Be careful what you wish for" would be to his desires. After a long flight home, and a short Christmas with his family, he headed to Virginia Beach to meet up with the SEALs and Chapman.

In Fayetteville, John was home after receiving confirmation that he was to join up with Andy and the two of them would deploy with Slab's team. He had only days left to spend with the three ladies in his life, so between preparing for war at work and packing at home, he made the most of them. John and Val treated his deployment as "nothing new." "I knew he was going on a mission," Valerie recalls matter-of-factly, "but he didn't give me any details. We were both used to it."

On his final morning at home, as he kissed Madison and Brianna goodbye, he spotted two of their pink hair ties. He picked them up, gently rubbing them between his calloused fingers, and tucked them into his breast pocket—tiny mementos to remind him of his little loves. Valerie drove him to the JSOC compound, dropping him at the gate. With a quick kiss and an "I'm out," he smiled and waved as he walked past JSOC's tight security. Her in-home nursing assignments were waiting, so she turned the car around and drove off. They were so used to him coming and going, and the hazards of CCT at the 24. "It was just business as usual for us. I didn't realize it was the last time I was going to see him."

At SEAL Team Six in the Red Team sniper section, it was anything *but* business as usual. Most of the men had yet to deploy, none having tasted battle in the manner they desired: to kill the terrorists responsible for 9/11 and their supporters, particularly the Taliban. The two CCT completed the team, giving them an even dozen men for the deployment.

For John, his desire to join the mission was tempered by the rust that had formed on his counterterrorist skill sets. He'd been on the survey team for two years, with only periodic combat training. Compounding the issue was his age; he was older (now approaching thirty-seven) than almost every other "shooter" on the team and was worried about his ability to keep up. It concerned him enough that he confided in Slab, who reassured him, "Don't worry, you'll do fine." But he also was conflicted by something else—as much as he needed this mission to validate his career, having two little girls at home who adored him had changed his perspective. Life was not about killing—except at the 24 and SEAL Team Six when you're getting ready to go to war.

The day finally came in late January. All their gear had been staged and transported to Naval Air Station Oceana to meet their waiting

C-17s. Like Viking longboats of a thousand years before, these air-crafts' purpose was to ferry them across the Atlantic to a savage land and battle.

The men gathered behind the sniper shop inside SEAL Team Six's compound. They were waiting, all of them dressed in anonymous gray Air Force flight suits, with small backpacks for the long flight. The late afternoon was cool but not cold enough for jackets, and there was only small talk among the team. As the blue Navy buses pulled up to take them to the plane, Slab gathered his men around him. "Look," he said, and all eyes turned to him, sensing he had some-thing more than flight movement schedules on his mind. "Things are going to happen on this trip. Number one—every one of you is going to kill somebody. Number two—you're all coming back alive."

For Andy Martin, anxious to get his first kill, it was the pregame speech he'd waited for. *Fuck yeah!* was his only thought. He scanned the men around him, some nodding, others wearing stoic looks, but all were in agreement, *Fuck yeah!* . . . until his eyes fell on John, his expression a cross between realization and dismay. "I think it was the first time the gravity of the situation hit him," he recalls. "To be told something like that by somebody you respect as a leader isn't to be taken lightly." Adds Andy, "When you're out of the game for a while, there's a cognitive dissonance of how things are. What we do. It's not that he wasn't capable. I just think it hit him pretty hard in the respect that it was 'game on.'"

The two men let the moment pass and never spoke of it. The bus doors opened, and the team climbed aboard, leaving America for their war.

CHAPTER

8

—

February 2002

WHEN THE SEALS AND THE TWO CONTROLLERS LANDED IN AFGHANISTAN, along with an entire SEAL Team Six command and control force structure, it was clear Bagram Airfield was no longer the battleground it had been just two months before. Transformed by the relentless might of the US military's logistical magicians, with what to the impoverished Afghans seemed like endless supplies and equipment, not to mention ceaseless airplanes, it now resembled a major commercial airport of the developed world.

The only real signs one was in Afghanistan were the desolate snowcapped mountains that surrounded the base, the bland low-slung architecture of the city, and the February winds rushing down from the Hindu Kush, slicing through heavy clothing and singeing exposed skin, promising frigid combat for the men offloading the C-17s fresh from Virginia Beach.

Operations were still ramping up in-country, and SEAL Team Six wasted no time getting in on the action. The snipers, along with Andy and John, moved into a tent city made of heavy vinyl with large heating and air-conditioning units plugged into the sides to combat the extreme temperatures. John stayed with Slab, while Andy was assigned to the number-two enlisted sniper leader, a SEAL known as Goody. Inside, the men made the most of their personal space: a cot and crates for storing kits or, for some lucky ones, unfinished pine shelves crafted from crates. Tent city living was old hat to the SEALs and Controllers, and little note was made about the living quarters. They were there to hunt men.

They soon planned their first safari: for the elusive Taliban founder, Mullah Omar (code name Objective Bear), a one-eyed former mujahideen and the de facto head of Afghanistan from the time of the Taliban's rise in the mid-'90s until the American invasion displaced him. He was rumored to be in the remote mountains of the Bamyan Province, northwest of Kabul, home of the giant cliff-carved Buddhas that would eventually be destroyed by Taliban forces. Intelligence from the CIA indicated he was holed up in a village, moving from one secure location to another.

The planned mission was to catch him in transit between his safe houses, using an eighty-man local partisan force for security and guidance through the mountainous terrain. For the operation, a six-man British Special Boat Service unit was to accompany the SEALs and CCT. The mission's call sign was Mako-30—Red sniper's standard. On 15 February, the nineteen Americans and Brits climbed aboard three 160th MH-47s for the hundred-mile flight to Bamyan. Slab and John, with a handful of SEALs, were on Chalk 1 (the first helicopter), the Brits Chalk 2, and Andy and Goody on the last chalk. A Special Tactics combat search and rescue (CSAR, pronounced "sea-sar") team was aboard Andy's helicopter. Led by a PJ named Keary Miller, it had CCT Gabe Brown as its airstrike and coordination wizard. The CSAR was not part of the mission; they were only there in the unlikely event of an aircraft crash or a call for medevac by other SOFs operating that evening. Keary Miller and Gabe Brown could not have known their destinies would converge with John

Chapman again on a mountain summit the name of which none of them had yet heard uttered—Takur Ghar.

On the LZ in the dark, the men quickly unloaded and stepped onto an anonymous valley floor high in the mountains next to a small mud-hut village. When the helicopters had departed, Slab and the SBS leader met with the local partisan leaders and discussed the situation. One thing was certain, the Afghans were not going to lead the Americans anywhere in the dark. "We ended up in a defensive posture, staying in a goat pen, waiting for sunrise so we could wrangle the partisan force," recalls Andy.

The sunrise brought a surprise. The Afghan partisans had brought donkeys to carry supplies and the Americans' rucksacks, because they were going to walk twenty-two kilometers to a position above the village where they claimed Omar was coordinating the Taliban's campaign. Andy and John looked dubiously at the donkeys. According to Andy, "They looked like German shepherds, they were that small. And we were laughing because we're thinking, 'Yeah right, these things are going to die under the loads we've got.'" Duly loaded by the expert Afghan mule wranglers, the hundred-man and donkey force set off for the distant target, trudging higher into the mountains on a narrow single-track footpath. Continues Andy, "Well, within about half an hour, those little donkey bastards were out of sight ahead of us." The men watched with varying degrees of dismay as they lost control and sight of their ammo, survival gear, and batteries.

The long day led into night as the force moved into assault position on ridgelines towering above another nondescript and nameless village—Omar's purported redoubt. Unfortunately the weather had moved back in, closing down visibility as darkness descended upon them. "The weather drops to zero-zero visibility, absolute dogshit for airplanes," remembers Andy. The partisans were telling Slab and the Brit leader that Omar was definitely in the village, but in the freezing mountain storm, the Afghans weren't willing to move forward, and the allies agreed to retreat to another nearby village and wait out the inclement weather.

Through their interpreter and the partisans, each of the Mako-30 elements was lodged with a separate local family—involuntarily. John and Slab went to one with a handful of SEALs, the Brits a second, and Andy with more SEALs to a third. "They'd never seen a Westerner before, and the only other foreigners they'd seen were Soviet troops. They were terrified," recalls Andy. Who could blame them? The Americans, vigilant to the very real possibility of an ambush, and suspicious of their reluctant "hosts," sent the men of the families out but kept watch on them. The partisans saw an opportunity and tried to push the women and children out as well, in order to stay inside where there was warmth. The heat source was minimal—no bigger than a coffee can—but heat nonetheless. When John saw what was happening, he stepped in. "No way. We are *not* putting women and children out in the cold. They stay. You go," he directed through the interpreter.

Pashtun hospitality demanded they feed and care for the dangerous-looking and heavily armed outsiders, so the family slaughtered goats and chickens, feeding the Americans significant portions of their winter stores. In return, Goody, Andy's SEAL team leader, tried to pay them in US dollars, but the family refused to accept the cash, even though they understood the value of American currency. The villagers slowly came to realize that the men were no threat and cautiously accepted them, in large part because of John's good nature. Slab would later state, "John's demeanor put them at ease, and I fully believe that helped keep us safe."

In John and Slab's house, the parents had two young boys and a tiny one-year-old daughter, a sun-darkened beauty with huge chocolate-colored eyes, darkly arched eyebrows, and a disarming smile. As Slab got on his Toughbook laptop to communicate with

SEAL Team Six HQ in Bagram, John was reminded of his own daughters, Madison and Brianna, who weren't that much older, and formed an instant connection. Cognizant of how much they were putting these modest people out, John was as respectful and helpful as he could be; not that the others weren't, but John was purposeful about it. On one of the nights, while they were waiting for the storm to pass, the little girl's mother showed how much John had won her over when she placed her daughter in his lap. Realizing the significance of the moment, a rarity given the culture in which no male outside of the family is allowed to touch a female, he asked Slab to retrieve his disposable camera and snap a shot. The resulting black-and-white photo captures the juxtaposition of the warrior and the man—a kind soul in a foreign land, there to do a rough job but whose love of family and children transcended fear and hostility—to freeze-frame a poignant moment when two humans silently bonded across language and culture. John's kind eyes, gazing directly into the camera, belie the warrior beneath.

For two days the team remained ensconced in Afghan hospitality while the partisan force held the possibility of ambush at bay. Finally, the force moved silently into position above the suspected Mullah Omar refuge. The partisans wanted the Americans to take the village down, yet something seemed off. Slab and Goody conferred, and as Andy observed, "We needed to rethink this." In the village below, there were mostly women and children going about their day. "No combat power whatsoever." And no sign of Omar.

Slab turned to his Combat Controllers. "Can you order up a show of force?" He wanted something that would shake the village and possibly the truth out of the situation they and the locals found themselves in. Andy got on the net and contacted Kmart, the combined forces air component commander (CFACC, in charge of airpower in theater), and explained what he wanted. Kmart (so named for convenient one-stop shopping) had just the item, a B-1 bomber, coming off another mission and heading home. "Perfect," declared the Controller.

"He called me fifty miles out and inbound at high Mach down through the valley," recalls the Controller. Andy gave the pilot an entry and exit point above the unsuspecting village and cleared him for the very high-speed pass. "He comes down through the valley, maybe seven hundred feet above the ground, and he's got this air cone coming off of him that you only see in pictures," he recalls of the plane. As it passed, it pulled up and was already firing back to altitude like a bullet, "when the shock wave hit us; it sounded and felt like ten JDAMs going off all at once."

Unsurprisingly, the town's residents poured from their huts, stunned by the display, and sent two representatives to meet with the Americans and Brits. Through the interpreter, Slab—overall in command of the mission—realized that what they'd walked into *wasn't* the potential hiding place of the number-one Taliban target, but a village-on-village Afghan-style Hatfields-versus-McCoys feud. Omar had been there, some parties claimed, but had long since departed. The partisan force provided to Mako-30 saw the opportunity to settle a decade-long dispute. During discussions, which took hours to sort out, Andy continued his show of force with more aircraft passes, until Slab finally called a halt to the ear-shattering displays.

With no Omar, nor even any real indication that he was ever actually there, "We left after the show of force. A dry hole," Andy recalls of the wasted mission. John called back for exfil, and a lone MH-47 returned to retrieve them. Recognizing the burden they'd placed on the small village, he added a request to accompany the extraction helicopter. As the helo hovered into position on the steep mountainside, its nose and blades hanging out over precipitous space and its ramp dropped to retrieve the men, a cargo pallet was dragged onto the mountain by the team. Strapped securely to the top of the plywood was cooking oil, coal, stoves, and dry goods such as peanut butter and sugar for the village who'd taken them in. John, on his own initiative, had requested the provisions as a token for the family and the little girl who'd stolen his heart. It was a small gesture in a large war. Perhaps it made no real difference in a country shattered by decades of conflict, but it mattered to the Combat Controller.

With nothing to show for their efforts but potential misuse of American and British military might and a bit of goodwill, the men clambered aboard and disappeared into the dark. The CCT aspects of the mission, driven primarily by Andy, had also been a bust for John. He hoped his next mission would provide greater opportunity to demonstrate his value and capabilities.

PART II

ANACONDA

CHAPTER

9

---

16 January 2002

PETE BLABER TOOK IN HIS SURROUNDINGS AS HE SAT BACK IN A WORN, overstuffed chair in an upstairs meeting room inside a hotel in downtown Kabul. The hotel was an Afghan government–owned enterprise but had not conducted business as a publicly available lodging in many years. Prior to the American invasion, it was used by the Taliban for troop R & R, and during the Soviet campaign, the Russians had utilized it for similar purposes. Having rented the entire facility, the CIA was now sole proprietor of the square plug of a building that was surrounded by a ten-foot wall topped with concertina wire. The Agency used it to hold sway over most US activities taking place in-country at this stage of the war.

Blaber, a six-foot-two Delta Force lieutenant colonel with a passing resemblance to Kevin Costner, sported thick black hair and preferred a well-trimmed goatee to the standard "operator beard." Outfitted in cargo pants, long-sleeve shirt, and Afghan scarf, he blended comfortably into CIA space. He'd conducted previous clandestine operations in the Balkans in close collaboration with the Agency and was already on his second tour in Afghanistan.

The dusty room was furnished with large, threadbare chairs, a couch, and traditional, locally made rugs of muted greens and reds. The curtains were drawn, save a slim ray of light illuminating the interior, giving it the appearance of a nineteenth-century British gentlemen's club that had seen better days. Inside, representatives from the special operations community gathered around the CIA's deputy chief of station, a man named John who organized the daily select brain trust. Blaber and his operations officer, Jimmy Reese, were the only Delta Force leaders present. The other key leader in the room was Lieutenant Colonel Chris Haas, a giant man with a jovial disposition who was the Special Forces battalion commander for all of eastern Afghanistan. The day's meeting was focused on a shared problem: what to do next.

The Taliban's abandonment of the capital in November of the previous year allowed the Agency and SOF to occupy Kabul without a fight, a seemingly significant and early victory for the Americans. But the Taliban and their often-imperious purse-string-holding Arabian overseers hadn't truly been defeated, merely displaced. Even Tora Bora, Delta and Combat Control's shining opportunity to dispatch bin Laden, was another example of squeezing the enemy like a balloon, only to have it effuse to either side of the American fist. So the question remained—Where the hell were they?

The gathering was more a brainstorming session than a structured briefing, with the three principals (Blaber, Haas, and John) agreeing to informal information sharing and collaboration. No generals or formal chains of command were involved, only key leaders on the front lines. Blaber described the fusion: "The CIA provided the ability to produce and process intelligence, the Special Forces teams would train and equip the Afghans, and [Blaber's men] would operationalize the entire effort by conducting on-the-ground reconnaissance to find and destroy the enemy." The meeting broke up when Haas announced he had an obligation at his own compound. After he departed, the men stood, and John, whom Blaber described as sporting a "Jesus hairdo and beard," held the Delta operator back.

The spy walked to the curtains and drew them fully closed. "We're getting a lot of reports that Al Qaeda forces are regrouping in an area in the mountains between Gardez and Khowst," he said, leveling an even gaze at Blaber.

"What's it called?"

"Shahi Khot."

The name didn't register with the Delta operator but, given that John had whispered the word, even inside his own secure space, Blaber gave it the appropriate gravity and whispered back, "Can you spell that?"

"S-H-A-H-I-K-H-O-T," he said quietly as they parted. Blaber grabbed Jimmy, and the two stepped into a driving blizzard outside the compound as the former contemplated the implications of John's revelation.

Pete Blaber was a non-parochial and seasoned veteran of Delta Force. After serving as a Ranger, he'd joined the Unit (always referred to with a capital *U* by its members) in 1991 and, since then, had climbed the very narrow pyramid that existed for officers to command Delta's B Squadron. Along the way, he'd conducted manhunts in the Balkans and executed clandestine operations in a handful of other countries. After B Squadron, he had commanded a smaller element inside Delta focused exclusively on clandestine and low-visibility capabilities, so when it came time for Task Force 11 to select a leader for fusing the CIA and Special Forces, he was the natural, if reluctant, choice. Task Force 11 (TF-11) was the higher headquarters for an agglomeration of all "black" special operations in-country, including Delta, SEAL Team Six, and a few others. For Major General Dell Dailey and Brigadier General Greg Trebon, the commanders of TF-11, Blaber presented an opportunity as well as a challenge. His credentials weren't in question, it was his personality.

In addition to his well-known disdain for rigid military hierarchy, structure, and planning methodology, his forceful personality conflicted with Dailey's equally strong character. Still, in the weeks leading up to the 16 January meeting, he'd been given his orders, delivered by none other than General Tommy Franks, commander in chief of US Central Command and, therefore, all forces in Afghanistan. "Get some men out into the frontier to figure out what's going on." Simple enough, and that had led to the station meetings with Haas and the CIA. Yet what really mattered to Blaber was the coup de grâce to any conventional military thinking that might get in the way of the final directive Franks provided him: "Find the enemy, then kill or capture 'em."

He needed no further guidance and used his charter as a means to construct his much-preferred tactic: a joint team of the best operators in the world. To Pete, this meant Delta Force, SEAL Team Six, and, as events would later prove out, most critically for a campaign he had yet to wage or fully envision, Combat Control.

Two weeks later, Blaber and his growing composite force were living in a CIA safe-house compound in the eastern Afghanistan town of Gardez, a Pashtun population center of 70,000 people and the capital of Paktia Province. At 7,500 feet above sea level, surrounded by the southwest terminus of the Hindu Kush, Gardez enjoys an alpine atmosphere. Summers are hot and dry, and the little moisture it receives falls mainly in the winter and early spring in the form of snow. It is here that Afghanistan's legacy of conflict is made manifest. Now in ruins and resting above Gardez, foundations and crumbled walls can still be found marking Alexander the Great's easternmost outposts in his bid to conquer the known world. In the fourth century BC, against these same Hindu Kush mountains,

Alexander was turned back, to be followed by so many others in the millennia to come.

Like Alexander, AFO needed to position itself at the edge of the latest empire to sweep into Afghanistan. By the time of Blaber's arrival, the safe house had been running for some time, the cost underwritten by the CIA. As Blaber put it, "They were the only ones with money in-country at the time." The Army's Green Berets were already on-site as well, training a four-hundred-man Afghan tribal force referred to as the ATF. The ATF were the first installment of great hope for America's Afghanistan strategy, shouldering the burden of defeating the enemy in combat (under American direction and with American munitions) and establishing a Jeffersonian democracy in which girls could be educated and a viable, non-opium-based economy founded.

The late arrival of Blaber's team relegated them to tent living in the compound's courtyard. That suited Blaber just fine; he preferred the Spartan arrangement. The safe house itself was more fortress than dwelling, sporting a dirt floor, colored thirty-foot-high solid walls, and tile-roofed watchtowers that dominated its four corners. The masonry consisted of mud blocks that measured in feet not inches, creating the appearance of the base of an Egyptian pyramid. The building was elaborate enough in its construction that each watchtower was adorned with what appeared to be ruddy, reddish-brown cedar-tree designs instead of the usual undecorated mud-colored facing.

With no place left but the center of the 200-by-200-foot courtyard, Blaber and his men erected several Army standard GP (general purpose) medium tents capable of holding up to twenty men. The remainder of the open ground was consumed by vehicles and their maintenance, generators, and supplies. Massive hundred-foot G-11 cargo parachutes that sometimes draped over the walls were evidence of the weekly Air Force C-130 resupply airdrops of ammo, water, and other supplies. Stacked and tumbled everywhere in the compound's dirt interior were wooden crates of olive-drab green or unfinished pine filled with ammunition, grenades, mines, rockets, and mortars. Linked .50-cal and 7.62mm machine-gun ammo was strewn among the crates, evidence of men arming vehicles for heavy combat. Here and there were other signs American special ops were in town: the ubiquitous gym equipment, and sandbag stepping-stones leading from tents to interior corridors and rooms for when dirt turned to mud.

Inside the walls, the former residence took on its new identity as well. The CIA occupied the best digs, and Chris Haas's Green Berets took up the remaining space. The fused efforts of AFO, SF, and CIA could be seen in the tactical operations center, referred to as the TOC. Its unfinished mud walls were adorned with maps, charts, and imagery. Radios and laptops were powered by compound generators that, like the men, ran 24/7. At the TOC's heart, ostensibly running the show, but in reality one leg of a triad, was the CIA's lead, a man named Greg but whom everyone called Spider.

Spider's nickname stemmed from his appearance—six foot, thin and wiry. He and Blaber knew each other well. They'd worked together in Bosnia, hunting UN war criminals. Pete referred to him simply as "the best combat leader in the CIA. Spider was a living, breathing example of how good the CIA could be when they had their best leaders on the ground," and the respect was reciprocated. Spider was well aware of Delta's capability to hunt men. But the fight shaping up in the Shahi Khot Valley would differ from anything Delta and AFO had encountered before. This time, killing the enemy wasn't going to happen by means of a bullet from a Delta sniper's gun, but through the handset of a radio. And that handset would be gripped by a Combat Controller.

After setting up camp, Blaber's first order of business was to procure troops. The combined total of Americans in Gardez numbered about fifty, but most were divided between the CIA, with their role of obtaining intel, and the SF, whose job it was to train and equip the ATF. The Green Berets, centered on the efforts of ODA 510 (the Special Forces detachment responsible), were already training the Afghan militia, who were led by a warlord named Zia. The Agency had been there the longest and had already established a reliable intelligence network. What Blaber needed now was a special operator with a specific skill set if he was to fulfill his mission with regard to the enemy: corner and kill.

Blaber knew there was only one place to go to get the men he needed—B Squadron. Having been their former commander didn't negate his need for approval to bring them from the States, so he went to TF-11 and Brigadier General Trebon, who gave the green light for twelve men from the squadron's reconnaissance element. It took one call to Fort Bragg and Blaber was on the line with one of the best recce leaders in the business, Delta master sergeant Kris K. After he absorbed the information, Kris agreed to have his team ready to deploy to Afghanistan as quickly as possible. They loaded out with virtually everything their team had: SR-25s, M4s, M203 grenade launchers, winter gear, and multiple uniforms. However, they were missing one critical component that, under normal circumstances, they would have had: They didn't have a Combat Controller with them, and it would take time for one to arrive in-country.

Already inside AFO were operators from Delta's Navy counterpart, SEAL Team Six. Two SEALs, Hans and Nelson, were in Gardez and already working for Blaber. Hans, who led the SEAL contingent, had made it clear the Navy was "definitely not interested" in conducting the operations in the Shahi Khot that Blaber had in mind, so much so that heated exchanges took place among various parties.

Attached to the SEALs was a CCT by the name of Jay Hill. Hill was a thirty-one-year-old career airman. At six foot three and with a powerful physique, he had the requisite "operator" beard and long brown hair with sun-bleached bangs that swept across his face, like a surfer just out of the water from a morning set. He could easily be the poster image for Combat Control recruiting. Even his disposition struck many who knew him as "laid-back surfer," as if combat were nothing to get riled about. He'd joined the Air Force in 1989 for the college education it afforded and originally worked on aviation life support equipment at his first assignment at Pope AFB. While there, he began to run into Controllers playing volleyball, working out, and generally enjoying themselves. What struck him most was how fit and confident they were. Eventually he met a few, including an intense young CCT named Billy White (the very same Controller from Tora Bora). The interactions left him thinking that perhaps he was missing something and that, in his words, CCT "looked like a great job. Jumping, diving, everyone's in good shape. I was twenty-one and it seemed the manly thing to do. I need to do what those guys are doing." In the summer of 1992, he cross-trained and, after successfully navigating the brutal training pipe, returned to Pope in 1993, this time assigned to the 21st STS. A few years later, he set his sights on the 24.

Now he stood among the best of all the services. His attachment to Team Six was not a new experience, and like Blaber, he was on his second tour in Afghanistan. On 19 October 2001, he participated in the first combat jump of the war, Objective Rhino. Following that, he'd traversed southern Afghanistan with Delta's B Squadron, "looking for bad guys to kill." After a rotation home for a brief Christmas celebration, he returned to Bagram and embedded with the SEALs of Red Team (the assaulters led by Hans, not the sniper element led by Slab). It was a series of decisions, assignments, and tricks of fate that led Jay, like Blaber and everyone else at AFO, to Gardez.

When he saw the downward direction of relations between the SEALs and Blaber, he made a decision. Even if the SEALs couldn't see the value in the opportunity being presented (and they didn't), *he* most certainly could. He approached Blaber, intent on changing teams. To an outsider, it might appear extreme to suddenly switch over, but Controllers move so fluidly between forces like Delta, SEAL Team Six, and the SAS that he didn't give it a second thought. He also had a history with B Squadron and relished the chance to get outside the wire. As he recalls, "At the time, the SEALs had a pretty bad attitude about AFO. And I realized I didn't want to miss out on the chance to do some real damage to Al Qaeda." And just like that, after their short exchange, he was back with the Army, as soon as they could get there. Blaber couldn't have been happier. Though AFO was still a long way from hunting-safari ready, another key piece, CCT, had fallen into place.

Waiting to conduct recce missions didn't necessarily translate into idleness for the Combat Controller. Occasionally in the evenings, and especially during inclement weather, the safe house was subject to shelling by local militias not aligned with Zia and the Americans. Chris Haas, as the most senior Special Forces officer—and the officer with the strongest relations with the Afghans—asked Jay, "Can you do something about that?" Jay replied, "Yeah, man, sounds good." The exchange and plan were "very nonchalant," as he recalls, but in the end he wound up with the authority to conduct strikes. *Game on*, he thought.

For the Combat Controller it was easy. "I'd climb up on the roof at night with a couple of beacons, usually my microponder and an SST-181." There he'd work out where the tubes the Taliban set up were, using the beacons for his location, then provide the aircraft with a distance and direction along the lines of "eight hundred meters at zero eight six degrees," talking them onto the location starting with big descriptions for compounds or hilltops and then necking it down. "With the beacons, it worked well regardless of weather."

The Delta guys weren't even aware he was conducting strikes at night, saying things like, "What are you talking about? What beacon? That box with the little microponder?" "They'd say, 'Uh, dinner's at eight, can you come down from the roof?' They had no clue, it was quite funny. They're very smart, but they're not; they just don't have the expertise in these other areas of combat."

The hostile militias never expected it. There were no indications Americans were in the vicinity, because they weren't, and the weather was believed to provide security from American airstrikes, just as it had with the Soviets before them. The system worked well, eventually causing incoming fire to drop off completely. "It shut 'em up. They never expected that, what with the crappy weather we had all the time."

CHAPTER

10

——

THE MORNING OF 10 FEBRUARY WAS COLD AND CLEAR. THE FRIGID WIND announced the proximity of the Hindu Kush as two dozen men from a handful of units and government agencies pulled out of the safe house in a convoy heading southeast of the city. The lead vehicle slowed to a stop on a barren stretch of the valley floor.

Kris K. and his fellow Delta recce teammates had departed the US on 9 February. While they were winging their way toward Afghanistan, another reminder of their purpose took place at the Gardez safe house. Shortly after 9/11, Delta's B Squadron had conducted a social exchange and patch trade with members of the New York Fire Department in Manhattan. A few returned with pieces of the World Trade Center as mementos. Inevitably some of these made their way to Afghanistan, their physical heft serving as raw energy to fuel the men in their pursuit of those responsible. A Delta operator named Kevin ferried one over with the intent of leaving this piece of America in the land that spawned the attacks.

Bundling themselves against the cold, the informal group assembled around the senior CIA officer in Gardez as two men dug a small hole and placed the World Trade Center remnant in the shallow grave.

The CIA officer spoke a few words, followed by the senior NCO from 5th Special Forces. Their memorial is buried at approximate latitude 33°33′5.X″ N and longitude 69°15′8.X″ E. To Jay Hill, even though he was on his second tour, the ceremony brought back a sense of the surreal. "Afghanistan was the last place on earth you'd expect to be."

For Blaber, it was another example of their modus operandi. "Spider, Chris [Haas], and I, we had the time to set aside for this. It just sort of happened, another self-organizing activity. No one really set out a hierarchical structure. We just organized and executed; it was our distilled essence."

While Jay's SEALs wanted out, at least one other SEAL wanted in on Blaber's operations. Homer was a former member of SEAL Team Six, currently on a joint assignment, who arrived shortly after the Trade Center ceremony, and "like a lot of guys, he was looking to get in on the action," according to Blaber. He became Blaber's sidekick in his travels around Gardez. Essentially, Homer's job was to "make stuff happen. He could get anything by trade or trickery, and he was also a good sniper/recce advisor." His combat experience extended back at least a decade to Somalia, where he and a Combat Controller jointly saved the life of his sniper team partner during the operation that came to be known as Black Hawk Down.

The arrival of Kris and his team completed the AFO force. At the safe house, they separated into two elements, I Team and J Team (I and J were used interchangeably with their phonetic India and Juliet). Kris would lead J, while another sniper, nicknamed Speedy, would lead the other team. Jay Hill wasted no time plugging in to his new team, and Kris welcomed the Controller's expertise.

Planning began immediately, led by J Team. Their mission, as directed by Blaber, was threefold: Establish observation posts in enemy territory in the Shahi Khot Valley to confirm or deny the presence of senior Al Qaeda leaders; scout designated helicopter landing zones for a pending mission tentatively named Operation Anaconda; and finally, call in airstrikes on enemy positions when identified. With close collaboration between the CIA and Spider in place, this last objective was shaping up to have a significant impact on the American effort. US intelligence estimated enemy numbers at approximately two hundred in the Shahi Khot Valley in the mountainous region east of Gardez. Inside the Gardez TOC, between the CIA and AFO, it was believed the numbers were at least double that. As the teams began their in-depth analysis of the terrain and the enemy's historical tactics, they had no idea the actual force they were facing numbered between 1,000 and 1,500 in the valley, while an additional 700 staged in the valleys farther to the east toward Khowst.

The first question facing the teams heading into enemy territory was how to get there. As Americans, their obvious first choice was the ubiquitous helicopter. Thanks to the CIA, AFO had access to Russian-made Mi-17s, a common sight throughout Afghanistan that didn't raise eyebrows the same way US helicopters did. There was, however, a downside to employing any helo, even Russian birds: Weather and high altitudes were significant restrictors to their use. And if one *was* used to successfully insert a team, there was no guarantee, given the same challenges, you could rely on it to get them out, forcing you to gamble lives on the odds. Additionally, Blaber stood in strong opposition to helicopters for lift. This mindset stemmed from the necessity of AFO masking their presence inside the Shahi Khot Valley but was rooted in a deeper understanding of the very nature of their use. The history surrounding mission failure in helicopter-borne operations stretched back to their inception in Vietnam, through Somalia, and up to "dry hole" raids conducted early on in Afghanistan. After Somalia, a personal experience for Delta Force and CCT, Blaber's assessment was that "every despot, drug kingpin, and dictator who had any reason to believe that the United States might be coming for him expected that when and if we actually came, we'd come in helicopters."[8]

With the US default choice a nonstarter, the team turned to vehicle drop-off, known as VDO, as a means to get close enough to their objectives for them to hike or climb the remainder of the way. As a test of the VDO concept and to get a feel for the enemy situation, Kris, Jay, and two other Delta operators, Bill and Dave, set out for an abandoned town ten kilometers east of Gardez. It was called Dara and was a gateway to the team's early choice for an OP some twenty kilometers farther into the mountains. This was the first time Americans had traversed enemy terrain in the area. They used civilian Toyota Hilux pickups, a sort of low-grade version of a Tacoma, and they were accompanied by fifteen ATF fighters who piled into the open back of the pickups for use as security. Just as important, the Afghans could be used to gather information from locals and the environment. In this, the ATF were indispensable.

Clothed for the frigid February temperatures, their ATF escorts huddled in the back sporting brand-new CIA-supplied sage-green winter coats and AK-47s, the team set off for the mountains. They got as far as the ghost town before the deepening snow halted all progress, well short of the distance necessary for the team to haul their supplies and packs to their OP. Their mud-caked trucks could not get any farther through the snow and ice on the steep mountain slopes.

The reality of what they'd be facing in the coming weeks dropped on the men like a mountain avalanche. In front of them towered a massive 12,000-foot-high peak that would have been an expedition by itself. Even the terrain in front of the numerous summits left

---

8   Barely a year later, the Iraqi army would circulate copies of the movie *Black Hawk Down* as a primer on how to defeat US forces.

them "uncertain that we would even be able to get over some of the cliffs that were en route," according to one operator. Conferring in the snow, Jay and the Delta operators realized they wouldn't make it to their OP without getting resupplied, whether they encountered enemy forces or not. Furthermore, trucks were now no more an option than helicopters.

As the Delta operators continued to revise and shape their infiltration plan, Jay was experimenting with overhead air support. On the early missions, this usually took the form of a Navy P-3 Orion. Originally designed for antisubmarine warfare, the 1960s-era plane had four turboprop-driven engines and carried a suite of electronic tracking equipment designed expressly for finding subsurface signatures and, therefore, lacking the sophistication of other airborne systems coming online in newer platforms. SOF troops had been using them as a poor man's ISR (intelligence, surveillance, and reconnaissance, the term referred to any overhead surveillance) for over a decade. Without sophisticated electronics and optics for ground terrain, they nevertheless provided a presence and coordination platform in the event of a crisis.

Better still were the armed MQ-1 Predators beginning to roam the Afghan-Pakistan frontier. These had been purpose-built for the CIA and US Air Force a few years earlier as a low-cost, remotely piloted surveillance platform and were available in armed and unarmed versions, with the former eventually comprising the majority of the fielded fleet.

In the early days of the war, the potential for fratricide was an ever-present danger to unconventional forces. Driving civilian trucks stuffed with Afghans in the back and similar to Al Qaeda's, the AFO shunned US fatigues, and separating them from the enemy was an elusive task even on the best coordinated of missions. Pilots simply weren't used to identifying American forces not in uniform, especially when they were riding in nonmilitary vehicles.

The responsibility fell to Jay, as the lone CCT on the team, to manage and direct any aircraft. The eastern Afghan frontier remained the Wild West, even in the skies overhead. Controlling that air traffic with its multinational composition—diverse and often fragmented by competing missions—and the pilots' limited understanding of conditions on the contested turf kept the Combat Controller on high alert whenever the team traveled. Jay's reality, with hundreds of sorties per day spanning the country (any one of which could find itself overhead on short notice), made it equally impossible for him to maintain a complete air picture. It was critical, though, that he take control of the airspace directly overhead in the event they came into contact with the enemy or were ambushed.

On the next recce test foray, a drive between Gardez and Khowst, an armed Predator began tracking them as hostiles. Even though he succeeded in establishing contact, the team was nearly fired upon by their own country because they were traveling in a suspect convoy. It was becoming painfully clear that getting to their objective, as challenging as it was proving to be, was only a fraction of their problems.

———

The two original AFO SEALs, Hans and Nelson, had participated in some of the recce trips, but tensions between them and the Delta operators came to a head on one mission when the Delta team leader pushed the four-man Army/Navy patrol mercilessly, to determine their ability to move in steep, high-altitude terrain. Broadcasting his displeasure, Hans stated: "This is bullshit." After they returned to Gardez, more discussions took place directly addressing the disparity of approach to missions and attitudes, which Delta felt was unsatisfactory on the part of the Navy. In the end, Blaber let them know, "Hey, guys, it's not working out." So he chopped them to Chris Haas's Green Berets, where "they were happy to go on to something else." This cemented the decision and effectively cut the two SEALs from the AFO mission.

Even as his two former SEAL teammates were exiting the scene, Homer understood the potential of the unfolding operations. One night, while he and Blaber were checking on the safe-house guards and perimeter, he mentioned that recce SEALs from ST6 were restless in Bagram. They felt imprisoned by the constraints of TF-11 targeting and planning. "They're chomping at the bit to get out of their barracks and into the hunt."

Blaber was in a quandary. He needed more troops, as he'd known even before they launched their first mission. But his relationship with the TF-11 commander was becoming more strained as he continued to form a force and operations extracurricular to TF-11's core mission of targeting high-value individuals. These were personified most publicly in the form of bin Laden and al-Zawahiri, the number-two Al Qaeda leader. But Blaber believed that was not AFO's only purpose. He recognized the disproportionate and decisive impact a handful of the world's best operators, well positioned and hidden among the enemy, would have on the coming battle. Some in the TF-11 operations center had taken to referring to Blaber as "Peter the Great" or "Colonel Kurtz," in reference to the movie *Apocalypse Now*, for his obvious "gone native" immersion. But Blaber saw "skepticism and sarcasm as net positives," because "it was far better to be doubted than micromanaged." It was clear any request for additional Delta Force troops would be unsuccessful, yet there was another option, especially for a non-parochial opportunist such as he. Just because the previous SEALs in AFO weren't interested, it didn't necessarily translate to the rest of SEAL Team Six. There were SEALs already in-country, largely locked up inside their Bagram base due to TF-11's mentality. That group included a frustrated Slab and his CCT, John Chapman.

Blaber recalls, "The SEALs weren't interested in doing AFO at the time. They thought it was a waste of manpower. At one point I had a sixty-minute VTC with [TF-11 commander] General Dailey and he was not interested in what we were doing. Not interested in giving more manpower. But I persisted. Basically, with a minute to go on the VTC, he said, 'Fine, I'll give you some SEALs,' and then signed off." Those SEALs were from Team Six and therefore belonged to the unit's commander, Captain Joe Kernan.

Kernan tasked the only SEAL snipers under his command based in Bagram, which meant Slab's men from Red Team, along with John Chapman and Andy Martin. But the tasking didn't clarify who would be moving a hundred miles south to Gardez and who would stay in the hope of killing HVTs (high-value targets) with TF-11. Kernan only agreed to send half a dozen men with one Controller.

Slab was of the opinion that TF-11's Bagram mission construct was more likely to produce confirmed kills. He had a dozen men, including the two CCT, broken into two elements. Slab himself led the first element, designated Mako-30. The second element, designated Mako-31, was led by the operator called Goody. As Controllers, Chapman and Martin took their call signs from their respective assigned elements but used an additional designation. CCT on the battlefield and in published communication matrices were almost always identified by a *C* suffix, pronounced phonetically in transmissions as "Charlie." This distinct designation allowed leaders, gunships, helicopters, and other CCT to readily identify them as Controllers. In practice, the designation expedited close airstrikes because fighters, bombers, and gunships knew any "Charlie" call sign would belong to an experienced and expert strike director. When the two Controllers on Slab's team separated, Chapman's call sign, working for Slab, was always Mako Three Zero Charlie and Martin, working for Goody, was Mako Three One Charlie.

The decision on who to send was Slab's to make as team leader, and he elected to send Goody's four SEALs and Andy Martin, choosing to hold the HVT mission for himself. With orders given to relocate, Andy and his SEALs began to pack and prepare for extended mountain operations, some of them grumbling about relegation to the "B-team" mission.

Having seen the value and action in his previous non-HVT missions, Andy took the opposite position. "I was motivated."

Goody, taking the decision in stride and in keeping with his reputation as easygoing, went about prepping his men without complaint, but asked the Controller, "You ready for this?"

Not prone to statements of ambiguity, Martin replied, "Fuck yeah!"

CHAPTER

11

—

23 February

BACK IN GARDEZ, JAY HILL AND J TEAM CONTINUED TO EXPERIMENT with insertion methods. This sometimes took on humorous facets as the men considered all options. In the vicinity of Gardez, there were large numbers of jackasses, so the men brought a few inside the compound and tried variations of pack configurations. The animals proved to be so unruly and difficult to manage that the option was quickly abandoned, and they returned to vehicles as the most viable insertion means.

Their next test reconnaissance took the men closer to a large humpback mountain named Tergul Ghar but universally referred to by American forces as "the Whale" for its rounded humpback shape. They traveled the main road south out of Gardez, this time with a larger ATF contingent wedged in the back of their trucks due to the increased Al Qaeda numbers believed to be in the area. Their destination was another valley, called Peanut, to the east of the Whale, near a mountain called Takur Ghar.

As they neared the entrance to Peanut valley, their interpreter, an Afghan they called Engineer because he'd been trained as one before the latest war to tear his country apart, announced that there were "two AQ bases up the valley and the AQ were watching them at that time." To the Americans, the ATF's ability to determine Al Qaeda at a distance and by location was sometimes uncanny. When Kris asked Engineer how he could distinguish local Afghans from foreigners like Al Qaeda, he said, "It's easy, and I can tell from one kilometer away by the way they act, look, and walk." This ability was proved time and again, and once saved a 5th Group Special Forces patrol when Engineer correctly identified, specifically, Chechens and Uzbeks at a distance and prevented the ODA from being ambushed.

On the journey, Jay had a Predator overhead and ensured the surrounding terrain was under surveillance. As they considered Peanut, the Predator "picked up seven vehicles and twenty pax [personnel] moving three kilometers east of Takur Ghar mountain." The team discussed their options, still hoping to penetrate the valley for a better view of the mountains closer to their intended OPs. They conferred with Engineer, asking what they'd need to go any farther. The answer: a hundred men, and aircraft dropping bombs in front of them. They turned for Gardez without incident, but their eyes followed the mountains receding in the distance, with the challenges and unknown enemy numbers still masked by the snowy summits.

Jay's team made one more excursion to test their methods and abilities only forty-eight hours before Operation Anaconda was to begin. This time, again in the mountains east of Gardez, they were dropped off and hiked in on foot, assessing the steep terrain for its ability to support the use of all-terrain vehicles (ATVs). "We went in, looked, listened, absorbed atmospherics, and froze our butts off up in the mountains...It was snowing, raining, freezing cold." They equipped themselves with the best gear available: large mountaineering packs (spray-painted by the men in individual patterns of khaki and tan) to better distribute loads; desert camo Gore-Tex to blend in and also to protect from the elements; and even more critically, they brought Afghan scarves and blankets to mask their American appearance from a distance. They left body armor behind because it was physically impossible to add the extra weight (upwards of twenty pounds in early 2002). They brought one sleeping bag among the entire team, solely as a lifesaving measure should someone go hypothermic. Otherwise, they had "Norwegians," a thin and light-weight insulation layer they combined with a Gore-Tex shell for the few hours they could attempt to sleep. These two items, when separated, served a more important purpose than semi-warmth for sleep: They could be molded to pad and sound-dampen equipment like radios and batteries, the bulk of their load.

Several key realizations came from the trip. The first was that tents were an absolute necessity at 10,000 feet in the snow and low temperatures if they were to stay out for any duration. Also paramount was the diminished life expectancy of batteries, which they quickly discovered was half the normal battery life in the subfreezing temperatures. This information was critical to Jay if he was to keep them adequately in communication with HQ and aircraft. The most important of these batteries were the BA-5590s that powered the PRC-117, their primary SATCOM and CAS radio. Each battery added two and a quarter pounds of dead weight to the operator, but also a critical handful of hours of operating time, which could save countless lives in combat.

With 120-plus pounds of gear each, they learned the team could move only two to three kilometers a night. To understand the sheer physical and psychological stress on Jay and the other AFO forces, imagine standing at the base of a towering 10,000-foot mountain on a frigid winter night, the temperature already below freezing and be-ginning its nightly plummet to near zero degrees Fahrenheit. Heave two fifty-pound sacks of concrete onto your back while your chest and arms are loaded down with a weapon, batteries, radios, GPS, knife, and an emergency medical pouch. Step forward with your right foot and immediately posthole into the snow, each step a strain on your back and body, your lungs searing as they gasp for oxygen in the thin atmosphere and you know there will be no sleep tonight or possibly even tomorrow. Top it all off with an uncomfortable head harness or helmet for your NVGs, which will be squeezing your cranium for the fourteen hours of darkness that lie ahead, during which you will attempt to scale two miles of snowy rocky mountain. Furthermore, there are only four of you and, should you encounter an enemy force of any significance, your limited numbers and ammunition and all your superior expertise will not hold out for long. For Jay Hill, besides the immense physical load and discomfort, there is the added burden of being the lone warrior who can change the outcome of the battle using his expertise to bring American airpower to bear, saving everyone or, if he fails, carrying that failure for life. So as a rule he carried as many batteries as he physically could.

As the AFO men recovered to the safe house, affectionately proclaimed to be HOTEL GARDYEZ by a sign posted adjacent to the main entrance to the TOC, Andy Martin and Mako-31 were loading out vehicles for the daylong drive. They arrived late in the afternoon under a fading, steel-gray sky in mid-February, the first time the entire Delta, SEAL, and CCT force of AFO joined under Blaber. The men, most of them familiar with each other, shook hands and hugged in greeting and took stock of one another and what lay ahead. For Jay and Andy, it was a joyous reunion. The two friends had worked together for years and shared a passion for practical jokes, usually at each other's expense.

With all his forces assembled, Blaber prepared for what was to come. Operation Anaconda was shaping up to be the largest operation of the war, a classic "hammer and anvil." Staging from the safe house, the hammer would consist of four hundred of General Zia's

ATF and additional Afghan units, augmented by Chris Haas's Green Berets, along with CCT Bill Sprake. This force would push south from Gardez around the Whale and focus on the center of the Shahi Khot Valley, driving the enemy toward the anvil.

The preponderance of US forces for Anaconda were commanded by Major General Franklin Hagenbeck, a combination of 10th Mountain and 101st Airborne Divisions. They would form the anvil against the mountains leading east toward Pakistan, their enemy's predicted escape route as they fled the might of heliborne troops and massed Afghan forces . . . Or so the US Army believed.

Blaber intended to put the three AFO teams now under his command—J, I, and Mako-31—in the field and positioned at well-chosen and concealed OPs to report enemy locations and movements. Once situated, his Combat Controllers could call in airstrikes to kill as many enemy as possible.

For Martin and the SEALs of Mako-31, it was instant mission immersion. Delta and Jay had conducted all the reconnaissance and analysis and enjoyed the advantage of a couple weeks' acclimatization. Mako-31 would have none of this, *and* Blaber had a surprise in store for them: Of the three OPs going out, Mako-31's location was considered the most critical. Centered between the two Delta teams and proximal to Takur Ghar, it commanded the best view of the air corridor that the conventional forces would be using. With little advance notification and few details, Blaber's surprise came as a shock. According to Martin, they learned they could expect "to be walking between nine and twelve thousand feet, and don't expect medical exfil or any kind of fire support prior [to H-hour] if you guys get fired up. We'll try to help you as best we can, but we're not going to burn this mission." They would have the longest distance to infil in the least familiar terrain, because the AFO recces were simply unable to get close to their OP.

Goody absorbed this all calmly. As he and his team were conducting their mission preparations, Blaber asked his newest team leader, "So what do you think?"

"Sir, this is one hell of a mission. I really appreciate you bringing us out here to be part of it," said the SEAL, paying more attention to his gear than to the Delta officer.

Blaber nudged his shoulder to ensure he had the SEAL's attention. "Goody, the success or failure of your mission will predicate the success or failure of the entire operation. You have to make it to that OP before H-hour."

"Sir, I'll make it to my OP come hell or high water. If we're hurting on time, we'll drop our rucks. If we're still having problems, we'll keep dropping gear until five naked guys with guns are standing on the OP at H-hour."

Blaber remembers thinking clearly: *Where do we get such men?* It was just what the AFO commander was looking for, and what he expected from the best.

———

In Bagram, two other Combat Controllers, John Wylie (call sign Jaguar-11) and Jim Hotaling (call sign Jaguar-12), had also received short-notice taskings from their own commander. In this case, it was to join the famed Australian Special Air Service Regiment (known by the acronym SAS or alternatively SASR) to serve below the Whale and Takur Ghar as safeguards against escape routes through the southern end of the valley. Two six-man teams (including their CCT) would be inserted by separate Mi-17s and establish independent OPs where they would report enemy movement and call airstrikes. Established under its own separate task force, designated TF-64, it was the Aussies' first opportunity to put its most elite force into action in any significant operation in the new war. For them, it was a chance to build on the legacy they'd started with America in

Vietnam. TF-64 worked directly for the 10th Mountain Division and Major General Hagenbeck, and therefore had no direct connection to the AFO forces, with one exception—Combat Control.

▬

Back at Gardez, with everything set for AFO to infil, the men of I Team, J Team, and Mako-31 spent their last night indoors, to a man thinking about the ground operations to come. There was one exception. Jay Hill was considering the three-dimensional battlefield picture, but it was incomplete. "You have to remember, Operation Anaconda was planned in a vacuum from [an AFO] standpoint. And air planning was an afterthought, as the whole thing was planned by the [conventional] Army. I should have flown to Bagram for more information, but we didn't know there wasn't a deliberate air plan."

The Combat Controllers of AFO were about to learn just how little the Army had considered their role or the need for airpower.

CHAPTER

12

—

28 February

DUSK

JAY HILL ASSESSED HIS ATV, A HONDA FOUR-WHEELER SPECIALLY outfitted by Delta's mechanics with a beefier suspension, a winch for recoveries, infrared headlights, and most important, a "quiet run" exhaust to muffle the throaty sounds of the vehicle. There were only four ATVs for the five men on Juliet Team—three Delta operators (Kris, Bill, and Dave) and a signals intelligence operator named Jason, whose job it was to intercept enemy transmissions to identify targets for the team to destroy and also to relay the raw intelligence to the TOC. Jay was the fifth member, and even though he had more equipment and weight than anyone else, there was no way a Delta operator was going to have a signals guy riding "bitch," so it fell to Jay to haul Jason to their OP.

Looking at the rig, Jay decided it wasn't a pretty picture. He had his rucksack, jammed with a PRC-117 (the backbone of every Controller's close air support, the radio was the size of two heavy dictionaries lying spine to spine and weighed ten pounds without batteries), ten BA-5590 batteries, two handheld MBITR radios (another multispectrum radio but smaller and less capable than a PRC-117) as backups for the PRC-117 (with batteries), a Panasonic

Toughbook laptop with batteries and cables, a portable DMC-120 satellite antenna, an SMP2000 microponder beacon (used for beacon bombing in inclement weather), infrared (IR) strobes for positive identification at night by other forces and aircraft, a laser range-finder, two types of IZLID laser pointers for marking targets with infrared, and various additional marking devices. To this, he added two Nalgene quart plastic bottles for melting snow against his body when he slept (he had no stove) and a handful of MREs. With so much necessary gear, he ran out of room and was forced to leave most of his comfort items, such as additional clothing layers, behind. He had no sleeping bag, merely a bivvy shell, using his "puffy" Combs jacket for insulation. In the end, his gear was heavier and bulkier than anyone else's on the team and his creature comforts fewer.

Jay's other critical items were carried on his body: three GPS units (a small Garmin, a large—and heavy—PLGR military type, and a small wrist mount), his M4 and five magazines containing thirty rounds each, a conventional compass, an NVG compass, and a VS-17 panel for daylight marking. All of these items were carried in his Rhodesian vest in addition to a first aid kit and knife. He used a helmet, they all did, but they weren't ballistically significant—quite the opposite. The men used cut-down versions of the plastic Pro-Tec skate helmet, modified by hand to remove the over-ear portions. The operators then added pile Velcro to the shell to attach items such as IR strobe lights and glint tape (for AC-130 identification) and, most important, snaps for affixing NVGs.

Mounted on the front cargo rack of the ATV was an X-wing antenna (basically, a foot-high, three-inch-diameter mast with a four-blade radiator fan from an import economy car glued across the top) that allowed him to switch between satellite and line-of-sight (LOS) communications without changing antennas. This was critical if they made enemy contact while driving. There'd be no time to switch out equipment if he was both calling in airstrikes and driving the

ATV. It was a massive load for the commercial ATV, and he hadn't even added his passenger on the back yet, but as an "Air Force guy," Jay was reluctant to pawn off weight on teammates lest they view him as weak. Every Controller was constantly on guard against this perception. In actuality, one of the second-order effects of this dynamic was a pressure to perform at the top of every competition and during every operation. It manifested itself in the respect most CCT earned in training and combat. The other effect, as in this case, was an inordinate burden, not only the weight of lone responsibility but gross weight itself. On the morning of 28 February 2002, the reality for Jay was clear: Some batteries would have to be distributed among the others.

Like the pounds he carried, Jay's duties as a Controller were largely invisible to Delta. To them, the Controller's actions were merely FM—fucking magic; things just happened, if they even realized they took place at all.

As he configured the maxed-out ATV, Jay was faced with his first challenge before even engaging the ignition: FalconView, a mapping software for laptops developed by Georgia Tech Research Institute tech geeks using C++ language for the Air National Guard in 1993. It allowed users to track identified targets (friend and foe) and themselves on a moving map. It also allowed users to switch between several types of maps, such as aeronautical charts, US Geological Survey topographic maps, and even satellite imagery. FalconView was still nascent in its development, and only the Air Force, which meant only CCT, had it on the battlefield.

Jay's challenge was how to configure his Toughbook so he could access the software while the team was en route. With Jason jammed behind him, he'd be pushed up against the gas tank between his legs, but that was the only place the laptop could be situated for ease of access. After trying various configurations, he settled on a combination of black Velcro strips glued to the tank and laptop and held in place against vibrations and potential rollovers by bungee cords as they ascended the treacherous slopes of the mountains framing the Shahi Khot Valley.

Unfortunately, FalconView was not compatible with NVGs. In order to view maps, Jay would have to stop his vehicle, kick Jason off the back, and open and fire up the Toughbook while Delta pulled security for him. He'd then have to yank his poncho "sleeping bag" from a cargo pocket and drape it over his head to guard against the bright screen compromising their position. To connect the laptop remotely, he had a small helmet-mounted hockey-puck-shaped antenna connected via Bluetooth. Nearly two decades later, it may seem commonplace or even simple, but shortly after the turn of the century, the configuration was cutting edge, particularly on the outer fringe of possibility under combat conditions.

In all, there was no more room on man or machine for additional weight or gear. Looking over the line of ATVs, Jay shook his head; gear hung everywhere, piled dangerously high on the vehicles, making them top-heavy and all the more dangerous on the mountain slopes. "We looked like gypsies. It was pretty comical."

As the day advanced, heavy skies loomed and rain began to turn to snow. Predictably, the temperature dropped accordingly. Kris, the Delta team leader of J Team, checked with the TOC while the others made their final preparations. "Just before leaving, a source reported to the CIA that the majority of the enemy was in the mountains and to the east of Sahi Kot [sic]," he recalled later. More good news: Their route also took them past a dangerously hostile village called Menjawar, which was "still an AQ holdout" that they most assuredly would need to give a wide berth due to the latest news. Capping it off was the announcement by the 5th Group Green Berets training Zia's militia, who were known to have Al Qaeda sympathizers within their four-hundred-man ranks, that they hadn't told the Afghan commander about the mission until twelve hours earlier, fearing a leak. Nevertheless, Kris learned, "Shortly after notifying Zia, the AQ knew Sahi Kot [sic] was going to be attacked." The news was met with shrugs. The teams were already going deep into enemy territory. Another confirmation of the enemy's awareness wouldn't change the tactics or dynamics of the operators.

The infil plan was conceived to get all three teams, J, I, and Mako-31, inserted in one movement. To do this, they were all prepped and staged together. J Team had the only ATV riders, and the other two teams would conduct their own vehicle drop-offs after J Team peeled off. Two Hilux pickups led the convoy, each with a MAG 58 7.62mm machine gun and a SAW, a lighter-weight 5.56mm weapon with a higher cyclic rate. These were manned by the infil insertion team, led by John B., a Delta captain well respected among the senior NCOs of the Unit. Three more Delta operators and the now-excluded SEAL, Hans, rounded out the infil insertion team. Fifteen ATF fighters jammed into the back of the trucks for security and additional firepower. The ATVs of J Team brought up the rear. In the event of contact, the trucks had the heaviest firepower.

Andy Martin had his gear prepped and staged with his SEAL teammates. A very type-A personality, he was ready to get on the mountain and kill Al Qaeda, certain that when the time came, the killing would be almost exclusively his domain. This would not turn out to be the case, but he had no way of knowing that Mako-31's mission would be the most difficult, dangerous, and decisive of the three.

At the rear of the convoy, Jay observed his Delta teammates and felt confident in his abilities and their plan, and remembers thinking, *These are the guys you want to do this with. This is why I'm in the 24 and why we did all those winter warfare training trips and ATV training.* But he knew this was no easy infil and the mission outcome was anything but certain, nor was it fully within their control. Still, Jay, who'd spent years preparing, thought, *This is what I was meant to do. We're going to put eyes on the valley and wreak havoc.* Recalling the moment, he states, "Everything came together as a Controller. It was literally a CCT mission."

Go time. They rolled out of the compound gate in the dark just after 1900 and traveled south along the Zurmat road, where the mountains' presence in the distance was more felt than seen. At the drop-off point, J Team bade their farewells, wishing the other teams luck, and turned east. On their own, they broke into pairs: Bill in the lead with Dave behind; Kris and Jay, with his human cargo Jason, bringing up the rear. Everyone was connected by interteam radio via headsets under their helmets.

For the Combat Controller, it was the start of days of nonstop communication and responsibility. The Delta operators were solely on their designated interteam radio net, whereas Jay had three separate nets coming through his Peltor headset. Peltors were green, dual-ear hearing aids and communications sets that doubled as ear protection from gunfire or eardrum-damaging explosions. They cut off all sound above a certain decibel and simultaneously enhanced ambient noise, allowing the men to enjoy a sort of "bionic man" hearing. Jay was on interteam like everyone else, in addition to being plugged in to their designated SATCOM frequency, or freq, to remain connected with Pete Blaber. He was also dialed in to an air-to-ground freq that he used to establish communication with a JSTARS aircraft overhead.

Joint Surveillance and Target Attack Radar System was the full name for the Air Force's Boeing 707 conversion used for ground surveillance, battle management, and command and control. It had powerful radar systems, allowing it to track hundreds of targets, and could vector and manage dozens of fighters or bombers while assisting with on-the-ground pictures during combat.

The four-wheelers crept around their next threat, a village called Cine, and started up the slopes of a mountain named Wac Sakh Ghar. Their route was to take them over the top of Sakh Ghar's ridgelike summit via one of several passes they believed were accessible, which allowed them to bypass Menjawar, the village known to have as many as two hundred Al Qaeda fighters who'd moved into the region in anticipation of the fight. On the other side of Sakh Ghar, they would travel south toward the north end of Shahi Khot Valley to their OP.

As they ascended the lower slopes, however, they learned another hard truth regarding Afghan terrain and maps: 1:100,000 US maps had very little detail, Russian 1:50,000 topo maps were never as accurate or reliable as their US counterparts (which didn't exist for the region anyway), and satellite imagery was inadequate for the man on the ground. Even Jay's FalconView was only as good as the images loaded into the program. The trails and navigable terrain they'd planned around were proving impassable as the meters added up behind their vehicles.

"We continued to move south trying to find a way over the mountain, getting closer and closer to Menjawar."

Eventually, they stopped and discussed the situation, using Jay's FalconView under the poncho. It was clear their carefully planned route was now blocked. They had a choice to make. They could drop back down the mountain, travel south along the lower slopes of Sakh Ghar, and attempt to pass through an enemy-occupied town to make their OP, or they could turn back and notify Blaber they would be unable to reach their OP and, therefore, not accomplish their mission, compromising the upcoming operation involving more than a thousand US troops and personnel. Ultimately, there was no choice.

"It was now obvious that we were going to have to go through Menjawar to get to our OP."

They rolled to a stop before the village, tires crunching loudly over rocks and their exhausts advertising their presence, or so it felt to the men. They watched the silent village intently for obvious threats. When nothing revealed itself and their choice was made, "we slowly moved through the town with streets as wide as six feet and saw no one, only a lot of dogs barking." The dogs set the men on edge, their Peltors amplifying the potential threat that the barking would bring Taliban or Al Qaeda forces out into the night. They prayed the Delta-modified exhausts would mask their passing. The main thoroughfare was no more than an alley, darkly claustrophobic. Every low-slung mud building had weapons behind its walls; every blackened window masked a potential AK-47 barrel. "It was about 2200 hours, and it was a good thing that when it gets dark, the Afghanis appear to bed down for the night. The thing that worried us most was an unexpected checkpoint, but we never saw any." The men had their weapons slung in front of them for easy reach, fingers ready to grab pistol grips and return ambush fire—a no-win situation since their right hands were required to work the ATV throttles. If fired upon, they could return fire or flee, but not both.

"It was just above freezing, there's no snow on the ground but it's muddy, so you can see the tracks . . . You're not making that much noise but at the same time you're just waiting for somebody to appear over the top of the wall and go 'Aha! Here's our guys!' because they knew we were coming, that Americans were pouring into the Shahi Khot, that they were going to do some sort of major operation."

With their biggest threat to that point behind them, they finally found a route over the mountain to the east. Turning south, they began to feel their way in the right direction, until along the trail, "we eventually came across a bunch of rocks piled across the road with one big rock that had an X painted on it." This meant the road was mined. So, "we figured: (1) we were very lucky, (2) the road was mined with [anti-tank] mines and the ATVs were not heavy enough to set them off, (3) we moved in the center of the trail and the mines were on the tire paths only, or (4) the area was falsely marked as mined to scare people off." As is so often the case in life, and particularly in combat, luck and events moved in unpredictable and unknowable ways. Jay concludes, "So we were thinking it wasn't the smartest idea to go through the middle of Menjawar. And then we end up in a damn minefield because you can't really tell the difference on the rock colors on Nods (NVGs)." J Team had dodged their second bullet of a mission that was only six hours old.

———

Ten miles to the south, I Team and Mako-31 were winding their way toward their vehicle drop-offs along the route reconnoitered by I Team only a few days earlier. The going was little better than on J Team's travels. "Because of the rugged, broken terrain, which caused the trucks to bottom out frequently, [I Team and Mako-31] dismounted some 2.5 kilometers short of their intended drop-off."

John B. repeated his delayed departure procedure, watching the eight phantoms disappear single file into the night, each of them burdened by more than a hundred pounds, like lethal pack mules. When enough time had elapsed, he turned his pickups for Gardez.

I Team and Mako-31 trudged together through the night for four kilometers along the valley floor, heading east along a creek named Zawar Khwar, and then I Team turned north for their OP another seven kilometers distant, leaving Andy and the SEALs with a movement ahead of them that was more than twice as long.

Neither team had much to say when they parted; it was a serious night and all of them were now deep in enemy-controlled territory. For Mako-31 it was doubly daunting. Not only had they missed the hard-earned lessons learned on the recce missions, but there was also something to be said for the personal experience of having previously walked the terrain. What they lacked in local exposure, though, they made up for with skill, experience, and intent. Andy and Goody had no intention of failing to make their objective or an impact on the overall operation.

To ensure they arrived at their OP unobserved, they'd deliberately plotted a circuitous infiltration route nearly twenty-two kilometers long. Though the least acclimated, Mako-31 also had to double their movement rate, reducing the time and ability to identify the enemy before the enemy might identify them. It was a *huge* risk. Still, they continued through snow that began to reach their knees, each step a posthole except where exposed rocky terrain provided some respite. Their painfully challenging progress was exacerbated by the snow that began to fall. Their misery did have one silver lining: No one in their right mind was out on a night such as this.

———

While Mako-31 slogged through the night, Bill, J Team's lead rider, was making a lifesaving leap from his ATV. The team had been climbing through increasingly deep snow on steepening slopes as they neared their OP. As the three others climbed the trail behind him, Bill's ATV suddenly stood upright under the heavy load and forty-five-degree slope and tipped backward. Bill flung himself off just as eight hundred pounds toppled. Dumped in the snow, he and the others watched helplessly as the rig and his equipment tumbled end over end "for over a hundred meters before it stopped." Gear was strewn down the slope. While his teammates collected the equipment, Bill righted his ATV, checked it over, and hit the starter. The engine quietly came to life. Once again, they were grateful for their specialized equipment and the superb skills of the vehicle crews.

When his rig was put back together, the men continued carefully across the steep terrain, eventually arriving at their primary OP site. But, as Kris recounted, "after conducting a recon, we decided it was not a good site. We would have to leave the ATVs out of site [*sic*] with no good hiding place for them." They studied Jay's FalconView screen, then "loaded back on the ATVs and headed toward another site we had seen from the top of the mountain we were just on."

To reach their secondary OP, they were forced to travel down into the northern end of the Shahi Khot before cutting across the toes of some ridgelines and due east into another small valley that "was the one with the confirmed cave and reported ADA [air defense artillery] and artillery pieces." The team ended up closer than they'd antici-pated, only "turning around about three hundred meters before the cave and moving back to the mouth of the valley," as Kris recalled. From there, they found a secure ATV hide site, which they masked with camo netting brought along expressly for that purpose. After nine intense and grueling hours, they finally stopped. Saddlesore but grateful, they removed their helmets and spent an hour doing a "look, listen, and smell" of their new base. On 1 March at 0447, J Team reported back to Pete Blaber that they were in position and open for business.

———

As Andy and his team continued their "heinous" route along a 9,400-foot ridgeline, AFO's approach to the enemy and their historic tactics and daily rhythm was proving well-thought-out. It was un-likely any Al Qaeda believed the soft-bellied Americans would be out in misery such as this or in terrain so forbidding and remote. Both served Mako-31 well and were critical since, as Andy observed, "the whole way in, based on the terrain, we always had at least ninety degrees, if not more, of masking where anybody could come up over the ridgeline, so [we were] really, really shit out of luck most of the time."

Despite their relentless march, the dawn beat them to their objective and they stopped as a steel-gray sky greeted the exhausted warriors. With no choice, they established a hide site a mere thousand meters from their objective.

In Bagram, John Chapman listened on the SATCOM net as his 24 teammates passed information or exchanged messages via Toughbook. He'd managed to get to the war, but his only mission had been a bust. Now he was sidelined, again, tantalizingly close but still a lifetime's distance from the operations going down.

CHAPTER

13

—

1 March

"WE WILL RETREAT TO THE MOUNTAINS AND BEGIN A LONG GUERRILLA *war to reclaim our pure land from infidels and free our country like we did against the Soviets. The Soviets were a brave enemy and their soldiers could withstand tough conditions. The Americans are creatures of comfort. They will not be able to sustain the harsh conditions that await them.*" So predicted Jalaluddin Haqqani on 29 October 2001.[9] Haqqani was a Taliban mujahideen commander, and his forces were already in retreat as he spoke these words from a Pakistani hideout where he would remain for over a decade. His words reflected the beliefs of most of the combatants arrayed against the pending Operation Anaconda forces. He also had the distinction of having been a commander during the Soviet campaign, and more important, its effort in the Shahi Khot Valley.

Haqqani based his opinion on broad perceptions built up over the previous decade and reinforced by events in Somalia and Haiti,

---

9   Haqqani's prediction appeared in the *Laissez Faire City Times* in an article titled "Afghanistan: An American Graveyard?" by Richard S. Ehrlich.

where it seemed Americans could be driven from one's lands by inflicting a few casualties. His assessment, though, was based on US foreign policy and not on the actual troops on the ground. Ironically, this "creatures of comfort" analyst was himself a creature of habit, and his forces now awaiting the Americans were repeating their tactics of more than a decade prior. Blaber's and AFO's study of the history and geography of their battlefield was about to determine whether "habit" or "comfort" would win the day.

Haqqani's understanding of where and when the first major confrontation was going to take place was solidified, thanks in part to the tip-off delivered by traitors within the American-allied ATF's ranks. But even before this confirmation of American intent, the Taliban and Al Qaeda had recognized the looming fight's location. From the enemy:

Our early presence in it [Shahi Khot] gave us sufficient experience and much knowledge of it inside and out, its dangerous parts and the ways out of them, and allowed us to master their use— by the bounty of Allah the Most High—for our operations with the Americans when Allah caused them to encounter us in that area. Maulawi Jawad was Saif-ur-Rahman Mansoor's military commander for the duration of the previous phase of battles. He had been involved in preparing the bases and occupied with arranging and fixing ambushes. We planted land mines accurately in the main roads, which led to the village [Serkhankhel, in the center of the Shahi Khot Valley], and we set up heavy artillery on the surrounding mountain peaks.

In the early days, we spent all our time preparing the area. Our numbers totaled 440 mujahideen in all, comprising 175 Afghan mujahideen from Saif-ur-Rahman Mansoor's group, 190 mujahideen from the Islamic Movement of Uzbekistan under the command of Qari Muhammad Tahir Jan (this was the largest group), and about 75 Arab mujahideen, the majority of whom had previous military knowledge and training.[10]

By 1 March, more fighters had poured into the valley and were fortifying the surrounding mountains, preparing for jihad. J Team had already survived two of Maulawi Jawad's preparations: the forces housed and staged in Menjawar, and at least one minefield. As the men adapted to their new surroundings and improved their OP, the next threat came to them.

Satisfied the location was sound from a defensive consideration, with good lines of sight on the valley to their south and the surrounding mountains, they stashed the ATVs behind a ten-foot embankment situated below the OP in the riverbed they'd followed. According to Jay the OP itself was bifurcated: One position was the mission support site, known as an MSS, where they set up their lone tent so two men could rest or eat; and the second was the actual observation post, "a hundred meters straight up the side of a ledge," where the three others would conduct operations. The way they'd situated it, "one guy would watch the rear and the pair [of men] on the rest plan. One guy would watch the target area, and the other would do the reporting and pull security." The two positions maintained communications by way of MBITR.

At noon, the Taliban came, single file.

They appeared from the cave area the men had passed hours

---

10 All enemy excerpts describing their participation in and impressions of Operation Anaconda originated on the Taliban website www.azzam.com and were generated by at least three individuals. Originally posted in 2003, they inevitably and eventually took on a predictable propagandist cast as the site was revised over the years. However, the author was able to corroborate original (2003) versions with friendly and enemy sources of information, such that the passages appearing on these pages most closely reflect eyewitness accounts by enemy combatants at the time. However, no passage should be read as accurate reporting of battle events but rather as insight into the disposition and mindset of enemy combatants.

earlier, traveling down the valley J Team had left behind. They all appeared to be Afghans, not Arabs or Uzbeks, and "they all had weapons to include RPGs." They were following the ATV tracks and "stopped right where our tracks went up from the valley to our ATVs."

Kris and Jay, who were manning the OP, observed them intently. Were they tracking J Team? Was it merely a small patrol or the advance element of a much larger force? Kris had Bill and Dave take up positions, but neither could see the enemy, and further movement would only likely give away their position.

J Team's tracks were "all over the place," so following the team's trail would prove difficult unless they happened upon the ATVs and the two Delta snipers hidden nearby. Then the Taliban sniffed out the tracks leading toward the ATVs. When they closed to two hundred meters, Kris knew they were in trouble. "Some of the thought process going on at this time was: these five personnel could be a point element for a larger force. If we shoot them, we would now be on the run by foot; if we shoot them, the mission could be compromised; if we let them go, they might bring back a larger force; and all the ATV tracks might have confused them and they had no idea what was going on. As they continued to move inch-by-inch toward the ATVs, we got ready to engage them at the last possible minute."

Jay sighted through the ACOG (Advanced Combat Optical Gunsight) scope of his suppressed M4 as the men approached. The Taliban below had no idea they were in the crosshairs of some of the deadliest shots in the world. The Delta snipers and Jay held the shot. Triggers brushed with the contact of each shooter's finger, poised to squeeze. At less than two hundred meters, kills were foregone conclusions for the Americans. "You're watching this guy in your scope, thinking, 'I'm going to have to shoot this guy,' and if you do it's going to echo across the entire valley and then you're done." With Jay and Kris above and the other two below, Kris kept the team in check even as the enemy closed to within 150 feet of the ATVs. The prospects weighed heavily on Jay's mind. "With your scope you could see they were talking about it, 'Hey, what is this?' and pointing at [the tracks]. They'd walked away and then came back."

Kris, Jay, and the snipers below weren't sure if they were compromised or not, but it seemed likely. Jay got on the net and brought in ISR to scan the surrounding terrain and cover likely avenues of approach. For good measure, he coordinated for close air to be on standby in case the men were attacked. While Jay was working the airwaves, Kris called Blaber on the radio, using the whisper mode (which amplified the transmitter's voice so the receiver heard it clearly), and relayed the situation.

Blaber responded, "What's your recommendation?"

"Well, if we kill 'em now, the whole valley will know we're up here, and we'll lose the element of surprise. Let me see what they do next. I'll call you back."

Kris describes what happened next: "Just as we got ready to fire, they stopped and paused for a few seconds, then talked to one another and then just turned around and continued to walk out into the Sahi Kot [sic] valley. One of them stayed back and went out of site [sic] for about 5 minutes. We believe he walked back up toward the area from behind a rock that was in front of us but, because of the 10 ft embankment could not see anything. Finally we saw him walk back out and link up with the other 4 personnel."

Kris called Blaber back after the enemy departed, explaining, "We've plotted the grid for the cave entrance they walked out of and [Jay] will coordinate a bombing mission on it at H-hour."

The others broke down the tent and began hauling the remainder of the gear up to the OP. There would no longer be a lower position; all the men would remain on the higher ground. The sun rose but the weather closed as a gale-force snowstorm blew in. Nearly two feet of snow fell, allowing them to work their relocation (something they'd normally only accomplish in the dark) throughout a tense day.

By nightfall, fresh snow had covered all the ATV and Taliban tracks, providing additional anonymity and security for the team. Anyone moving about now would be exposed by fresh tracks in the snow. The team felt safe and, with the immediate threat diminished, continued to consider their location. Further scouting revealed a small draw farther upslope with superior views of Tergul Ghar, the Whale. So they repeated the process of relocation throughout the night of 1 March, electing to leave the extra gear from the ATVs at the temporary OP and putting more distance between them and the ATVs. As a security measure, Dave and Bill set a claymore mine booby trap with a trip wire to guard the downstream approach to the ATVs and to serve as an early warning from their rear, before leaving them behind for the duration of the mission.

The new site provided another advantage in terrain dominance and masking should a larger force return. J Team would be able to effectively attack with plunging fire. It also closed the distance between the MSS and OP to fifty feet, strengthening their mutual support. The site itself, though, was more exposed. All rock face with six-to-ten-foot ledges across the face and backside, there was sparse foliage, only scattered ankle-high brush. Jay recalls, "How we were positioned, we were not as concealed as you'd think you would be in the mountains of Afghanistan. I had a leaf suit on, but underneath a blue North Face coat. [And] it was not just that, I had a VS-17 panel out for IFF [Identification, Friend or Foe]. So if somebody flew over and saw us, an Apache or something like that, it wouldn't shoot at us." Theoretically. This was a real concern among the team. The unknown was how well the pilots flying across hundreds of miles and dozens of mountains and valleys were briefed on three small and autonomous groups of Americans deep in enemy territory.

Considering the close call with the Taliban, the men decided it was not all negative. It had unearthed their point of origin, the cave. Without realizing it during their wanderings through the terrain on infil, the team ended up no more than seven hundred meters from what was clearly a significant enemy position, much closer than they cared to be for an operation spanning more than a week. Looking through their sniper scopes, buildings could be seen as well.[11]

With his first target identified, Jay got to work planning a pre-H-hour strike on the cave complex. For his first strike, he wasted no time on subtleties. He was going to announce the American campaign to Al Qaeda with an earth-shattering bang. The cave complex was to be the recipient of a Blu-118/B 2,000-pound thermobaric laser-guided bomb, courtesy of a B-1 bomber crew. It would be the inaugural use of the newly redesigned and improved ordnance.

As J Team settled in and began reporting enemy positions and movements, Andy Martin and Mako-31 were waiting for daylight to wane in order to continue their infiltration. The waypoint afforded them a direct view of Shahi Khot's center and the village there. Before the morning's storm moved in and eliminated all visibility, the team "observed some Afghans fleeing the area with two camels in tow, overloaded with their possessions." If there were lingering doubts about knowledge of the pending operation, the hasty departure of locals removed them. Not taking any chances, Goody held his team in place till sunset, when they hefted their gear once again and moved

---

11   The cave complex, as it came to be known, would later be revealed to have housed Osama bin Laden before his relocation to Tora Bora in December 2001. Kris's after-action report supported the notion: "Based on all the security positions overwatching the cave, all the mule feces and signs of occupation, I would say there was a good chance of this being true."

out under cover of thick fog, hoping to make it to their OP. The night's "hump" proved more difficult than the first. The terrain was extreme, and sheer drop-offs and crevasses created obstacles along their mountain trail. In six hours of movement, they managed barely three kilometers.

———

As Mako-31 were beginning their second day, CCT Jim Hotaling, along with six Australian SAS troopers, sat freezing and huddled with his gear in the rear of another CIA-operated Mi-17. He watched the valleys and peaks pass underneath in the Afghan twilight, thinking about the mission he'd received in Kandahar three days prior, with no notice or fanfare, from Major Terry Maki, the commander of the 22nd STS. He'd had only twenty minutes to prepare before relocating to Bagram and meeting up with his team and their leader, Matt B.

Hotaling was a thirty-three-year-old reservist CCT. He'd been on active duty for several years before transferring into the Individual Mobilization Augmentee (IMA) program, which afforded former CCT who didn't wish to be under the formal obligations of the Air National Guard the opportunity to remain in the community. IMA allowed him to train with the 22nd STS at McChord AFB in Washington State, where he worked full-time as a state highway patrolman. At five eleven, he had a round, stocky build with tightly cropped coarse brown hair and jovial facial features, earning him the nickname "Fozzie Bear." When the war kicked off, he'd been mobilized and then deployed to Afghanistan in October.

Upon arrival, he and another Controller by the name of John Wylie were immediately assigned to the SAS. For the next three months he "mission whored," a term that described jumping from unit to unit and mission to mission. It was the best opportunity to get in on action and airstrikes, and he bounced among the Aussie

SAS's 1 Squadron, the Norwegian Marinejegerkommandoen (MJK) special forces, German Kommando Spezialkräfte (KSK), and both B and C troops of SEAL Team Three. This ability to move freely among units, services, and allies, sometimes from week to week or even on a daily turn, is unique to CCT, again demonstrating the need to be competent and proficient across the spectrum of skills required in special operations tactics on a wholly global scale. Hotaling had done eight previous missions with the Aussies, including one other high-altitude patrol.

The SAS had endeavored to find a role in Anaconda and success-fully lobbied for the opportunity to uphold a portion of the mission. For their efforts, they were rewarded with two patrols assigned to cover the south end of the Shahi Khot to prevent escape. The Aussies, recognizing their inexperience with US air and airstrikes in general, immediately requested the two Controllers they were familiar with.

Pre-mission planning had been a whirlwind of coordination and packing for both Controllers, neither of whom had worked with their assigned US or SAS teams before. Short-notice assignments to unfamiliar units were nothing new, but both men knew the stakes in this particular situation were elevated. Not only did the SAS highly value their participation, but each Controller carried the weight not just of the Air Force but of the entire nation.[12]

The Aussies tended to pack more heavily than their US counter-parts so, as a result, Hotaling's ruck weighed 110 pounds. Unlike Jay Hill with Delta (who was reluctant to push weight onto his team), the Aussies ensured that the ruck of each man on the mission was within two pounds of his teammates'. Still, to this, Hotaling added

---

12   Based in part on Operation Anaconda, the Royal Australian Air Force, recogniz-ing the need for a comparable capability Down Under, initiated the creation of its first Combat Control Team in 2006. Designated B Flight, No. 4 Squadron RAAF, it now operates from RAAF Base Williamtown, deploying Aussie CCT in support of Australian SOF worldwide.

thirty pounds of "combat load," including a vest with ammo, first aid, water, signaling devices, an M4 with suppressor and ACOG scope, and NVGs.

The hour-long flight from Bagram was uneventful, but the men in back were keyed up—like the SEALs, they'd had no recce experience in the mountains east of Gardez. The helo set down in the dark five kilometers south of the Shahi Khot Valley, and the men struggled off the ramp under the weight of their packs. They trudged into the night and directly onto their intended OP, which had a commanding view of the approach and departure routes. Unlike Blaber's AFO teams, the Aussies, like the rest of the US and allied military, had no reservations about using rotary lift to insert, in this case right on top of the OP. It was also the reason the team was inclined to pack heavy; they did not intend to move or be resupplied, a decision they would soon regret.

———

Half a dozen kilometers to the north, Andy and the SEALs were anxious to arrive at their targeted location and acutely aware of their promise to Blaber. They moved out at 1430, still almost two kilometers from their OP, and the terrain between them and their objective was more challenging than the night before. This night completely drained the team, and they managed only 1,100 meters up the mountainous slope, finishing at nearly 11,000 feet above sea level and 600 meters short of their OP. As they moved, sweat poured from their bodies, soaking their shirts under their crushing loads. Pausing in the frigid mountain air, even for a few moments, caused them to freeze. It was something almost impossible to avoid, so although thighs burned with each heavy footfall and lungs ached with each gasp, it was better to keep moving than to stop.

They occupied a hide site and established security, catching their breath and stretching their aching shoulders and backs. There was precious little time to take personal stock; it was close to midnight. H-hour, the time at which 10th Mountain and the 101st Airborne were scheduled to land on the valley floor, was set for 0630 the following day. If they were to get eyes on the valley before sunrise, they'd never get there as a team burdened with their packs and equipment. With little choice, Goody sent two SEAL snipers, Chris and Eric, forward to scout their final OP while Andy established comms with AFO HQ.

The two SEALs, free of their rucks, crept stealthily forward through a snow squall, scanning their surroundings for Al Qaeda as they went. Two hundred meters forward of Mako-31's position, they were confronted by a gray-green five-man tent wedged beneath a rock outcropping a few feet from a cliff's edge. Complete with a tin chimney protruding from one corner, it was exactly where the team planned to place their own OP. Al Qaeda had arrived at the same conclusion, beating them to it by days.

Chris, who'd been a SEAL for over a decade and was the twin brother of a Combat Controller named Preston, pulled a Nikon Coolpix camera with an 8X lens from his mini pack to capture some shots for Andy to pass back, when Eric motioned for his attention. On the ridgeline fifteen meters above the tent was the unmistakable silhouette of a tripod-mounted Russian DShK-38 12.7mm antiaircraft machine gun, protected from the elements by a blue plastic tarp wrapped tightly around the barrel and receiver. Chris snapped some shots and then confirmed the weapon's location using his laser rangefinder and GPS.

The discovery was fortuitous. The position dominated the entire 700-meter-wide approach corridor the TF-Rakkasan helicopters were to use for insertion in little more than twenty-four hours. The DShK's 3,000-meter range placed the entire assault force in "duck shoot" range. The two men watched the position for signs of fighters, but nobody showed themselves in the cold, so they silently withdrew back across the snow-covered ridgeline to report their findings, careful not to dislodge any rocks as the squall covered their withdrawal.

Andy relayed a short message outlining what they'd discovered. At the AFO safe house Blaber read the message, absorbing the new information, the first concrete evidence of enemy preparation for the assault.

The SEALs went back for a second look in the light of day to determine whether the site was occupied and to get better photos, this time with Goody accompanying them. What they saw gave them pause. Two men were in the open. The first was a short, dark-haired, and bearded Mongol wearing typical Afghan tan "man jammies" and a sleeveless jacket of gray, red, and blue, topped by a brown wool hat. But it was the other man that caught the SEALs' attention. A tall, clean-shaven Caucasian with a full head of reddish collar-length hair, he was dressed for the elements in a heavy red Gore-Tex jacket, Polartec fleece liner, and Russian pattern camo pants. This man was clearly in charge of their fighting position. He'd carefully arranged ammunition in an arc around the DShK's pit for rapid reloading when the time came. Both men seemed fit and healthy, the Caucasian occasionally shadowboxing with himself and strolling between the DShK and the tent.

At first, they assumed he was Uzbek, but the longer they watched, the less sure they were that they had his ethnicity pegged. At the hide site, Andy downloaded the photos onto his Toughbook.

Andy was the team's communications expert, but it was Goody's mission to lead. He quickly typed a message for Blaber and the SEAL Team Six HQ, attached the photos, and hit send. Although Blaber was their immediate commander, the SEALs of Mako-31 were also reporting their actions directly to their chain of command in Bagram and excluding Blaber from these back-channel messages. This would have far-reaching and tragic consequences in the coming hours and days.

Because of this, John Chapman in Bagram and Jay Hill across the valley were oblivious to the message traffic, which would also have consequences when Mako-31 began reporting more enemy locations in the coming hours, including on Takur Ghar.

Goody designated his message "eyes only" for Blaber and included the assessment that there may be as many as five fighters. The day-time photos clearly showed the Caucasian in his mountain redoubt with the TF-Rakkasan insertion corridor stretching panoramically into the distance behind him. Mako-31's other concern was the possible presence of other allied forces. The Aussies were already in the south, so Goody asked Blaber, "Are the Brits up here?" It was possible. The Mako-31 team looked nothing like an American force, and who knew if the Brits were similarly outfitted and using locals as part of some uncoordinated operation?

The photos conveyed more detail and impact than any written report could. It was clear to Blaber that the Uzbeks and other foreign fighters were ready for a fight. Blaber assured Goody there were no Brits or other forces in their vicinity and immediately passed the message to Bagram. It caused concern among the planners, who had been assured by the broader Army and intelligence organizations, supported by dedicated satellites, surveillance aircraft, and even a CIA Mi-17 video flyover just the previous day, that threats to the in-sertion force simply didn't exist. Before they'd even reached their OP, Mako-31, and by extension Blaber's entire AFO force and concept, were changing the looming battle.

Goody, Andy, and the others needed to outline a plan. The DShK would need to be eliminated before TF-Rakkasan entered the valley, and it was impossible to say whether the weapon and fighters, now only six hundred feet from their position, were reinforced by a larger contingent tucked into the mountains nearby. But their mission was not to directly engage the enemy; they simply weren't equipped for any type of direct assault or sustained firefight. And there was the question of what Blaber might say. But some action *had* to happen; they simply couldn't allow the DShK to stand. Even if TF-Rakkasan did modify their plan, Andy couldn't call in airstrikes from the current OP with an enemy force a stone's throw away. Eventually they'd be discovered. The SEALs and Andy, all of them trained snipers, were not inclined to leave an enemy force standing, and they believed they could take them, but would Blaber agree?

After further discussion, Goody got on his laptop and asked Blaber for guidance. Instead of providing direction, he asked the SEAL, "What's your recommendation?" To the SEALs and Andy, who were beginning to appreciate the Delta officer's leadership style, it was manna from heaven.

Blaber, who was acutely aware of the precarious position of his teams, waited while his team leader absorbed the question.

"I want to make sure we maintain the element of surprise as close to H-hour as possible. I will wait until H minus two [hours]. At H minus two I will start moving; that will allow me to take my time getting into position. I'll engage at H minus one, and then [have Andy] follow up with AC-130."

For good measure, Goody followed that immediately with, "I understand that you have to make the decision on this and I'll support any decision you make."

Blaber, always one with a flair for the dramatic and not wishing to miss an opportunity, sent back, "Good hunting," smiling at the exchange.

On a mountain deep in enemy territory, five men, seriously out-numbered and unsupported, smiled too. For the men of Mako-31, an opportunity such as this is why each became a Combat Controller or a SEAL.

———

At TF-11, everything was not smiles as Blaber's early reports and photos circulated. Some of the staff believed Blaber was exceeding his mission. Mako-31 "did not have sufficient men to attack the position, nor even 'doctrinal authority' to conduct a direct action," according to one TF-11 staffer. "Peter the Great" was at it again, scoffed another. Also taking note of the increased message traffic, and the impact of AFO, was the commander of SEAL Team Six, Captain Joe Kernan, and his ops officer, a SEAL named Tim Szymanski. Two of their men may have excluded themselves from AFO, but half of Slab's Red Team sniper element was now decisively engaged in a big opportunity. For Slab and the rest of the SEALs in Bagram, nothing was happening, and everyone in TF-11 was now fixating on Blaber's three teams in the field as Operation Anaconda began to spin up in preparation for combat operations. Wheels began to spin in the minds of the SEAL leaders.

Back in Gardez, Blaber sent a final message to Goody, a four-word mission statement: "Terminate with extreme prejudice."

Falling back on his Navy vernacular, the SEAL acknowledged with a simple "Aye, aye," before signing off.

Blaber looked at a map on the wall of the safe house. All three of his teams were in and "open for business," ready for H-hour. He was extremely proud of what the small, elite joint force was doing in the field and confident in their abilities. The enemy had a vote in what happened next, of course, and conditions remained perilous for the Delta, SEAL, and Combat Control operators, but he knew there was no one else in the world who could perform better in the days to come.

At TF-11's JOC (Joint Operations Center) in Bagram, Brigadier General Trebon, the deputy TF-11 commander, was just finishing a conversation with Six's Captain Kernan. He picked up the phone to dial the AFO commander with some news.

CHAPTER

14

—

2 March

BEFORE SUNRISE

THE SECOND OF MARCH DAWNED WITH BETTER VISIBILITY AND WEATHER for the AFO teams as temperatures approached a much-welcomed 32 degrees Fahrenheit. Jay Hill and the Delta snipers were settled into their OP and had established a battle rhythm for reporting on the enemy. There was plenty to report. In addition to civilians fleeing the valley, positions were being fortified across the Whale, and forces could be seen mustering and repositioning. It was going to be a good day for killing.

The mission was Delta-led, with Kris delivering the reports to Blaber while Bill and Dave did most of the scope-spotting. The mission's statement and core, however, were all CCT. In preparation for orchestrating bomb strikes and gun runs (helicopters and fighters), Jay had two MBITRs and his PRC-117, which, when combined with his FalconView expertise, gave the team an unprecedented suite of lethality with which to decimate the enemy forces.

"I had my radios all set up, superior comms through the entire valley. Kris would make the calls to [Blaber] and I'd worry about range-finding, running down all the different targets, and nominating them." The day was well spent, "reporting back potential targets

163

to Pete [Blaber], who would relay to Bagram who would...well, Trebon and those folks I'm sure were listening too, on SAT alpha [the designated AFO satellite frequency]. Everything was set up so we could talk to everybody. And we were in a good position where we had the entire valley covered." All he needed now were planes and bombs.

Below him, in the center of the valley, the enemy's preparations, advance warning, and superior numbers did provide them certain advantages, but could they use them effectively? Intercepted requests revealed their concerns as well as their strategy: "The traitors and their American allies are going to attack soon, we need to bring reinforcements to the village."

Maulawi Saif-ur-Rahman Nasrullah Mansoor was the commander responsible for fielding such requests and for shaping the overall strategy. With hundreds of mujahideen under his command, his assessment did not agree with his subordinate's request. Based on his experience as a subcommander under Haqqani in the Soviet campaign, during which they were victorious, he replied, "There is no need. We were in Shahi Khot during the first Afghan jihad [against the Soviets]. There were six mujahideen in total and we were surrounded by ten tanks. Over five air attacks were staged on us in a single day, and there were about one hundred Soviet soldiers who attacked us from the land. But all praise belongs to Allah alone— they were not able to set foot on a single hand-span of the village, and we remained in this same state for about one week." Convinced the high ground, coupled with mortars and antiaircraft systems throughout the valley (along with Allah's blessing) and the hundreds of fighters who'd fled from the north, was adequate to defeat the "soft" Americans, they waited, reciting their daily prayers.

The stage was set for the morning's US-led invasion of the Shahi Khot. Three postage-stamp-size elements of America's finest troops, thirteen men in all, waited to battle a thousand to fifteen hundred hardened and experienced fighters of the jihad who were arrayed across two hundred square miles of fortified fighting positions. They were armed with heavy machine guns, antiaircraft weapons, mortars, and artillery and occupied the vast majority of the high ground surrounding the Shahi Khot Valley. Yet for all AFO's capability and experience, Blaber's troops were merely peripheral to Operation Anaconda's main thrust.

The plan to eliminate the enemy was simple. The US Army intended to drop a few hundred infantry troops from the 10th Mountain and 101st Airborne onto the valley floor. They would then establish blocking positions against the mountains to serve as an anvil against which the (theoretically) terrified Al Qaeda fighters fleeing ATF forces (augmented by Chris Haas's Green Berets) would be crushed. But Army planners did not have accurate enemy numbers, nor did they understand the enemy's intention. They also fundamentally misunderstood their foe, as evidenced by Mansoor's directives. The Al Qaeda field commander correctly assessed where the Americans would land and began moving troops into position accordingly.

As the hours ticked down for the operation to commence, Juliet Team continued to "report enemy activity and waited for H-hour. The plan was, prior to H-hour, we would have control of fires [airstrikes] and, after H-hour, the 101st would have control." Jay was steadily building his target list, double-checking distances and locations with his Delta teammates and occasionally exchanging information with Andy. He could feel the tension rising from the valley. Al Qaeda and the Taliban could be seen on the Whale to his southwest and in the villages in the valley. Strangely (or not, as it would turn out), the latter had very few locals and none of the activity one would expect of daily Afghan life. Everywhere they looked were, exclusively, adult males moving with purpose. Other prominent sites, including the peak of Takur Ghar to the south, also revealed enemy activity. In the valley, J Team reported that the Army's HLZs remained clear of obstacles and enemy fortifications. This wasn't surprising, since the HLZs, centered in the valley and on level ground in front of the mountain peaks, afforded no tactical advantage, save as level landing sites for the giant and slow CH-47s. It was on the Whale that most enemy activity could be seen, and Jay took particular note of the mortar pits.

For J Team, their initial role during the operation's kickoff was simple. According to Kris, "[Jay's B-1] that was striking the cave next to us was supposed to check in with us prior to dropping. The 101st would land and establish blocking positions while the ATF came into [Shahi Khot] and did the dirty work. There was supposed to be a good fire support plan for mass bombing of the Tergul Ghar [the Whale] and Takur Ghar mountains. At H-3:00 we were cleared to engage targets." As day turned to night, and the night turned cold, the team took their last opportunity to attempt sleep while waiting for killing time to begin.

On their OP, Jay had arrayed his CAS equipment ergonomically around him: radios, scope, laser rangefinder, IZLID IR pointer. He tried to get some sleep, "maybe an hour and a half, because you were . . . You didn't want to go to sleep. One, it was cold as hell. Two, it was the excitement pouring through your veins. 'I get to do some Combat Control shit here.'" Still, with an unknown number of straight combat days before him, "we were trying." Thinking, "If there's a time to sleep, you better do it now because you've got to conserve yourself for the next couple days. This thing is going to be a long time. But we had to take shifts with sleeping and it never really worked out." The men sat, as silent as the night was dark. Watching. Waiting. Knowing.

———

As Jay froze in the pre-morning light, stuffed inside his puffy jacket, Andy and Mako-31 were already executing their pre-operation strike. Shortly after midnight, they had quietly jammed all their items into rucksacks (ensuring nothing would "rattle or clang" and betray them), picked up, and moved in the direction of the DShK while Chris traveled ahead of the others to find a site to stash their packs. When the rest arrived and dropped their rucks, Goody, Chris, and Eric began their slow approach toward the enemy's position.

Andy stayed with the equipment, not for security but to ensure he didn't give away their position when he began his airstrike coordination. He opened the top of his ruck to access the screen of his PRC-117 radio, turned it on, and configured it for operations. He then pulled the DMC-120 SATCOM antenna from inside and quickly assembled it, directing it at the appropriate satellite. He did a quick comm check on the net. Satisfied he was on the "bird," he pulled out the tools of Combat Control's trade (nearly identical to Jay's, nine kilometers to the north). Andy went through his mental checklist, comparing it with his plan to remove the DShK after the SEALs killed the Al Qaeda team leader they had seen outside the tent earlier. He finalized his preparations and sat back. Around him, the mountains were eerily silent. The SEALs made no sound as they closed in for the kill. He checked his watch; a little more than an hour to go. A sound reached his ears, the low, steady drone of a lone turboprop plane overhead. He looked through his NVGs at the reassuring shadow, invisible to the naked eye, that was making slow "two-minute turns" (orbits) in the distance. Andy smiled to himself. The first of the aerial predators had arrived: Grim-31, an H-model AC-130 "Spectre" gunship. It was Andy's favorite execution tool for conditions such as this. He shivered in the cold and thought, *It's going to be a good day.*

Chris led the other SEALs as they crept toward the enemy camp. Clouds came and went, alternately illuminating and then masking the terrain. They slid their way to a ridgeline and he realized they were only sixty feet from the darkened tent. Chris was in front, the other two behind him to minimize their profile against the sky. The snipers double-checked their rifles, two Stoner SR-25s and an M4, and marked the time: It was now two hours before TF-Rakkasan forces were to land in the valley, H-2:00.

Chris recalls what happened next: "I observed a man come over the top of the ridge and look down into the valley; he came from the direction of the tent that we could not observe at the time. I then realized how close we were to the site. The individual returned to the tent, and we continued to wait. The clouds cleared, and we could now hear the gunships overhead [there were two in the valley]. I observed the same sentry come out to the same spot; he was looking out to the west again. I slowly crouched down and tried to get the attention of [Goody and Eric]. Before I could, the sentry looked our way just as Eric stood up. Due to the illumination, he easily spotted the movement and turned and ran toward the tent."

The SEALs had compromised themselves. Left with no choice, Goody ordered the attack. The sentry was shouting at his comrades to wake as the three SEALs charged over the ridge. Chris stopped and fired one shot before his rifle jammed. Goody took a knee and had fired his first round into the tent when his rifle also jammed. Both men were shooting the SR-25s, each with a suppressor (providing muzzle-flash masking as well as sound reduction), and both had iced up.

The two men frantically worked to clear their weapons. The sentry, by then inside the tent, unloaded a full magazine from his AK-47 at them. The SEALs could see the blinding muzzle flash from between the folds of the tent flaps. They'd stirred up a veritable hornet's nest as men poured out of the tent with weapons in hand. One, a Chechen, charged Chris, who had finally cleared his jam. Chris pumped several rounds into the chest of his assailant, dropping him in the snow mere feet away. A second broke right, lunging toward the DShK, but was blasted by Chris and Goody simultaneously.

Their problems were just beginning. From the team's left, a fighter was flanking them. Eric dispatched the AQ soldier as Goody got on the radio to Andy, who was already moving toward the gunfire. The difference between the American and Al Qaeda weapons is very easily distinguished, and it sounded to the Controller like his men were on the losing side, based on the volume of hostile fire. As if in confirmation, a sustained burst of 7.62 passed just over his head, the telltale tracer rounds carving a slow-motion arc in front of the silent, starry backdrop.

Grim-31, fully briefed by Andy, was moving overhead at 20,000 feet above mean sea level (less than 10,000 feet above the team's mountainous ridge), its 40mm Bofors cannon and 105mm howitzer ready and trained on the DShK and tent. The pilot reported to Andy they had "two enemy bodies just outside the tent and another wounded and crawling away."

Andy and the SEALs met halfway. As he was telling Chris they needed to pull back so he could destroy the DShK position, Grim-31 announced through Andy's headset that there were "two other figures moving north of Mako Three One trying to get on their left flank." The flankers were only seventy-five meters away and appeared to be emplacing a machine gun. When a sustained burst of 7.62 PKM fire raked the ridge near the team's position, it obviated the need for further confirmation.

They were in serious trouble. An H-model gunship's "danger close" for its 40mm Bofors was 125 meters; for the 105mm it was 600 meters. The team was well under 100 meters from the DShK, and more fighters were appearing from the night, attempting to engage Mako-31. Relief was up to Andy, who had Grim-31 poised with an "at my command" weapons release.

The team continued its retreat as Grim-31 waited to hear the words that would authorize the unleashing of the first 33-pound, 1,550-foot-per-second, high-explosive shell. While the men tumbled across the rough terrain, pursued by tracer fire, Andy uttered them. "Cleared hot," he stated in a steady but winded voice.

The weapons of an AC-130 can only be fired by the pilot, who always sits in the left seat, the same side as its deadly cannons and sensors. As soon as the pilot, Major D. J. Turner, heard the clearance, he checked his sensor operators in the rear to ensure his "friendlies" were clear, and then pulled the trigger. It took the 105 round a little less than seven seconds to travel the distance, sticking its landing with a thud and *whump* felt by Andy and the team.

Back inside the AC-130, the 105 gunners ejected the spent brass casing as soon as the recoil had finished and had the next 33-pound round in the breech in less than five seconds.

As soon as they called, "Gun ready!" Turner hit it again. This was the type of mission gunship crews lived for: killing bad guys when their brothers-in-arms were in dire straits, knowing full well no other fixed-wing aircraft was as decisive an edge.[13]

The pilots and sensor operators watched with satisfaction as the rounds killed the two machine gunners instantly. Having been pre-cleared by Andy for the rest of the target, they trained their weapons on the tent, shredding it with multiple 105 rounds and strewing the contents across the rock face.

As the members of Mako-31 collected at their rucks, Grim-31 fired

---

13   D. J. Turner's crew would play a critical role in the coming hours and days. For Haas's men and the ATF, they would be involved in a friendly-fire incident less than an hour after striking the DShK. But as events developed on Takur Ghar forty-eight hours later, it was Turner who would find himself over the mountain when the battle there unfolded.

on yet another flanker, killing him outright. They waited till the gunship finished its work, then moved carefully back to the DShK position to conduct a battle damage assessment, certain in their movement thanks to the watchful eyes overhead.

At the DShK and tent, they found five bodies cooling in the early morning air. Inside the tent was a treasure-trove of Cyrillic documents confirming the fighters' Chechen ethnicity, as well as a few Arabic papers. The most significant find came from inspecting the DShK. It was clean and serviceable, freshly oiled, with two thousand rounds stacked conveniently around it. Goody reported, "The AQ had built a makeshift traverse and elevation mechanism allowing it to hit targets out to 3000 meters and to easily cover the flight routes of the US helicopters which would arrive shortly." The position also had an RPG launcher with seven rounds, a Russian Dragunov 7.62mm sniper rifle, multiple AK-47s, and the PKM machine gun that the Chechens had used in their attempt to flank the team.

Mako-31 occupied their adversary's former position, making it their new OP, and planned to remain for the duration of the operation. When TF-Rakkasan flew into the valley fifty minutes later, the SEAL team leader tracked their approach through the DShK's gunsights.

CHAPTER

15

—

2 March

NIGHTTIME

THROUGHOUT THE VALLEY, GRIM-31'S EXPLOSIVE DISPLAY ANNOUNCED the Americans' presence like a bullhorn in church, eliminating the need for further verification by the enemy. Both sides knew "it was on," and that realization had the fortuitous consequence of unsettling many of the Al Qaeda fighters. On the Whale, many took to firing their weapons blindly into the darkened sky, exposing them to the watchful eyes of J Team, who, like everyone else, had observed the display to their south. Jay listened in on the same "fires" freq Andy used to kill off the DShK element.[14]

As fast as he could, Jay, using the entire team to help with distances and coordinates, began logging previously unknown positions for later strikes. They counted down the minutes until their own "first strike," when the B-1 with the 2,000-pound thermobaric bomb arrived at H-:30.

---

14 Every Combat Controller used the same "fires" frequency for strikes in the Shahi Khot. Not only did this allow for sequencing and handoffs, it crucially prevented fratricide. Despite the coming battles and dozens of "danger close" airstrikes conducted by CCT during Anaconda, not one instance of friendly fire took place under their control.

173

Sitting in the OP with his radios arrayed around him, but primarily concerned only with his MBITR on the fires freq, Jay watched and waited for the B-1. As soon as it made contact (known as "checking in"), he would verify the nine-line brief to ensure ground and air were synchronized.[15]

Jay was ready. As soon as the bomber dropped the thermobaric and destroyed the closest threat, he hoped to move him to the Whale to drop a handful of 1,000-pound JDAMs. These were bombs that had been converted from dumb bombs (unguided except by gravity) to all-weather smart bombs. A "bolt-on" fin kit allowed the ordnance to be steered to a target by inertial guidance and GPS or laser energy.

Jay gazed out across the valley in the early morning twilight, his NVGs stored back in the ruck and a wool hat inadequately keeping the cold at bay. To the west, he was beginning to make out terrain features on the Whale, where the fighting positions they'd mapped in the dark were taking shape, when an explosion behind him rocked the entire OP, shaking the earth beneath them. The Al Qaeda cave had blown up. Wide-eyed shock and disbelief were exchanged wordlessly on the OP.

A mushroom cloud of coal-black smoke enveloped a fireball where the cave entrance sat an instant before, the sound still reverberating across the early morning calm. The B-1 had dropped without checking. J Team, less than seven hundred meters from the target, was just beyond the "danger close" distance of five hundred meters for a 2,000-pounder, but the men were pissed. This was just the kind of miscommunication that could get them killed in the coming hours and days. Suppose they'd moved closer to recon activity, or

---

15 The nine-line brief is used by all US, NATO, and allied fighters and bombers to receive information from the individual controlling the strike or bomb drop on the ground. It is conducted upon first contact, usually over a predetermined geographic point known as the Initial Point but referred to as IP.

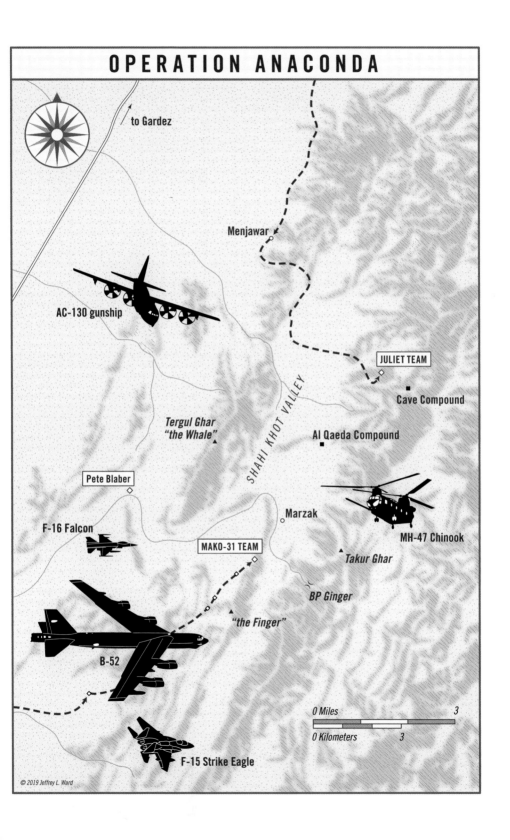

OPERATION ANACONDA

to Gardez

AC-130 gunship

Menjawar

JULIET TEAM

Cave Compound

SHAHI KHOT VALLEY

Tergul Ghar
"the Whale"

Al Qaeda Compound

Pete Blaber

Marzak

MH-47 Chinook

F-16 Falcon

MAKO-31 TEAM

Takur Ghar

BP Ginger

"the Finger"

B-52

F-15 Strike Eagle

0 Miles 3
0 Kilometers 3

© 2019 Jeffrey L. Ward

AFGHANISTAN

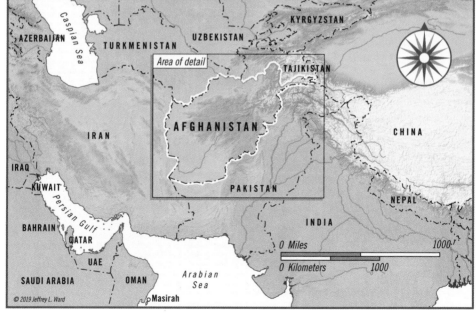

John Chapman in 1968 with a World War I veteran. *Courtesy of Lori Longfritz*

John with his friend Mary Tersavich. *Courtesy of Lori Longfritz*

Airstrike called in by Jim Stanford in northern Laos. (Images of airstrikes would later become emblematic of Combat Control.) *Courtesy of Catherine Bond*

CCT Jim Stanford and his O-1 Bird Dog in Laos, 1966. *Courtesy of Catherine Bond*

John at diving practice, 1981.
Courtesy of Lori Longfritz

A young Airman
Chapman with his
prized Le Mans in 1986.
Courtesy of Lori Longfritz

The Desert One CCT of
Brand X just prior to the
ill-fated mission, 1980.
Courtesy of Mike Lampe

John Chapman after graduating from OL-H indoctrination in 1989. *Courtesy of Lori Longfritz*

John and fellow pipeline survivor Joe Maynor, CCS graduation day, 1990. *Courtesy of Joe Maynor*

Mr. and Mrs. John and Valerie Chapman on their wedding day, 1992. *Courtesy of Lori Longfritz*

24 STS Green Team 1996 conducting urban warfare training. John is front row left. Keary Miller, who would later recover John's body, is back row second from left. Pat Elko is back row third from left. *Courtesy of Pat Elko*

Calvin Markham spotting targets for airstrikes in Afghanistan, 2001. *Courtesy of Calvin Markham*

Combat Controllers Bill White, Marcus Millard, and Calvin Markham in front of the still shuttered US embassy, Kabul, 2001. *Courtesy of Calvin Markham*

Joe O'Keefe (right) and two Delta personnel on a Soviet MiG, Bagram Airfield, 2001. *Courtesy of Joe O'Keefe*

Mike Stockdale and two Delta personnel inside a Taliban arms depot tunnel, Tora Bora, December 2001. *Courtesy of Mike Stockdale*

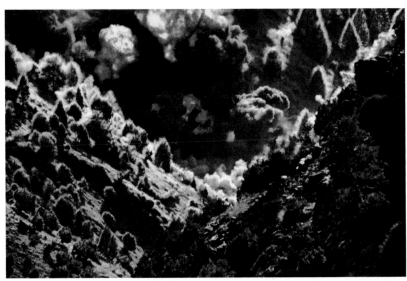

Airstrike by Combat Controllers during the hunt for Osama bin Laden in Tora Bora, December 2011. *Courtesy of Joe O'Keefe*

John, Val, and the girls on their annual vacation to Virginia Beach, summer of 2001.
Courtesy of Lori Longfritz

John on his cot in Bagram.
Courtesy of Lori Longfritz

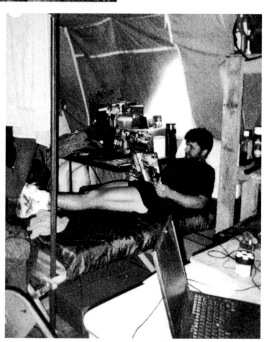

John and baby inside the Afghan home the team was placed in during the Mullah Omar mission. The photo would go on to become the iconic image of his life, juxtaposing the warrior with the compassionate humanitarian underneath.
Courtesy of Lori Longfritz

John in an Afghan village while on patrol. *Courtesy of Lori Longfritz*

After the storm in the mountains.
Courtesy of Andy Martin

SEALs and CCT moving by foot into the mountains in pursuit of Omar. *Courtesy of Andy Martin*

Andy Martin making a SATCOM call while John looks dubiously at their mules. *Courtesy of Andy Martin*

More fortress than residence, the Gardez safe house. *Courtesy of Jay Hill*

Testing and probing the areas surrounding Gardez prior to AFO infiltrating the mountains. *Courtesy of Jay Hill*

Jay Hill on his ATV in enemy territory.
Courtesy of Jay Hill

The enemy camp as
captured by Mako-31.
Courtesy of Andy Martin

Early morning airstrike using
airburst ordnance against
enemy troops in the open.
Courtesy of Andy Martin

The Australian OP with
CCT Jim Hotaling targeting
enemy positions. *Courtesy of
Jim Hotaling*

Andy Martin in Mako-31's second OP. *Courtesy of Andy Martin*

One of the Apaches that nearly mistook the team for enemy forces as it rolls in on a target for Andy Martin. *Courtesy of Andy Martin*

Jay Hill next to his spotting scope during J Team's nonstop onslaught. *Courtesy of Jay Hill*

The summit of Takur Ghar mountain. *Department of Defense*

Razor-03's crash site shortly after the mission and before the aircraft was destroyed in place. *Department of Defense*

Bunker 2 on Takur Ghar. *Department of Defense*

The DShK position atop Takur Ghar Chapman prevented from destroying the QRF. *Department of Defense*

The Special Tactics CSAR team of (from left to right) PJ Keary Miller, PJ Jason Cunningham, and CCT Gabe Brown days before their fateful mission. *Courtesy of Gabe Brown*

Takur Ghar as seen from overhead shortly after the battle. Razor-01 would later be destroyed in place by AC-130 fire like Razor-03. *Department of Defense*

An airstrike on the Whale during Anaconda. *Department of Defense*

Bagram memorial for the seven men killed on Takur Ghar. *Courtesy of Lori Longfritz*

Madison at the stern of the MV *TSgt John A. Chapman* after its christening in 2005. *Courtesy of Lori Longfritz*

The SEAL Team Six memorial where John was the first non-SEAL to be added. (His name is at the bottom of the left column.) *Courtesy of Lori Longfritz*

Valerie between coauthors Dan Schilling and Lori Longfritz at the White House with John's Medal of Honor. *Courtesy of Dan Schilling*

worse, the GPS coordinates were off? With no nine-line, it was a bit of Russian roulette, with dozens of aircraft "barrels" pointed at the AFO teams. According to Kris, the initial strikes comprised the following: "Eight JDAMs were dropped on the Whale and only one JDAM on Takur Ghar. The AC-130 also fired at the bunker [on the Whale] and that was pretty much it for the 'great' fire support plan. The Whale should have been carpet-bombed based on the disposition of the enemy forces. Takur Ghar should have been bombed more as well. Once again [AFO] intel had previously identified enemy positions on Takur Ghar. This would come back to haunt the US forces soon after."

With the reverberations of the explosion still echoing across the mountains, everyone in the valley—Al Qaeda, AFO, and any remaining civilians—was well aware that a battle, whose shape had yet to fully develop, had commenced.

At 0630, three CH-47s swept into the northern end of the valley below J Team, the *thump thump thump* of their heavy rotors echoing off the mountain slopes. Inside each were forty combat troops from the Army's 101st Airborne Division. The infantrymen's battalion commander, Lieutenant Colonel "Chip" Preysler, who was responsible for all of them and for the northern portion of the operation, was crammed near the front of the cargo compartment in one of the helicopters.

Inside the helo, a door gunner called out a warning: "Two minutes!" One of the senior infantry NCOs shouted the first order for the young soldiers inside: "Lock and load!" Simultaneously, forty-plus sounds of M4s, SAWs, and M240 machine guns chambering rounds could be heard over the din of rotor and engine noise, various *clack clack*s on the machine guns and *chick klunk*s on the M4s. "Thirty seconds!" came shortly after. The soldiers fingered their weapons nervously, almost none of them having seen combat and many having no real idea of what to expect.

At 0633, Preysler's helicopter touched down. As it settled and the landing gear absorbed the load, the men shouldered their rucksacks and stood as one mass. Led by a 240 gunner, they charged down the helicopter's ramp, moving to the sounds of comrades shouting, "Go! Go! Move! Move!" They ducked under the low roof at the hinge and stepped into the Shahi Khot . . . straight into enemy fire.

———

To the south, a similar scene was unfolding, only this time it was 120 men from the 10th Mountain Division. Lieutenant Colonel Paul LaCamera was in charge of the southern blocking positions—the anvil.

Colonel Frank Wiercinski, commander of the 3rd Brigade—the Rakkasans, from which TF-Rakkasan drew its name—was in charge of all the allied forces in the valley. The two-battalion movement, essentially a brigade-size air assault, had happened only one other time since Vietnam. Wiercinski was aware of the lives under his command and of the history that would be made on this day, one way or another.

As the blocking forces were inserting to the north and south, he orbited inside the rear of a flight of two Black Hawk helicopters, looking for a place to insert his tactical command team, known as the TAC. He planned to land near a geographic feature called the Finger, which lay at the base of Mako-31's new OP, remain on the ground only long enough to determine the operation's progress, and then fly back to Bagram. His chief task today was to assist his boss, Hagenbeck, with managing expectations at CENTCOM and in Washington, DC, where President George W. Bush and Defense Secretary Donald Rumsfeld remained intimately connected to the campaign.

Spotting a tactically desirable cleft in the rocky terrain, he keyed the microphone on his headset. "Put us down there," he told the pilots. The space was tight and Wiercinski's pilot missed his approach, forcing the helo to go around and line up a second time. The second Black Hawk managed to squeeze in, missing the rock ledge with its rotor by two feet, dumping the TAC's security and radio team.

As Wiercinski's helo circled back and lowered into the draw, an Al Qaeda fighter stepped from a rock outcropping with an RPG and leveled it at the slow-moving Black Hawk. He squeezed the trigger, and the grenade punched out of the launch tube, streaking up toward the exposed underbelly of the helicopter, scoring a direct hit against the chin bubble. A second fighter, wielding an AK-47, took aim at the "winged duck" and unleashed an entire banana clip. His aim was good as he perforated the length of the helo's tail boom, damaging the tail rotor hub and nicking a push-pull rod inside that is critical to countering the main rotor's torque. "If that thing had severed, we'd have lost tail rotor control, and we'd have been gone," recalled Jim Marye, the air mission commander on board.

The TAC was taking fire even before Wiercinski's team touched the ground, but he'd chosen the site well and it was masked from the enemy. Bullets were striking against the rocks above the soldiers as the two Black Hawks limped off in the morning light. They appeared to be safe from direct fire . . . for the moment.

As they established Operation Anaconda's battlefield command and control position, the same could not be said for the 10th Mountain and 101st Airborne troops moving off their LZs. Even before the tail rotor strike, Wiercinski was listening to radio calls from the blocking positions regarding casualties and fierce enemy resistance. TF-Rakkasan was learning what Blaber and the men of AFO had already suspected: The enemy was well armed, well positioned, and hungering for a fight. There were no fleeing jihadis and there was no organized retreat. Al Qaeda was here to fight.

As the TAC got their bearings and established a more secure perimeter, they were surprised to look up and find a corpse hanging off the ridge above them. Without knowing it, they were staring straight up at Mako-31 and the aftermath of their firefight, including the bodies of the enemy.

By this time, the second wave of heavy-lift CH-47s was landing with more infantry, but the TF-Hammer (General Hagenbeck's main thrust) forces had stalled. Grim-31 had moved over their convoy and, in a tragic incident, had fired on them in the confusion, killing one American Green Beret and several ATF. Because of the attack and lack of concerted bombing of enemy positions, TF-Hammer had retreated under the demands of a frustrated and angry Afghan Commander Zia, leaving the US infantry to carry on the fight alone. TF-Hammer also stranded Blaber, who was attempting to get into the mountains to better track the battle and assist his teams in the field.

Soon after the rest of TF-Rakkasan had inserted, the infantry had secured all the blocking positions except one, identified in the battle plan as Ginger. Ginger sat just below Takur Ghar mountain and was fiercely defended by a concentration of Al Qaeda troops. With the mountains and high ground surrounding the Rakkasan troops, and the enemy refusing to flee, the infantry began its assault against the enemy positions firing down on them. The majority of fire originated from the Whale but also seemed to be coming from the mountains to the north and east.

Things turned deadly for Mako-31 when they began to receive direct fire—not from Al Qaeda but from the Rakkasans, even though Andy had placed several VS-17 panels around their position when the fighting started. Roughly two foot by six foot, VS-17s were tough but pliable panels with parachute-cord tie-downs along the edges and at each corner. They were orange on one side and vibrant cerise on the other, and were used for marking virtually anything· on the battlefield as friendly. As the team took cover, Andy manned the radio and found the TAC's freq and call sign, diverting the friendly fire "to a more prominent ridgeline" east of the team.

Soon after, hostile 82mm mortar rounds began to drop onto their position from a ridge just south of Takur Ghar. The first rounds landed short, but the team couldn't see the enemy tube. When the next rounds landed long, the team was effectively bracketed; incoming enemy or friendly fire could be managed, but not both. Goody made the decision to leave their OP. With all the shit that was going on, there was only one place to relocate, the Rakkasan TAC. It was a surprise to the conventional Army troops when Mako-31 walked into their beleaguered position (they too were taking more and accurate fire as the morning progressed) and introduced themselves simply as "recon and surveillance snipers." Andy and Goody briefed Colonel Wiercinski, and then Andy joined forces with the TAC air liaison officer, an Air Force F-16 pilot assigned to assist with air support, while the other snipers beefed up the perimeter.

In the north, Jay watched as the 101st was taking casualties. They were also returning the favor, pumping out 82mm and 120mm mortar rounds and engaging in pitched gunfights and mortar duels with enemy positions on the Whale.

Kris continues their observations:

Because the AQ had been tipped off about the attack 24 hours prior, they were now waiting for the ATF to come into their AO [area of operations]. The AQ knew exactly which way the ATF assault force was coming in because they were set up east-to-west, facing south, and on line waiting in shooting positions. We saw them from our OP and they were dressed in military kit: LBE [Load-Bearing Equipment], small rucks, weapons, and even a guidon [a symbolic flag, carried by soldiers since the Roman legions and used to identify units and inspire troops]. Dave was on the scope and watched the AQ occupy positions as their commander used hand and arm signals to stage them. Once in position, the commander motioned the guidon bearer to move to him and then directed him to move to a building in the town of Serkhankhel.

We had observation of 101st troops and they were moving right toward the AQ. [Jay] called a B-52 in with JDAMs to strike the AQ positions and within minutes he dropped them right on top of the AQ, killing several to include the commander. The 101st called us and asked who gave us permission to drop the JDAMs because they were about one kilometer away. We explained the situation and they understood but told them we needed to make another pass. After the first pass two guys got up and drug the commander's body down into some low ground. In this low ground more AQ were moving in and out. The 101st wanted to get farther out of the way, but instead moved directly toward where we were going to drop the next set of bombs. After the confusion of getting them moving in the right direction, [Jay] dropped right where the AQ were last seen and saw no movement from that area for about two hours. Then the AQ reoccupied the same positions again and [Jay] dropped JDAMs on them once more. After the third JDAM strike that day, they reoccupied the position and had JDAMs dropped on them and they never came back to it again. It appeared that they had a bunker or command post of some type in the low ground, because the AQ would come out of this area after each strike and drag off the dead. Even the survivors of the bombings, who must have been wounded, would always assist in dragging the dead away.

Jay was in his element as a Combat Controller and, by every measure, was enjoying the most significant day of his career.[16] At the TAC, Andy was alternating between airstrikes in conjunction with Major Dino Murray, the air liaison officer, referred to by the acronym ALO, and the action taking place around their position. Chris, the SEAL sniper, had spotted an advancing force of ten to twelve fighters. "They moved every few minutes from position to position, each time pausing just long enough to take a few shots [at us]. Several with RPGs and a few, who appeared to be leaders, with hand-held radios waving their arms and motioning still others over the ridgeline to come join the fight."

The SEALs discussed the situation and, along with Andy, formed a line and moved forward, closing the distance with the enemy. An airstrike was out of the question—too close. Chris and Eric opened fire, killing several of the Al Qaeda countersnipers outright.

Andy and Goody crouched down and ran along a rock wall that masked their movement. Andy was also a trained sniper, a certification Controllers could pursue in the course of their career if they desired. The two snipers popped up and rapidly engaged one target after another, killing half the enemy force. Recalls the Controller, "The engagement was a one-sided affair."

Four men "eliminated the direct fire threat that had pinned down the Rakkasan soldiers, killing eleven AQ and wounding another five. They then moved back to the ridgeline, providing 'overwatch' for the conventional forces, while [Andy] Martin began calling in CAS and AH-64s on the enemy mortar positions detected by SEAL snipers," according to one AFO after-action report.

The engagement didn't end there. Andy continued to wield B-52s

---

16   The guidon-fielding commander observed by J Team would turn out to be none other than Maulawi Saif-ur-Rahman Nasrullah Mansoor, who had refused to consider his subordinate's request for reinforcements.

and B-1s, as the Rakkasan and Al Qaeda mortar teams traded salvos. The TAC was also being targeted during the exchanges, with the enemy effectively walking mortar rounds to within fifty meters of the beleaguered position.

———

Several kilometers farther south, Hotaling and his SAS team were watching events unfold through sniper and spotting scopes, the details relayed through the Combat Controller's radio as his CCT brother destroyed enemy positions and fighters by the score. Unfortunately, at the far southern end of the valley, no engagements or fleeing enemy forces presented themselves. The SAS had labored and pressed their American ally hard for inclusion, so watching the action from the bleachers as the day wore on and hearing the friendly casualty count mount was simply not acceptable.

As they talked it over, Matt, the team leader, was adamant; they needed to reposition closer to the action. The team pored over their maps and Hotaling's FalconView, identifying a new OP to the north that was close enough for them to provide support to the battle. Hotaling got on the net and requested pickup. Overloaded as they were, patrolling their way to the new location was out of the question. After some negotiation, one of two nearby CIA Mi-17 helos was promised for the mission.

The team packed up their gear and prepped for pickup. Shortly after 1800, Hotaling heard the CIA bird on a helo frequency. It was the same pilots from their insertion, and the unwieldy bird flew in ponderously, landing next to the team. They climbed up into the oil-streaked interior, passing their rucks inside. Unlike Chinooks, the Russian helicopters had no ramps. Instead, equipment and men had to be hoisted up to the floor, three and a half feet above the ground. When everyone had clambered aboard, the helicopter lifted off for the short hop to their new site. Four minutes later the team offloaded and the lumbering helo disappeared into the sky.

No sooner had it departed than it became clear they had been deposited in the wrong place. Not only were they *not* on their objective, they were no closer than they'd been before they were picked up. Trying to get the Mi-17 back was futile; it was already on its next mission. The SAS was stranded on an eluvial plateau, the mouth of a dry stream bed emanating from between two peaks. Using GPS and their maps, the men determined their objective was up the water course.

Walking the course without analysis or intel on enemy locations was asking to be ambushed. Recalls Hotaling, "After the CIA dumped us not where we needed to be and we'd mapped the course, it led straight up the creek. The terrain on both sides of the creek bed was masked. There was no way to know what was up there or between us and our OP. Plus the distance was a motherfucker."

They had no idea how long it was going to take to make the movement, but there was no doubt they were going to do it. Hotaling got on the net again, this time hoping for something that could serve as an ISR platform, at least a P-3. He contacted an orbiting AWACS, the best source for airspace coordination and requests, hoping for an AC-130, but all the gunships were prioritized in support of the actual fight taking place to their north. Instead, what appeared overhead was a Predator, an armed CIA drone in this case, call sign Wildfire. "We're good," he informed Matt. The men shouldered their packs and stepped off into an uninviting darkness, their NVGs in place and weapons ready. It was going to be a long night.

———

For Blaber, the long night had already stretched into an even longer day. When TF-Hammer had gone bust, the Americans had returned to the safe house. On the battlefield, his teams were proving to be more of a decisive influence than the main force, who were taking it to the enemy in mortar duels and small-arms engagements but weren't destroying the majority of the targets and had suffered significant casualties. At TF-11, Brigadier General Trebon stated, "The good news was that TF-11 OPs performed their CAS function exceptionally well, inflicting 60 percent of the total enemy casualty count."

At the heart of those words were a few Combat Controllers. Of the day's events, Blaber recalls, "Jay Hill is in the field with Juliet Team and he's creating kill boxes on the fly. It was just incredible. These guys [CCT] are some of the most well-rounded, all-purpose guys. If I was going to Mars on a mission, I'd definitely take one. It's a critical and serious decision to trade off a Delta shooter when mission space is tight, not to be taken lightly, but, well, there you have it. I never go without one and every one I've had was a stud."

The damage AFO was inflicting was welcome news for the Delta officer. The doubters and obstacles were silenced or removed, and what remained was continuing to prosecute the mission to the fullest and ensuring he did everything he could to support and supply his men, who were hanging it out in the mountains.

As if to emphasize the point, at TF-11, congratulatory messages and calls came in from Major General Hagenbeck and General Tommy Franks, the CENTCOM commander. President Bush and Defense Secretary Rumsfeld had seen Mako-31's DShK photos before they were twelve hours old. Inside "tent city," Slab and Chapman caught the news as it unfolded, realizing that by holding out for a high-value target mission, they were missing the main show. During the run-up to Blaber's AFO missions and Anaconda's execution, they'd not actioned a single target.

Inside the Gardez TOC, Blaber's satellite phone rang. He heard Brigadier General Trebon's familiar voice on the line. "Pete, wonderful job. Look, we can't ask you guys to continue this; you're not set for that. What I want to do is turn this over to the SEALs. Let them command it, and let them continue prosecuting the fight. You and AFO need to be out looking for the next battlefield. I want to send some SEALs down and I want you to get these guys in there as quick as you can."

Blaber was stunned. Nothing about Trebon's suggestion made sense. How the Air Force general officer and pilot would conclude there was an immediate need for more troops in the field was a mystery to him. He had little time to dwell on the subject, though, because all three teams were decisively engaged, and every minute of the twenty-four-hour battle was critical, including Blaber's time.

"Sir, my teams are fine for at least another forty-eight hours; I recommend that any team going into the valley goes through the same routine as the three teams already in the valley. Before they infiltrate they need to spend time at Gardez so they can acclimate to the altitude and study the terrain and the history of the Shahi Khot. They need to talk to the CIA, the Special Forces, and the Afghan militiamen who have been working in the area." He searched his mind for anything else that might dissuade Trebon, landing on what he thought would settle the matter for any senior leader with troops in combat. "Sir, sending those teams in without any time to prepare for the environment doesn't make sense; it's setting them up for failure."

The call ended without a definitive course of action. Blaber turned to his AFO intelligence officer, Glenn, who'd been with AFO from the beginning and had developed much of the plan that shaped the picture everyone in the safe house had come to rely on—AFO, CIA, and Special Forces alike. The Delta intel veteran shook his head with concern, his eyes bloodshot from lack of sleep. "I knew it; they have no idea how much preparation we put in to ensure those teams could operate in this environment." The two Delta officers locked eyes and then returned to their responsibilities. Something was going on at TF-11, but there was no time for solving that mystery.

As he put on his headset and switched to the AFO SATCOM frequency, Blaber had no idea how right he was about his mission preparation-time assessment. In less than forty-eight hours, others would pay a heavier cost in the absence of preparation, and for a few TF-11 men, the price would be the ultimate.

CHAPTER

16

---

2 March

MIDNIGHT

THE PERIOD OF DARKNESS (POD) ON THE NIGHT OF 2 MARCH STRETCHED on for everyone in the Shahi Khot Valley, including Al Qaeda. From the enemy:

We spent our night alert and on guard, to deter any more air-drops throughout the night, as was expected. Before performing the morning Fajr prayer, we divided the brothers into three groups: the first joined the group of Maulawi Saif-ur-Rahman Mansoor, for he needed more people; the second took position where the Shilka ZSU-23 antiaircraft cannon was situated, at the entrance of the valley; which left myself, along with three other brothers, as support for any of the groups that needed more men. To begin with, we headed toward the location of the Shilka and took our positions in the rear, to help curb the aerial bombardment which had increased significantly. During the entire period, the enemy did not cease to spray the mountain peaks and valleys with the lava of bombs and missiles, while machine guns sprayed their bullets in every direction. The martyrs were too many to count. Many of the Afghans were now martyrs. One brother tried to hide

in a trench from the bombs, but the trench was full to the top with
dead Uzbeks.

For Combat Controllers Jay Hill and Andy Martin, the POD was a nonstop airstrike fest, each Controller sequencing aircraft, handing them back and forth, or sharing with TF-Rakkasan. The strikes were so frequent and numerous that the numbers and aircraft blurred. The devastation and relentlessness revealed in their after-action reports are impressive. Sometimes the strikes were identified by the aircraft or munition, other times they describe merely the outcome.

Jay: OP site and bunker (2-3 KIA)—AC-130

Andy: Enemy squad (11 KIA, 5 WIA)—2 x F-16s

Jay: Fighting position (4 KIA)—JDAMs [He reported over SATCOM, "If anyone was on the ridgeline they aren't now."]

Andy: Mortar position (unk KIA—poss 2-3, target suppressed)—4 GBU-31s

Jay: 3 x fighting positions (5 KIA)—JDAM bomb box

Andy: Hilltop fighting position w/poss mortars (unk KIA—poss 2-3, target suppressed)—4 GBU-31s— B-52

Jay: OP (3 KIA, 2-5 probable KIA)—JDAM bomb box

Jay again: Bunker (3 KIA)—JDAM bomb box

Andy: Congregation of enemy on ridge (unk KIA—poss 2-3)—2 GBU-12s

Jay: Mortar position and 1 x DSHKA (7—KIA)—JDAM

Andy: Cave complex (2 KIA, unk damage to tunnels)— 8 GBU-31s—B-1

Jay: Sniper position (2 KIA)—Predator Hellfire

Andy: Mortar position (unk KIA—poss 2-3, target suppressed)—4 GBU-31s

Jay: Mortar position, 2 x Toyota PU trucks (4+ KIA)—
  MK-82

And so it went, through the entire night, without sleep, hands freezing on the mikes and handsets, changing radio and rangefinder batteries as they drained in the below-freezing temperatures. They suffered blurred vision and the pressure to ensure not only that each and every strike was on target but that there was also no confusion with friendly locations, since the entire battlefield was anything but static as units and enemy positions maneuvered and fought.

The two Controllers weren't alone; each was supported by his team. And though one mission was led by a SEAL and the other a Delta operator, the leadership roles reversed once they were engaged, as Jay explains:

A definite evolution, or change of mission responsibilities takes place after you first arrive. [Before then] there's more of them and they're taking care of certain things, "Hey, this is our OP. This is where we're going." They're getting you there, they're defining the area, you're doing your own stuff and your position hasn't percolated to the top yet because you're not talking to [aircraft]. But as soon as it does, well then you become the center point and you start tasking. "I need you to do this for me. I want you to verify my coordinates. Hey dude, I need you to check my math, make sure, because I'm literally bombing people off of FalconView and a laser rangefinder and they're three klicks away." The roles kind of get reversed.

It's really complex. To get your eyes on [target] and come up with a game plan of how you're going to get aircraft in and safely separate them, drop bombs, and do it at night with the gear and the sensors we were dealing with at the time, and they were just not adequate. Back then, we had to correlate coordinates off FalconView. If you say to a Controller today, "I was bombing off FalconView" he'd just shake his head in wonder. It was terrible, but it worked.

Because it had to. Each of the Controllers ultimately had the responsibility for life and death: life for the troops in contact and their respective teams, death for everyone else on the battlefield. The burden was heavy. Any slip when controlling such things as run-in bombing headings or restrictions, or incorrect coordinates (even those that were read back by the pilot), and there was only one man who'd be the target of the subsequent investigation and left with a lifetime of guilt, one man left holding the bag. Conversely, if you were good (and sometimes lucky), you moved forward knowing your efforts made all the difference.

―――

As Jay and Andy traded aircraft throughout a night of blurred hours, Jim Hotaling only had access to a single platform . . . but it was all his and its presence was critical. The CIA Predator shadowed and guided the SAS team as they worked to reposition themselves nearer the battle after the errant helo drop-off. The men progressed at an excruciatingly slow pace. To them, the Predator was a lifeline. Even though they were moving at night with NVGs, Al Qaeda forces were everywhere throughout the valley and its facing mountain slopes, exactly where they were traversing. Worse still, the terrain in every direction was higher ground, and they felt completely exposed. They had no place to maneuver along the creek bed, so an RPG or DShK emplaced along their route would make short work of them. Even more alarming, the men staggered under the immense 140-pound loads they carried, making it impossible to identify threats from above. They were too busy trying to maintain momentum without falling over and, like the AFO teams, stopping only led to freezing in the night, so it became a torturous tightrope balanced between exhaustion and cold.

Between breaths, Hotaling periodically talked with the pilot, who was sitting in a heated box, "most likely sipping coffee," mused the Controller. But he remained grateful to "have the Predator as our point man." When the drone approached "bingo" fuel, it would depart, replaced by another Wildfire. On occasion, there were gaps in coverage, and Hotaling would fill the intervening time with the AWACS air coordination platform (call sign Bossman), a poor substitute for men moving on the ground in rugged terrain, but still a source of continuity and comfort. When the next Wildfire arrived, Bossman handed it off to Hotaling for control.

His faith in the system wasn't misplaced, but Predators' reliability was susceptible to overestimation. Visual acuity for the pilot scanning the ground below was no more than 20/200, rendering certain angles and terrains a mystery, especially those with shadows. It's often noted that the operator's view was little better than staring through a straw from high altitude, so unless the focused lens passed directly over a threat, it was quite possible to miss the heavy machine gun or RPG position that could cost a life.

Furthermore, as would happen repeatedly from the time of their introduction into the modern battlefield, Predators and other drones, even those with improved acuity, fed into another dangerous condition. For leaders sitting far removed from the battlefield, the temptation to believe that drone footage provided adequate situational awareness led to increased micro- and mismanagement by general officers and higher headquarters. They felt their central operation centers, by virtue of information flow and video feed, somehow "knew better" than the men on the ground and their forward commanders. Combine that with the urge to "do something" when situations became dire, and it was inevitable for them to take control away and make decisions for the men on the ground. This would play out in Anaconda in tragic ways over the next twenty-four hours.

For now, though, the Aussies progressed with the belief they were at least more secure than if there was nothing overhead, and it allowed them to double the speed at which they would otherwise have traveled—which was still a snail's pace. As the 3 March sun rose in the east, they waited for its heat to clear the ridgeline so they could feel the warming rays of the fiery orb. When it finally reached the exhausted men, they stopped for something to eat and checked their location. After twelve hours of constant movement, they were only halfway to their new OP. The long night would now become an even longer and more dangerous day. At least the sun was shining on them from a clear, but cold, blue sky.

———

As Hotaling shouldered his ruck, Pete Blaber was hitting his own wall. Awake for fifty-five hours straight, he pulled the headset off his matted, unwashed hair and dropped onto his cot inside the AFO tent for two hours of well-deserved blackout. When his alarm went off, he was still fuzzy. He grabbed his Glock pistol from under his pillow, tucking it into his tan cargo pants, and stumbled out into the morning with his toothbrush in his mouth to take a piss. In the tent next to him, Led Zeppelin's "Kashmir" was prophetically playing. Ablutions complete, he headed toward the TOC, passing "a bunch of unfamiliar faces," only to be intercepted by Glenn, the Delta AFO officer and Blaber's right-hand man in Bagram. Speaking rapidly, his agitated intel analyst told him two teams of SEALs had arrived earlier and their officer in charge was waiting for him in the TOC.

Inside, Blaber found a Navy SEAL lieutenant commander named Vic and two teams of SEALs from SEAL Team Six's Red Team; Mako-30's Slab from the recce element; and one other team made up of assaulters—not reconnaissance experts—call sign Mako-21, led by a man named Al.

"What are you doing here?" Blaber asked Vic, who explained that Trebon had ordered him to Gardez to command and control the SEALs, and that he was to infiltrate the teams into the ongoing fight *that night*. Blaber was instantly pissed. Grabbing a satellite phone, he stepped out of the TOC and into the compound for some privacy, leaving the SEALs behind, and rang up Trebon.

"What's going on, sir?"

"Same thing I told you. I want these guys in the fight. Vic is in charge of the [SEALs], you just stay in charge of the AFO guys. And when do you think you can turn them over to Blue?"

"Sir, there's no need to shove these guys into the fight. I don't need to put two more teams in tonight. We control the valley, not them—"

Trebon cut him off. "Pete, put both SEAL teams into the fight tonight. That's an order." The general hung up. Blaber knew what was happening. With the sterile-sounding and effective airstrike calls being reported across the AFO SATCOM net, it appeared to the TF-11 leaders that putting more teams and Combat Controllers in the field was simple... Stick them in a helicopter, fly them to some high ground, put the Controller on the radio, make strikes. Easy.

But in Blaber's mind there was more to the situation. Trebon was an Air Force pilot and would never come up with the idea to push SEAL Team Six into the fight. It could only be coming from Kernan and Szymanski. Glenn had been right: Neither the SEAL Team Six leaders nor TF-11 generals understood conditions on the ground, and dropping men into the middle of the battle at the last moment without preparation was asking for disaster.

The irony of Szymanski and Kernan pushing Trebon from below was not lost on Blaber, who'd had to convince the SEALs of the mission's value and had even off-ramped others for poor attitude and performance. Now they didn't just want in, they wanted the entire show, and they had co-opted Trebon in Bagram to get it. When Blaber had asked Trebon in previous conversations whether the SEALs they intended to send down were going to conduct direct-action missions (which were their forte), the general had replied their missions were to be the same as Blaber's current teams'.

The two had not settled on a time frame, so when Trebon asked about timing, Blaber replied, "I can't give you a time." The general wasn't satisfied. "I want you to come back to me with when the exact time is that you're transitioning this to Blue." The one concession Blaber received was that Vic would serve as his number 2 until he turned over control.

Vic was a contentious candidate to lead the SEALs in AFO operations. Technically, he was the Red Team recce officer in charge, placing him in the Navy command chain between Slab, Goody, and now (by virtue of his inclusion in AFO) Al the assaulter, and their senior officers, Szymanski and Kernan back in Bagram. His few months in Afghanistan had been anything but quiet and had exposed poor judgment and leadership on two occasions. The first involved an unauthorized New Year's Eve vehicle movement between Bagram and Jalalabad, during which Vic and the SEALs in the SUV were stopped at a militia checkpoint. It resulted in shots being fired, injuring a SEAL and necessitating the team's rescue by a British helicopter. The second of what became known as "Vic's three strikes" inside the TF-11 command occurred during a "dry hole" raid he led in which an unarmed Afghan had been killed when he approached the team's location. From the darkness of the SEALs' hiding spot, the civilian had been told in English to stop. When he didn't stop, the man was shot through the eye and killed. The SEAL who shouted the English command and fired the round that killed him was Vic. There was an investigation but no charges, leaving an impression that extended up to the TF-11 commanding general, Dell Dailey. According to a TF-11 general officer familiar with both events, "[Vic] got as much of a fair hand as any other person would who ultimately showed, probably, not the right judgment." Defending Kernan's choice to continue allowing the junior SEAL officer to lead, he added, "You can't pick out a lousy judgment–type guy right off the bat." However, others were less forgiving, including SEALs within his own unit. When one Navy operator returned from the field to find Vic in the Gardez TOC that morning, he was stunned. "I got the feeling [Vic] was now running the show on the ground. Of course, he was out of his league."

But the decision to send Vic to run things and put teams in play was done. According to one official after-action report, Kernan "had already made the decision to insert."

For John Chapman, the drama surrounding who led the missions "back at the rear" in the Gardez safe house was immaterial. He had a new mission and set about prepping his gear, studying the AFO maps on the walls as well as talking with Glenn, the Delta intel officer. He was joined by Ben Miller, the Combat Controller assigned to Al's Mako-21 team. While the two CCT had similar responsibilities, the nature of the separate teams' composition, and the fact that they came from different elements, caused the two friends to implement their actions independent of each other and immerse themselves within the separate forces—just as Chappy and Andy had done previously during their early missions with Slab and Goody. A divide also existed between assault troops, with their direct-action mission, and the more low-key snipers of recce. Slab, as the senior recce team leader, personified these differences with his introspective and laconic approach to dealing with others.

As Slab and Chapman were making sense of their short-notice mission, the battle continued to rage at Mako-31's location, and another piece of the TF-11/SEAL puzzle fell into place. Between identifying and nailing down targets with his SEAL teammates and calling in airstrikes, Andy received an odd communication. It came from the

TF-Blue TOC in Bagram and didn't include anyone else in the AFO chain of command. Mako-31 had continued to provide their situation reports to TF-Blue, the SEAL Team Six element in Bagram. Of course, the two senior officers of the unit, Kernan and Szymanski, were also hearing Mako-31's transmissions on the AFO SATCOM channel. This message was different.

TF-Blue wanted Mako-31 to relocate to a new OP using one of the Agency's Mi-17s. That they would send the request directly to the team was new—and odd—but it was *where* they wanted the team to relocate that got his attention... Takur Ghar.

Andy showed the message to Goody. The team's reply did not take long to formulate. Takur Ghar was three kilometers away and had a commanding view of the valley, much better than their current location, but it had problems. Mako-31 responded with three points:

1. The team was perilously close to running out of ammo and batteries and would need resupply to execute.
2. With that in mind, they'd still need to go back to Gardez and then reinsert, but not on top of the mountain. They'd have to offset and walk their way up, which would take time.
3. Takur Ghar was crawling with bad guys, as evidenced by the airstrikes and the inability of the 10th Mountain troops to occupy BP [Blocking Position] Ginger at its base.

Goody turned them down with a push of the send button, which closed the matter for Mako-31. What was clear to Andy was, "They [Six's leaders] wanted us to insert on an Mi-17 with a single door-mounted M60 [machine gun]. They wanted it done now. That mission would have required multiple DAPs and SEAL boat crews to take the summit. [DAPs—Direct Action Penetrators—were specially modified MH-60s flown by the 160th SOAR. Essentially attack helicopters, they came equipped with variations of .50-cal, 7.62mm miniguns, and 2.75-inch rockets.] When we declined the mission, they moved it on to Slab's team instead."

———

For the broader Operation Anaconda, things were not going smoothly. TF-Rakkasan was in fights, with strikes taking place everywhere in the valley. It was also taking a beating as Al Qaeda forces continued to muster numbers and close with the Army.

With a handset to his ear, Jay watched from behind sunglasses and beneath his wool cap as yet another strike took out an Al Qaeda bunker. This strike, from a B-52, delivered a 2,000-pound GBU-31 (actual weight 2,036 pounds and a monstrous twelve feet long).

An airstrike has a strange and macabre beauty all its own. Massive ordnance detonations against ground targets produce the expected satisfaction of destroying your enemies in a vivid, billowing, black-and-orange ball of fire, smoke, and dust. At only three kilometers away, the initial violent explosion is followed by the reverberation as the radiating sound wave compresses air in every direction and reaches the ears a second later. As the sound fades and the black smoke billows upward and out, bits of rock, weapons, and human parts rain down in the immediate vicinity of the detonation. Finally, the last image is of dust, settling and spreading across the valley floor. It is mesmerizing to friend *and* foe.

JDAM airbursts used on enemies in open terrain are different. These produce a string of black aerial cauliflower blossoms in a line, puffs of deadly Fourth of July–type fireworks that, instead of celebrating a festive day, shred and mangle man and equipment below without the dirt and flying debris.

Jay and J Team continued to prosecute the mission, though things were not going smoothly for them either, despite their superior fields of view and, by now, seamless teamwork.

Like Mako-31, to ensure they weren't "fragged" by friendlies, the team did their best to mark themselves as American, but the task was made more difficult because "the bad guys had VS-17 panels as well, which we didn't know at the time, and they looked like us because they're wearing fatigue bottoms, North Face–type jackets, and civilian clothing, using Hilux trucks and whatnot. And many of them are Chechen or Uzbek or whatever, the point being they didn't look Arab or Afghan. [So] as far as on the mountaintop, we looked similar, and aircraft that were in the valley a lot, like the Apaches, might not know AFO was over here or there."[17]

As Apache attack helicopters swooped across the valley, interspersed with fighter and bomber airstrikes, Jay was just beginning to work a flight of two F-15 Strike Eagles to hit a target on the Whale when Kris announced they had something in front of them. Jay and the Delta snipers watched through binoculars as an ancient white Toyota Land Cruiser pickup truck stuffed with enemy fighters rolled to a stop in front of the foothills below their OP. He recalls, "We're watching this guy, asking, 'What's he doing?' He's looking right at us and then jumps out and sets up a mortar tube and starts firing at us. We all went, 'Fuck!' as the first couple rounds were inbound. It was quick."

Unfortunately for the Al Qaeda mortar men, Jay's Strike Eagles hadn't committed to their briefed target, and he rapidly lined them up with a new nine-line, diverting the flight to the enemy mortar position now bracketing J Team. With little time to spare and no pre-coordination, the Combat Controller did it the old-fashioned way—

---

17 This actually happened to Jay and Delta during the insertion of the main 101st forces earlier in the morning, when a flight of two AH-64 Apaches turned on J Team's OP, lining up for a gun/rocket run. Jay recalls all of them at the OP reflexively shouting "No! No!" as he grabbed for the handset and radio, rapidly switching to 243 MHz (the Guard frequency, used by all aircraft for emergencies and always monitored during operations), and called them off at the last second, saving the team and preventing a tragedy.

he talked them onto the mortar position using years of expertise in guiding pilots to the target via descriptions of landmarks and features. Using only Mk-82 500-pound dumb bombs (no laser or GPS guidance), Jay and the pilots "shacked" the truck, mortar tube, and its crew, killing a handful of Al Qaeda.

The jet fighters lived up to every bit of their name and reputation, leaving a shredded pickup and bits of human in their wake as the two Strike Eagles sped back to their base for fuel and more bombs.

CHAPTER

17

—

AS THE NIGHT OF 3 MARCH APPROACHED, THE MEN OF "REDBACK," THE Australian call sign (a reference to the deadly native spider of the same name), were dragging themselves up the few remaining steps of the near–cliff face to their OP. The final three hundred meters of their movement exhausted the last of their physical reserves.

Hotaling had reached his limits too, but as the rest of his team gratefully dropped their rucks and surveyed the immediate surroundings to determine the OP's defensibility and vulnerabilities, it was time for the Combat Controller to go to work. He placed his ruck near the top of a low saddle, opened it, and set about arraying his airstrike gear.

He thanked Wildfire for the escort and then called several other entities (among them Bossman, the AWACS; Kmart, the combined forces air component commander, who apportioned aircraft for use on the battlefield; and Tombstone, the TF-Mountain fire support center) before also dialing into the AFO SATCOM net. The question he really wanted answered was: What was going on in the other areas of the Shahi Khot? A great deal, as it turned out.

At the Gardez safe house, Vic, the newly arrived SEAL officer, was in a difficult position. He wasn't the ideal selection to lead SEAL Team Six's aspirational AFO operations in Anaconda, but the situation and directives were not of his creation. They came directly from his SEAL leadership in Bagram, who believed they understood the conditions in the Shahi Khot better than those who had been "boots on the ground" for days, or even weeks. The truth was, Six had never prepared for the long-duration and austere conditions under which AFO was operating. Delta's recce test missions had exposed this. Instead, SEAL leadership substituted prudent planning and preparation with a misplaced confidence in their men to overcome *any* obstacles without notice. In short, hubris.

It wasn't that SEAL Team Six operators weren't capable—Goody, Chris, and Eric were proving that, even as TF-Blue worked to rush the new teams into the fray. But to rush (particularly the assault SEALs, with or without CCT) was to invite disaster. Blaber, the only officer on the scene with the knowledge and experience in the Shahi Khot to make such judgments, had made this clear, going so far as pushing back against Major General Dailey and Brigadier General Trebon to the point that he'd been told the generals were on the verge of firing him and removing him from country.

But Vic lacked either the confidence or competence to fall in behind the ground-truth understanding of Blaber and the teams in the field. I Team, the all-Delta mission, had even weighed in on the subject via the AFO SATCOM frequency, stating: "It's unsafe, it's unsound, it makes no sense." So the Navy pressed ahead even though Kernan hadn't originally pushed for such an early transition. In the AFO official after-action report it's noted that, initially, Kernan "proposed to Trebon that the shift from TF-AFO [as it was known] to -Blue should take place over the next few days, with the TF-Blue TOC assuming command and control on 6 March." What changed was the realization by TF-Blue that the majority of the airstrike killing would be over by the end of the first week of March.

Whether to avoid Blaber's pushback or for some other undisclosed reason, Vic and the SEAL Team Six leadership in Bagram established a separate communications and chain-of-command structure for planning and implementing their missions. This meant two parallel command and control architectures would be in place, and Vic was the belly button of the second. In implementation, it meant other organizations that had a piece of the mission would be unaware of communications and unable to provide input. Furthermore, it prevented the SEALs from fully understanding not just the environment they were introducing their men into, but the roles of other key actors within Operation Anaconda too, including air assets and allied forces. Ultimately, the separate communication structure and refusal to incorporate Blaber's battlefield experience was negligent. The SEAL leadership placed ego before all else, including the safety of their men. This arrogance would prove deadly.

On the heels of Blaber's call with Trebon, Kernan called to clarify when Delta would be turning command over to the SEALs. With no option to retain command of the mission he'd built and run for nearly two months, Blaber suggested it happen when Mako-30 and -21 lifted off from Gardez to insert into the Shahi Khot, but the two men never finalized the actual handover. To Blaber, this meant he was in charge until such time as he declared the handover complete. In the meantime, Kernan told him Vic would function as his number 2—in effect, the deputy AFO commander.

What was clear to everyone in the Gardez safe house was that Mako-30 and Mako-21 were going in *that night*. The question was— Where? Because TF-Rakkasan was now concentrating its efforts in the north of the Shahi Khot, and TF-64, the Aussie SAS effort— which included both Hotaling's and Wylie's patrols and two other vehicle-mounted blocking positions—was shoring up the south, Vic and the SEALs looked to the north. Blaber recalls, "Due to the fact that they had to go in that night, walking was not an option, as you needed at least a day and a half, not counting the time it takes to do the terrain analysis."

That meant helicopters would be used, breaking AFO's standing rule. Blaber was concerned but consumed with running the current operations where his men were in enemy contact. Still, he took the time to walk Slab outside for a private word. Slab and Blaber had worked together in Bosnia when the former had run man-hunting missions there. Blaber had great faith in the quiet SEAL's sound judgment and extensive experience. He hoped perhaps Slab's seniority could sway Vic and the SEALs in Bagram from attempting to put the teams in so quickly. Away from Vic and the others, he said, "Slab, I'm really uncomfortable with you guys going right in. I want to make sure you get all the advantages the other guys had."

"I totally agree. But I do what I'm told, and we're being told to go in tonight," replied the SEAL in classic Slab understatement, ending the conversation.

With only a few hours to plan, Vic and the SEALs determined that Mako-21 would infil near the front line of TF-Rakkasan at an HLZ adjacent to J Team. And since they would infil onto an HLZ secured by the 101st Airborne, they would take a resupply to J Team, because Blaber intended to leave them in the field for another two nights. Of all the teams, they were the best equipped and most effective on the battlefield, due in large part to Jay's deft handling of airstrikes and aircraft coordination. Mako-21 would then move east on foot to another high-ground OP and cover a sector with a road that was suspected to serve as an east-west enemy supply route.

Meanwhile, Mako-30 would insert at the base of Takur Ghar and walk to the summit of the 10,469-foot peak. The teams would depart the Gardez safe house HLZ simultaneously on separate 160th SOAR MH-47s, after nightfall but early enough so that both teams could complete their movements before dawn. They would then join the airstrike "orgy," with their Combat Controllers directing even more strikes on the enemy, who continued to refute their defeat by fierce resistance. No position in the valley had yet given itself up to capture.

In order to make it safely up Takur Ghar, Slab knew he needed to infil as soon as possible, figuring that, to make the summit, he'd need four "AC-130 covered" hours to ascend 1,300 meters. Whether Slab tried to adjust their plan or influence the SEAL Team Six leaders remains in some dispute. Ben Miller, Mako-21's CCT, remembers Chapman going outside into the cold to use the laptop to connect with Bagram throughout the day, with Slab hovering over his shoulder. Inside the TOC it wasn't possible to use the portable SATCOM radios, because the roof interfered with the signal. The time before Chapman left Bagram was frenetic, as the SEALs and Controllers packed as best they could for the as yet to be fully defined missions. "I don't think Chappy'd had any sleep. He worked information and planning all day and was freezing out there. Slab too," recalls the other Controller. As the day wore on, there was some confusion with MH-47 timing, and Slab had Chapman working via the laptop with everything he had to coordinate their lift. Miller continues, "Everyone is wondering when the helos are coming in for our insertions. CCT can often find info faster than anyone else, and so John ended up the point guy trying to find out." It was not exactly cozy inside the safe house either—the only heat came from a sickly fire in the TOC—but Chapman was outside for most of the day, and his reserves were being sapped before the team even took its first step off the helo on infil. Additionally, he would not only be expected to retain all the call signs, frequencies, and airstrike "special instructions" procedures (called "spins," these complex restrictions and procedures were requirements for each Controller to memorize and be tested on before ever controlling a strike on every battlefield); he would also be packing the heaviest ruck. Miller could see it weighing on his friend. Since Slab was the senior enlisted SEAL and, therefore, the most experienced Navy operator in the safe house, it fell to him (and by extension Chappy, his CCT) to work the logistics and planning for both teams' missions. It was a difficult and heavy burden for both men.

When the plans were solidified, Vic approached Blaber as the latter was making his own preparations for the night's operations. Blaber intended to join the "new and improved" Green Beret/ATF convoy making its second attempt to hammer Al Qaeda. Inside his small SUV, Blaber had installed a laptop and a fixed X-wing SATCOM antenna with radios so he could remain in contact with all the teams in the field and across the communications spectrum while he was moving or even under fire.

At 2200, thirty minutes before the Mako-30 and -21 helicopters were scheduled to land at the HLZ adjacent to the safe house, Vic again approached Blaber in the compound as the AFO commander finished loading batteries and ammo, and broached the subject of changing Mako-30's HLZ from the bottom of the mountain to the summit itself. As Blaber recalls in *The Mission, the Men, and Me*, "He had brought the same idea up hours earlier, but both Slab and I had dismissed the concept for tactical reasons. Fully aware that Mako-30 was only thirty minutes away from moving to their [pickup zone], I cut right to the chase. 'There's nothing on the ground cueing us to make a change, so it doesn't make sense to change it.' I added that...the helicopter pilots would never consider any change at the eleventh hour; it was against their standard operation procedure. 'No problem,' he responded, not pressing the issue. We talked for a few more minutes about coordination for the night's operations, during which I reinforced to him that I would be running things from my vehicle near the fishhook and that if he had any questions or issues, he should call me." With that, Blaber climbed into his vehicle and departed. Vic was now in charge of the safe house and operations there. As it turned out, Vic never spoke to Blaber again that night, not even when helicopters began to plummet from the sky, riddled with bullets and RPG warheads—in a disaster of the SEALs' making.

Thirty minutes later, Slab, Chapman, and the rest of Mako-30, and Al, Ben, and the SEALs of Mako-21, moved to the HLZ, where they sat with their gear piled around them on the ground. The men were anxious to get started so, just before launching, patience was not their strong suit. Waiting around for helos was agitating...and things were about to get complicated.

In the air, Alan Mack led the two-ship flight of MH-47Es toward the Gardez HLZ. The sixteen-year Army chief warrant officer was also a seasoned veteran of the 160th and the most senior of the four pilots spread between the two helicopters, designating him the flight lead. MH-47 Chinooks are large and gangly-looking helicopters compared to the Black Hawks, Little Bird MHs, and AH-6s flown by the 160th. To the pilots who flew them, they were beautiful: faster than the others and with a broader performance envelope, which made them perfect for the high altitudes and heavy payloads required by Delta and SEAL Team Six missions in Afghanistan. This one was no exception. Mack descended slowly toward the Gardez HLZ—the Chinooks did nothing fast—and hovered just above the ground before finally settling onto the dirt, coating the SEALs and CCT with dust.

On the ground, he, Slab, and Chapman conducted a preflight brief confirming the plan. Mack and his crew would insert Mako-30 and use the aircraft call sign Razor-03, while the other helicopter, call sign Razor-04, would insert Mako-21. Both aircraft would depart together toward the Mako-21 insertion, and Razor-03 would then continue alone to the base of Takur Ghar. For the aircrews, it was just another night of insertions and did not appear to be a difficult or lengthy mission.

When both crews and teams were finished briefing, everyone loaded the Chinooks, which cranked and lifted off shortly thereafter. Razor-04 slid in behind Mack's helicopter. In front of them and overhead, Nail-21, an AC-130U (the latest version of the gunship, affectionately known as a U-boat) arrived above Takur Ghar and their designated HLZ near the bottom of the mountain. Its mission—to ensure the site was clear and cover Mako-30's infil.

Six minutes from landing, Nail-21 called Razor-03 on the radio and informed them that he "could not put 'eyes-on' target due to a CFACC strike, [and] was forced to clear the area until the strike was complete." It was another busy night in the Shahi Khot as Jay and Andy worked airstrikes with their infantry counterparts. For the Razors, remaining airborne while the strikes took place would burn precious fuel. In order to fly heavy and at high altitude and still leave some performance leeway in the aircraft, Mack loaded enough fuel for the flight, then added enough for fifteen extra minutes for contingencies. With no idea how long the strikes would take, he returned to Gardez.

Once on the ground, Mack "selected 97 percent rotor RPM to reduce fuel burn," which, essentially, put the aircraft into idle. As the strikes continued, Nail-21 informed them he was "bingo" fuel (empty) and departing but would soon be replaced by Nail-22 (who was also approaching minimum fuel) and shortly thereafter by Grim-32. Mack dropped the engines further to ground idle, the lowest fuel consumption configuration he could use with the engines still running. Then word came down that the 101st was conducting an air assault, forcing yet another delay, so Mack shut down the engines but left the auxiliary power unit (APU) running to provide power to restart.

Mack was sitting at the controls, biding his time, when Slab appeared. The SEAL was concerned. Each precious minute that ticked by brought him and his team closer to sunrise. Mack recalls, "He asked if it was at all possible to take him directly to his OP on top of the mountain. I told him I had the aircraft performance to do it, [but] told him I could not guarantee a suitable landing site [on top] since I had no imagery. Since we could not ensure the landing, we decided to stick with the original HLZ at the base of the mountain."

As the 101st assault wrapped up, Mack prepared to start engines, when Nail-22 called them. "He had 'eyes-on' our HLZs. They were clear." He passed the information to Slab on the intercom. Things were looking up.

Mack began his preflight checklist and started engine one, followed by engine two. But as soon as the second engine fired up, it "ran away," revving up uncontrollably until he was forced to perform an emergency shutdown. The problem, "exceeding several operational limits," made the aircraft no longer mission capable. For the crew and men of Mako-21 nearby, the engine problem was announced by a spectacular "ball of flame" shooting out the back of the engine. "I called the [TOC] and asked that a spare aircraft be flown down [and] informed the team leader."

Now Slab was in a bind. It would take at least another hour to get replacement birds to Gardez. Two were dispatched, because Razor-04 was also approaching critical fuel due to the delays.

He stepped off Mack's helicopter into the cold, the APU whine of the helicopter dominating the night. He moved away from the helicopter to think. The absolute earliest they would make it to their insertion HLZ was now 0300, three hours before morning nautical twilight—the time at which they would be visible to everyone—*if* everything went off without a hitch. As it stood, that seemed unlikely.

Slab found Vic and conferred. There simply would not be enough time to make it up the mountain before sunrise, and there was no way the SEAL was going to put himself and his team in the position of having to ascend the slopes in daylight, into an ambush that would likely cost them their lives. He asked for a twenty-four-hour delay, the only prudent decision, and relayed it through Razor-03's radio so Chapman wouldn't have to unpack his ruck. The recorded transmission in the TF-11 JOC log is "RAZOR-03 RELAYS TO SHARK 78: EARLIEST INFL IS 2215Z TO 2230Z THIS TIME WILL FORCE DAYLIGHT MOVE- MENT; ELEMENT AT RAZORS LOCATION REQUEST BUMP 24 HOURS; WHAT WOULD YOU LIKE TO TELL THE TEAM." In the log, the only recorded response is "STANDBY."

Vic needed to discuss the situation with his immediate superior, so he got on the satellite phone and made a call, but it wasn't to Blaber, who was already en route to the Shahi Khot. Instead, he called the TF-Blue TOC in Bagram. As the AFO rep in Bagram, Delta major Jimmy Reese notes in the official AFO after-action report, "Not once was [the situation] addressed with the AFO chain of command. We had no idea these conversations were going on. They were discussing this on the TF-Blue command net, instead of coming up on the AFO command net and discussing it with the ground force commander, Blaber." Vic's decision to exclude the standing AFO chain of command would have dire, far-reaching consequences.

Nowhere is it recorded to whom Vic spoke, and he's never identi- fied the individual by name. On his end of the call, Vic stated, "The earliest infiltration time possible is now 2:45 to 3:00 a.m." He then asked for instructions and was told, "We really need you to get in there tonight."[18]

With his orders now clearly spelled out, and with no other choice, Slab discussed the new plan with Mack while they waited for the

---

18   In light of events and the passage of time, there is no definitive answer as to which SEAL officer actually gave the implied order. Official accounts vary, as do the recollections of individuals involved, and nowhere are any names given. However, there are only two possibilities—Captain Kernan, the SEAL Team Six commander, or his operations officer, Commander Szymanski. Individuals with firsthand knowledge believe it was most likely Szymanski. In the official TF-11 JOC log, the call from Razor-03 on Slab's behalf received no official answer. The call sign acknowledging the call was Shark-78, the operations officer. Later, TF-Blue officers attempted to place the transmission's responsibility on the enlisted sailor manning the radio, but the Joint Operations Center log clearly shows the call as Shark-78, the TF-Blue operations officer, Szymanski.

replacement aircraft. They decided that the pilots would swap and fly the new helicopters with the enlisted gunners and crew who arrived in them—strictly a pilot swap, since they'd planned and flown the mission to that point, and further changes were only asking for trouble.

After talking about the summit, with its lack of imagery and planning, Slab asked Mack, "Well, what's it going to be, chief?"

"I'm willing to try if you are," replied Mack, but reiterated there was no way to determine if there was a suitable HLZ.

"Well, if you can't get us in, then you can just bring us home," replied the SEAL.

The replacement MH-47s arrived and the pilots swapped. They listened on SATCOM for any indications of further delays or disruptions, while the engines remained running and the two teams loaded. Razor-03 and -04 took off for the last time from Gardez at 0227 for the twenty-plus-minute flight to insert the Mako teams. Mack, sitting in the left seat, watched as Razor-04 dropped out of formation toward Mako-21's insertion site, an HLZ secured by the 101st Airborne, taking a resupply bundle with them to hand off to Jay Hill and J Team. Razor-03 continued toward Takur Ghar alone.

In Bagram, Jimmy Reese was sitting next to Major General Hagenbeck's desk in the latter's TF-Mountain TOC having a conversation with Brigadier General Gary Harrell, a former commander of Delta Force. States Reese, "We [AFO] in the mountain TOC would hear intermittent reports from the MH47s passing info back to [160th TOC]. That is how we heard the new HLZ location about a minute or two prior to the first insertion of Razor-03. They called in a proposed grid [the top of Takur Ghar] just as they were going inbound to the HLZ. It was the first we had heard the report and were surprised they were trying to insert on top of the OP."

At the same time, in his OP to the north of Takur Ghar, Jay heard some of the traffic on the AFO SATCOM net but paid little attention.

He was too busy working an AC-130 in support of the TF-Rakkasan air assault that caused the Razor-03/04 delay. He was frustrated by the multiple airstrikes diverted or confused in the complexities of the battlefield below. Twice he'd pointedly asked, "What is the deal with CAS?" Twice he'd called in strikes on a mortar position pummeling the 101st, and twice the aircraft had been called away. Finally, the planes—F-16s—returned, "but can't hit targets accurately."

While Jay was requesting different aircraft, "Something with JDAMs," J Team's team leader, Kris, was looking for clarification on Mako-21's infil and their linkup for the resupply they were promised: fifteen of the critical BA-5590 batteries, twenty-four MREs, five gallons of water, and sixty AA batteries (for NVGs, IR pointers, and other devices), material the team desperately needed if they were to stay in the field several more days, as directed by Blaber. Of the three teams in the field, theirs had so far been the deadliest and best placed.

Astonished, Jay saw them—two MH-47s flying from Gardez, materializing out of the night. "We're up there doing strikes, marking targets, the whole nine yards, but we're pretty smoked because we'd never gone to sleep. Then we hear the helicopters and I'm thinking, 'What the hell?' And I remember looking off our [position's] shoulder and going 'Hey, KO [Kris's initials], who's this? What's going on here, are they bringing in weapons?' I thought it was reinforcements for the 101st to be honest with you. I'm trying to drop bombs and I'm like, 'Hey guys, you can't drop bombs through helos, I need to know [if aircraft are inbound].'" The no-notice infil jeopardized ongoing strikes.

Kris had no idea either, and the team watched Razor-04 as it peeled off to land nearby. "We could hear two of them, and it was a huge shock when we saw where they were going because your eyes had adapted to the lighting, so you could see really well. And then they flew right into the place that we'd reported earlier that was bad. In fact, we'd put eyes on it earlier. We told [AFO], 'Hey man, that's "bad guy land,"' because you could clearly see the little bonsai tree and positions with personnel [on top]." As Kris documents in his after-action report, "The sad part about this whole thing is, at *no time* [emphasis added] did [TF-Blue] contact the OPs and ask them about the situation on the ground."[19]

Razor-03 continued its flight toward the mountain summit. "And then they turned in, and I remember that hook turn, the gray helicopter, they flew right to the top, and that's where it all went downhill. You see a huge flash, I can still see it clear as day, and then just explosions, like it was a TV show. You could hear gunfire, the Dishka [DShK] actually returning fire, shooting at the helo," Jay recalls.

And then Razor-03 was gone, lost to the night. In its wake, a short gunfight. Neil Roberts, having fallen from the helicopter and landed unharmed in the snow, was fighting for his life, his last moments uncaptured by any drone or gunship footage but witnessed by J Team. What is known is he was hit by enemy fire that caused extensive bleeding shortly after falling. His machine gun was found jammed, gummed with his blood. The fight did not last long; he was severely wounded during the initial exchange. Roberts never even pulled his pistol. His end came when one of the Chechens killed him close up with a single round to the head, execution style. After the bullet that ended the SEAL's life was fired, there was only silence on Takur Ghar.

---

19 Reporting on the enemy's disposition, or even its occupation of Takur Ghar prior to Razor-03's insertion of Mako-30, is a study in contradictions. Slab maintains they would never have inserted if informed about enemy forces. However, Glenn, the Delta intel analyst, claims to have briefed the threat. Additionally, members of both J Team and Mako-31 have stated they reported Takur Ghar's occupation by Al Qaeda. It is impossible to say where the critical disconnect was, but it was most likely within the SEALs' separate chain of command. It was another consequence of the SEAL senior leadership failure to communicate and coordinate their intentions and actions. What *is* clear: Mako-30 was not aware before insertion.

CHAPTER

18

—

4 March

0255 HOURS

AS THEY LURCHED FROM THE SUMMIT, AL MACK BARELY HAD CONTROL OF his MH-47. The cyclic and collective kept going "dead" in his hands. Each time they did, the helicopter became a 40,000-pound chunk of metal plummeting out of the sky. In the rear, Dan Madden was furiously opening quarts of hydraulic fluid with a beer-can opener that hung from a string on the wall, pouring them into the manual filling station and then quickly yanking the manual pressurization pump handle up and down to introduce the precious liquid into the system. Each time he did, the controls would sputter to life in Mack's hands. Yet as soon as Madden stopped pumping to spear another quart, the controls would seize as the helicopter bled out through the shredded lines, and the aircraft began to plummet once again. Madden only had four cans; after that, there would be no stopping the helo from falling out of the sky, killing them all. As it was, even when the hydraulics were topped off, the Chinook shuddered in flight as if the rotor heads and transmissions were going to come apart at any moment.

Leaving both a trail of fluid and a man behind on the mountain, Mack continued wrestling the controls with the help of his copilot,

Chief Warrant Officer Talbot. Impact was inevitable, it was merely a question of where. If he could keep the aircraft upright on impact, they *might* survive the crash. If it rolled, all of them would be crushed by inertia and the weight of the aircraft. Coming off the peak at over 10,000 feet it was just possible, with their momentum and downward flight angle, to reach the valley floor nearly 2,000 feet below. In fits and starts of hydraulic relief, he spotted some reasonable terrain in front of them at the exact moment the controls seized. Madden, pouring their last can into the reserve, saved the crew a final time as Mack fought to bring them down upright.

At ten feet, Mack stated, "I could not move the cyclic stick." The helicopter had flown seven kilometers from the lone SEAL on the mountain. It slammed into the ground on a fifteen-degree uphill slope and ten-degree cross slope but, miraculously, didn't roll. Both pilots jettisoned their doors and, collecting their maps and sensitive packet material, dropped to the ground, joining the survivors in the back. It was a remarkable feat of teamwork and airmanship to bring the crew and operators down alive. Without both pilots and Madden working the problem till they touched down, every man would have perished.

Once on the ground, Chapman immediately set about getting them an AC-130 for cover and to fend off potential adversaries should the threat prove real. Joined by the crew, some of whom were feeling bad about the crash, Chapman responded, "Aw, don't worry about it. I've felt harder PLFs [parachute landing falls]."

With his SATCOM and UHF ground-to-air radio up and running in a matter of seconds, the Controller wasted no time. "Any Grim, any Nail, this is Mako Three Zero Charlie. We've just had a crash landing and need some perimeter security," he announced on UHF.

All Grim call signs reflected AC-130H aircraft, while Nail was used by the newer model AC-130Us. That night the Anaconda operation was supported by two U-boats (Nail-21 and -22). However, at the time of the crash they had already departed and had been replaced by two older, but still capable, H-models with the call signs Grim-32 and -33. The problem was, with the changeover, the two arriving gunships had no pre-brief on the Mako-30 mission and no situational awareness of the immediate events. Their first inkling they were involved in a highly dynamic and soon-to-be confusing command and control situation manifested with Chapman's transmission. Hearing Chapman's call, the first H-model on station responded, "This is Grim Three Two, what can we do for you?"

"It looks like we lost somebody at the LZ," he stated and then passed Roberts's grid coordinates, communication and identification (MBITR and IR strobe) capabilities, and a probable call sign. In practice, the SEALs did not stress communication training to the extent their Delta counterparts did, relying more heavily on their embedded Combat Controllers. Mako-30 was no exception. Chapman loaded, programmed, and checked the entire team's radios, explaining, as he always did, how many clicks on the presets each SEAL would need to turn to reach different nets. For this reason, it was possible Roberts, known as Fifi to his teammates, might use any number of call signs or frequencies to identify himself.

Upon receiving the initial request, Grim-32, piloted by Major D. J. Turner, immediately diverted to Chapman's location. After a cursory scan to ensure the crew and SEALs were not at risk, it departed for Takur Ghar, coordinating with the second AC-130H, Grim-33, to take up position over Razor-03.

Meanwhile, believing their mountain objective was nearby, Slab put one of the SEALs on planning a foot movement back to Takur Ghar. He thought they could hike to the lost SEAL and then coordinate a pickup with another helicopter from there, using Chapman and the gunship to keep any problems at bay. While the other SEALs worked on it, Slab had Chapman relay their intent to HQ.

Chapman called the AFO deputy commander, Delta major Jimmy Reese, at Bagram, where he functioned as the AFO's link to the larger Army HQ that commanded Operation Anaconda. Because of the friction and disconnect between Blaber and Vic, Reese had learned of the unfortunate plan to insert directly onto Takur Ghar only moments before their tragic attempt. He acknowledged the team's plan.

The SEAL tasked with planning their foot route returned to his team leader and, regarding the mountain Slab had pointed out, announced, "That ain't it." He pointed to a distant peak in the dark, barely visible even with NVGs. "That's it over there. We ain't going to make it," he stated flatly.

When the calls started going out on SATCOM and UHF, other elements of AFO already on the ground began picking up the situation. Ben Miller and the SEALs of Mako-21 had themselves been on the ground for only a few minutes when the Combat Controller heard Chapman on the fire support frequency, furiously working to resolve their crash-site situation. "I heard him talking to all kinds of air. I didn't talk to him because I wanted to keep the mike fresh and net clear. But there was definitely a lot going on with their crash and rescue."

Powerless to assist, and with their own objective still many kilometers distant, they started their movement into enemy territory.

Also listening to the crisis unfold was Jay Hill. The two friends knew each other well, and Jay "was very familiar with Chappy's radio 'etiquette' and 'phraseology' as a Combat Controller," as well as the Mako-30C call sign he was using. The call sign Mako-30, when used without the C suffix, indicated the man on the radio was Slab. But Hill also knew Chapman's voice, and the two indicators told Hill exactly who was who on the AFO radio net.

At the crashed Chinook, Slab reversed his initial decision, electing to use the pickup helicopter Chapman had called in to retrieve them. Chapman immediately raised Razor-04, the sister ship of Razor-03, piloted by Jason Friel. "When you get here, what I want to do is, this crew will stay here. We'll fly up to the mountain and get Roberts and come back and get the crew, and we'll all get out of here."

Mack, still surging with adrenaline and standing out in a naked darkness, no longer commanding the night from a well-armed helicopter, told Slab he was willing to remain with his crew while Mako-30 conducted its rescue—on the condition Slab leave him someone to help defend their position. Slab, desperate to get to the mountain but loath to leave any shooters behind, offered Chapman, their ablest air support and best choice for a single individual to defend a tenuous position.

Chapman had other ideas. He refused to be left behind, and he and Slab had a heated exchange over the matter, during which Chapman stated definitively, "I'm part of the team, and if you're going, I am too." Faced with the Controller's intransigence, the SEAL acquiesced and elected to take everyone to the top, including the Razor-03 crew.

On the air, Friel refused, stating, "Naw, that's not going to happen."

Hearing the response on Chappy's radio, Slab took the handset from the Controller. "Put me there. You can do this."

"Not with that LZ under fire. I'm taking all of you to Gardez and we'll sort it out there."

When Razor-04 and Friel landed, the pilot greeted his good friend, Al Mack, happy to find him alive. Left with no alternative, a frustrated and anxious Slab and his team climbed aboard while Mack's crew stripped and sanitized Razor-03 of weapons, ammo, and sensitive material.

Razor-04 returned to the Gardez HLZ at 0434, and the team unloaded the helicopter. While they went inside, Friel kept the engines running and blades turning. At the remote outpost, if he shut down and had a mechanical problem—always a possibility in the overtaxed 47s—he'd be stranding the team and signing Roberts's death certificate. Yet although it increased the likelihood of the mission's flight, it was also burning precious fuel. Checking the gauges while Chapman and the SEALs were inside, he noted the helo was already on its reserve tanks. Calculating flight times to Takur Ghar and the nearest refuel point, he realized he was left with no margin for error or contingency; more good news to pass to the team when they came out.

Inside the high-walled safe-house compound, Chapman considered what was essential to execute the rescue. He'd need to move fast, and the only thing that mattered was the ability to talk to "air." He needed to think in three dimensions. The SEALs, like everyone else on the battlefield, thought strictly in 2-D: Point A to point B had this type of surface terrain, or a particular position afforded this or that advantage or disadvantage. But John didn't think that way, nor could he afford the luxury of its simplicity. His world was ruled by three axes, not two.

HQ, with their constant questions about status and location, had already proved to be an obstacle, not a solution, so long-haul SATCOM wasn't critical. He looked at his ruck and its full load for the original multiday mission. None of the food, water, spare batteries, and clothing mattered.

The only item of solid value he considered was the PRC-117 SATCOM radio. It doubled as his primary weapon for wielding airpower, with its twenty watts of power to push out transmissions, but it weighed ten pounds without batteries. As a seasoned Combat Controller, he never traveled without spare batts for every radio. It was one of the many reasons CCT had to be in better physical shape than sister-service spec ops forces they worked with; a Controller's ruck always weighed significantly more than anyone else's. The PRC-117 ran on two BA-5590 batteries weighing 2.25 pounds each. So taking his PRC-117, even in a pared-down ruck, would give him an additional 25 pounds to haul. On the run at 10,000 feet. In the snow. Under fire.

Chapman dispensed with the ruck entirely and opted to carry his MBITR, which would cover the frequency ranges he needed for air support but could push only five watts. In addition, he took a VS-17 signal panel and compass to back up his handheld GPS stuffed in his cargo pants. It would have to do. Besides, they were only going to be on the mountain long enough to rescue or recover "Fifi," for what... thirty minutes? They weren't even taking water with them. Snatch and grab, and kill everyone who got in the way, the latter being his job. He could do that.

He pared down every ounce he could, except his gaiters. No sense in getting snow in your boots running through a mountaintop gunfight. None of the SEALs or Chapman took body armor or ballistic helmets to the top. They'd left that gear in Bagram, preparing, as they had, for a long-range recce patrol.

Chapman didn't even add ammo to his Rhodesian vest. The uglier it got, the less likely he was to be shooting. It was the Controller way. When everyone else fired, he'd be on the radio that much more— turning back tides of rushing Al Qaeda, taking pressure off their own lines, or removing threats before they could inflict casualties. He and his radio were their last line of defense. Five watts would get him to Grim-32, already waiting for him at Takur Ghar. If they lost that, even twenty watts of transmission power wouldn't save them. As insurance, he did pack several Russian mini hand grenades. These were lighter (though less effective) than the M67 grenades carried by conventional US forces. He joined the others and Slab, who was busy fighting to convince HQ of their situation and intentions.

"I had this many when I left," Slab explained, and gave the names of the seven men on Mako-30 to the leaders at the Navy's TF-Blue TOC in Bagram. "Now I have this many," and he listed all but Roberts. But the questions and requests for numbers and confirmations kept coming while the clock ticked. In exasperation he concluded, "Look, we lost a guy. I have everybody except for Fifi. You have to believe me on this." He hung up and the men returned to the helicopter, where Friel told Slab, "I don't have too much gas." The closest FARP (forward area refueling point) was a site called Texaco, twenty miles away; Bagram was even farther. There were no options for the team leader. He asked the pilot to fly the mission anyway, and Friel agreed. It meant they'd be flying directly to the top, with no opportunity to scan the site to determine enemy numbers or even whether Roberts had managed to get to a defendable location.

Under the red lights of the MH-47 cargo space, Slab outlined what they knew and were going to do. With the turning blades and turbines making it difficult to hear, the team closed in around him to catch every word. The smell of fuel and hydraulics permeated the craft, mixed with the smell of men who'd been sweating and were infused with adrenaline.

"Okay, here's what I know. Reports have come across that the gunship saw a strobe up there. Four or six dudes are around Fifi. That was the last report I heard. The strobe is on. He is alive. Four to six dudes are with him. We can deal with that. We'll set up a strobe when we get there, identify ourselves, and anybody that is outside our circle, the gunship will light 'em up."

To a man, they realized that Fifi being surrounded did not bode well for their teammate. Slab continued, "We'll get a foothold up there. We'll find a place, clear it, and move onto it. We're going up there and the bird's going to land. We are getting off fast in pairs. Don't wait for the ramp to get all the way down. Get the hell off." The team nodded somberly as he spoke. At the end, Slab announced, "Hey, we're going back up there and killing every last one of those motherfuckers." It was something all agreed on.

Slab then pulled Chapman aside, explaining the two of them were a pair and would be the first off the helo. "Your sole job is to get to cover and get guns on. Do nothing else but get to cover and get on the radio. We'll take care of everything else. We need you on that radio," he said as the helo's engines spooled up for takeoff. There was no turning back for any of them.

The seventeen-mile flight from Gardez was short and intense. The SEALs stared out the Plexiglas windows, each anticipating the mission. Toward the rear, Chapman waited too, his mind a kaleidoscope of frequencies, procedures, and call signs. He would need to draw from them all if he was to keep the team alive and rescue his friend.

Slab was working to get pre-assault fires onto the mountain before they landed to give them a chance of getting established before being outgunned. The AFO commander, Pete Blaber, was also working the issue. Interestingly, Slab had chosen to call Blaber rather than Vic and his own Navy chain of command. The Delta AFO leader and SEAL each outlined scenarios for Grim-32, the AC-130 gunship now orbiting Takur Ghar, to fire on the mountain in support of the lost SEAL. The gunship, however, rightfully refused to entertain any of them, arguing that there was no way to determine which heat signature was Roberts and therefore any strikes targeted against individuals could inadvertently kill the very object of the mission. This meant no pre-assault.

On Takur Ghar, the Chechen who executed Roberts (and attempted, unsuccessfully, to decapitate him) moved within a bunker on the summit. Other Chechens and Al Qaeda had finished rooting through the SEAL's possessions and passing them around, including the IR strobe, and had dispersed. The leader, with years of separatist fighting against the Russians under his belt, knew the Americans would be back. They had a weakness for their own. He didn't know why the American they'd killed ended up alone on their mountain, but he was certain more would come back for him. And they would return in helicopters, probably many. He and his men were ready. Killing one lone American was not the satisfaction or glory he sought; he desired to kill many and meet Allah as a martyr to receive the blessings and rewards that were his due.

CHAPTER

19

___

4 March

0455 HOURS

AS MAKO-30 NEARED THE MOUNTAIN WITHOUT ANY PRE-ASSAULT FIRE support, frustration boiled over in the SEAL leader. "Motherfuckers!" Slab muttered regarding the gunship, and told Friel, "Go around," so he could get a look and perhaps induce the gunship to fire.

"Not going to happen," replied the pilot. Without even enough fuel for him to make a second pass, he declared a fuel emergency before they inserted.

Slab now had an impossible choice: Leave with the helicopter and abandon his teammate, possibly saving the lives of his remaining team and the helicopter crew, or go into the same HLZ as before without support, fully announcing their intentions to the enemy. It wasn't really a choice at all.

In the cockpit of Grim-32, frustrations were also growing. The pilot, Turner, couldn't fire, no matter how much ground forces begged. His responsibilities were equal parts destruction of the enemy in support of the operators and the prevention of fratricide. His situation was not uncommon among AC-130 crews. The men on the ground, with a very narrow view of the battle, often could not appreciate the ease with which locations and forces could be confused. Turner's fire control officer offered an opportunity when he announced, "Two guys have been walking around that rock all night and I know they are bad. Why don't we shoot them?" To do so required the concurrence of the entire crew. When one of the other officers on the flight deck voiced an objection, the last opportunity to force the enemy's head down vanished, as did all hope of Mako-30 getting on the ground without taking fire.

As the helicopter neared the landing, the final words Friel spoke to Slab were rhetorical: "It ain't going to be good."

At 0457, the MH-47 prepared to touch down in the exact spot where Razor-03 had met its fate. Its twin turbine engines spewed heat and noise from the back of the fuselage, defeating the mountain silence. Snow scattered in every direction in what remained of the night. Anyone within fifty feet of the helicopter would be blinded in the rotor-induced blizzard. The enemy was far enough away to allow an unobstructed view of the giant settling onto their summit, though the noise made it difficult to communicate. But communication was no longer necessary; they were all fully armed, the only means they needed to communicate with their most despised enemy.

For the men in back, the final seconds of infil were an unbearable eternity. Waiting for the helicopter to make its way sluggishly to the ground left them exposed, a terrible feeling of powerlessness for men of action. The crew doused the lights, leaving those in the back in complete darkness. Only the men's NVGs provided illumination, yet with the swirling snow and the narrow field of view out the ramp, nothing was visible. Chapman was pushed up against Slab almost as if the two were going to make a skydive out the back. His adrenaline was pumping, and he was anxious, as they all were, to get out of the thin-skinned death trap. He felt the helicopter jerk as it touched down.

When the wheels hit, Slab and Chapman launched themselves off the ramp. Slab took two steps in the knee-deep snow and plunged face forward, filling his NVGs with snow in the process and temporarily blinding himself. Chapman, second in line, wasted no time and went around the SEAL, heading to his left in search of high ground or shelter to begin orchestrating airpower with Grim-32. The four remaining SEALs spread out in two-man fire teams around their leader, who quickly recovered.

On the snow-covered slope, Chapman paused for a moment, orienting himself to the terrain. Fire was incoming but concentrated on the helicopter, even as it began lifting off, trailing smoke and dragging enemy fire along with it. Then it was gone, and the mountain went silent for a moment. The Chechens and Al Qaeda stopped firing, trying to determine what had happened in the blackness. The SEALs and Chapman had yet to fire a shot, and in the dark and confusion after the blowing snow and rotor noise, the enemy had no idea how many Americans were on the ground. Without NVGs, they were mostly blind . . . but only for another forty-five minutes.

The quiet was short-lived. Fire exploded all around the team as the enemy let loose a barrage. John made a snap decision and began running uphill, into the fire, without looking behind him to see if Slab had recovered or what the other SEALs were doing. He took a knee and began firing at the closest point where he could see muzzle flash and a fighting position in the first bunker, Bunker 1.

Twenty feet behind him the SEALs huddled, getting their bearings before splitting off in their two two-man fire teams. Slab, seeing Chappy upslope, stepped out in pursuit of the Combat Controller.

John could see the enemy had the advantage of high ground and dug-in terrain. There was no cover for him to set down and start calling airstrikes. That would have to wait. If he didn't do something *now*, there'd be no one left to call for air because there would be no one left.

His heart was pounding in the thin atmosphere at over 10,000 feet. Even Gardez was only 7,500 feet, and the extra elevation was attacking his cardio system as surely as the Al Qaeda were attacking the team. He stopped momentarily once again, then drove forward, breaking trail through the snow, which rose past his gaiters to his knees. As his boots plunged through the snow, he held his M4 pulled against his shoulder, barrel pointed forward at an angle into the slope. He stopped for a breath, brought his weapon up, and, sighting on Bunker 1 using his laser and NVGs, snapped off a few shots. Then he ran again, lungs aching, to his right. As he surged uphill, the bunker moved up and down through his NVGs, but outside the circle of illumination, all was dark, creating the effect of images swimming.

Behind him, Slab moved to catch up as Chapman stopped again, took a knee, and snapped off another three- to five-round burst. Before the SEAL could catch him, Chapman was up and moving again, his knees and feet blazing a trail in the virgin snow, increasing the distance between them again. It was as if the Controller was a man possessed. He never looked back at Slab, just fired and moved like a machine into the enemy's fire. Slab stopped, getting the lay of the land and checking the rest of his team.

Two of the SEALs (who would come to be the upper fire team) had moved left and uphill a few feet from the original huddle and stopped, firing upward at the invisible enemy. The final two SEALs of Mako-30, the lower fire team, had spread out near the huddle and were searching for targets. The team was taking fire from three directions—east, west, and north—the most effective of which was raining down from the hilltop to the north, directly in front of Chapman. Slab turned and looked uphill at the Controller, now twenty feet ahead of him, and watched in disbelief as John again charged at the enemy, snapping off shots.

Still the Controller never looked behind him to see if Slab had caught up. The fire from Bunker 1 was cracking as it passed him and the team. He couldn't believe he hadn't been hit. Between heaving breaths he looked through his NVGs, the muzzle flash from the AK-47 fire blinding due to the light amplification of his optics. He didn't wait; he launched himself—stumbling through postholing snow would be a more accurate description—headlong at the bunker.

Bunker 1 was arrayed in an arc under a ten-foot-tall bonsai-shaped tree. The defensive position was well constructed, having been improved by the Chechens and Al Qaeda fighters from its original construction by their mujahideen predecessors during battles with the Soviets twenty years earlier. Inside were two Chechens, well protected and masked by the tree overhead and a large rock outcrop to the left that covered their flank. Twenty-five feet behind them sat a second bunker, Bunker 2, filled with more fighters, including Roberts's executioner, a PKM heavy machine gun, and several RPG tubes with a stockpile of rounds.

The two Chechen fighters were spraying the team below them. They could hear the Americans, but they were difficult to identify in the dark, a problem compounded by the blinding effects of their own weapons and their lack of night vision devices. They felt they had the upper hand: They'd shot down one helicopter already, and this second one had limped off. Plus, they'd tasted their first kill for the glory of Allah, the reason they'd traveled through Pakistan to the rugged peaks of Afghanistan. And had He not delivered to the mujahideen an American for them to kill and his gear to pillage? One of the fighters was already wearing the American's Gore-Tex pants, another his black woolen watch cap. Allah would surely give them more Americans to sacrifice and desecrate. They fired their weapons, fear and excitement driving them.

It was the last action for the two dirty and ill-equipped fighters.

John appeared, lungs burning, in front of the bunker's berm and between it and the flanking rock. Taking advantage of his NVGs and laser he killed first one, then the other in as many seconds. Shocked by the American materializing from the black, both went to Allah without another shot. John had been on Takur Ghar for exactly two minutes and had now killed the first men in his thirty-six years of living.

Slab was still behind him but closing the distance. Below, fire team one, saved from the deadliest fire by Chapman's one-man onslaught, began charging up the steep slope toward the rock outcropping, ignoring the wild fire from the west flank to their left. The two SEALs were intent on getting into the fight, finding Fifi if he was still alive, and killing every single motherfucker on the mountain.

John, now in command of the bunker, oriented himself to his new surroundings, looking for a place to establish his airstrike position. Fire continued to pour in from the next bunker and off to his right. He engaged both directions, changing out at least one magazine in the process, as Slab finally joined him under the tree. The two shared an instant before Slab engaged Bunker 2, loosing several three-round bursts.

Chapman dropped to a knee next to the tree's trunk. To his left, Slab was facing Bunker 2 when a burst of fire from that position split the few feet between the two teammates. Slab slid behind the rock outcrop farther to his left and yelled, "What do you have?"

"I'm not sure," replied the Controller.

Slab returned his attention to Bunker 2 and tried firing a couple 40mm grenade rounds from the M203 launcher slung beneath his Stoner SR-25 .308-caliber sniper rifle, but the twenty-foot distance to the next bunker was so close, one grenade failed to arm before impact and rolled down the hill. It exploded without effect. The second detonated, but the fire kept coming.

Slab moved to his left against the security of the base of the rock outcropping. A grenade thrown by the enemy in Bunker 2 detonated in the snow half the distance to the two Americans but failed to inflict any damage. Slab didn't realize it, but the very reason for them being on the mountain lay mere feet from his position. Focused on staying alive, the SEAL never saw Roberts's body.

Farther to his left, fire team one arrived at the rock outcropping and was taking fire from Bunker 2 and the heavy DShK antiaircraft gun behind it. The two SEALs pressed themselves into the snow, attempting to lower their profile from the vicious raking. Below them, fire team two continued their attempt to flank to the right but couldn't beat back the fire pouring down, so they withdrew another thirty feet downslope.

John was now concentrating his fire on Bunker 2. He stepped up, exposing himself to deadly fire again. The close range and blinding flames from the PKM machine gun made it impossible to ignore. He was sweating from his push up the hill, still trying to catch his breath. Luckily there was no need to take aim through his scope; he merely centered the laser point on the muzzle flashes. Years of training alongside the best combat shooters in the world, Delta Force and SEAL Team Six, put him on autopilot. Despite the adrenaline and physiological stress, he exhaled, then smoothly pulled the trigger until the suppressed weapon coughed, but he was not rewarded with seeing the impact.

An Al Qaeda fighter charged him from his right side to counter-flank the Americans, firing wildly. John shot his assailant from a few feet away, stopping him and knocking the man over. Before he could pick another target, he was suddenly slammed in the torso and knocked backward. "Where'd that come from?" he yelled to Slab over the sound of the machine gun. But he never heard the answer, toppling back and onto his side. His world went dark.

Slab heard the shout but didn't respond. He saw Chapman ten feet away, the NVGs' green glow illuminating his face and his laser pointing against a tree, rising and falling with his breathing. The Controller's legs were crumpled beneath him, but he was alive.

The mountain was exploding around Slab and his two remaining fire teams. To his left, the first man of fire team one arrived, with the other SEAL hot on his heels. The latter had their only crew-served firepower, an M60, and he scuttled around behind his teammate with the rock masking him, so he and Slab could huddle. Slab looked over at Chappy, but the laser, while still on, didn't appear to be moving, and he concluded the Combat Controller must be dead. He was now down two men. "Get on top of the rock and fire point-blank in the bunker," he told his 60 gunner. Slab needed to put an end to Bunker 2 quickly if they were to survive.

"Roger that," replied the other, who climbed the half dozen feet to the top and began firing from a knee. When he couldn't get a good-enough angle into the bunker, he stood up and began pouring sustained fire into the position. As he did, Slab moved to the other fire-team-one member in preparation for a sweep to the left to finish off the resistance, when a frag grenade, thrown from the bunker in the face of the 60 gunner's withering fire, exploded near the SEAL's feet. It was followed by another determined fighter exposing himself to return the point-blank barrage with his AK-47, striking the 60 gunner's thighs. The SEAL rolled off the rock, calling out, "I'm hit!" as he collapsed at Slab's feet.

The two SEALs held another rapid discussion while the first member of fire team one continued to fire from the left side of the rock. At least the enemy wasn't charging them. Slab had no idea of the numbers of Al Qaeda and Chechens on the mountain, but if they rallied in force, the SEALs, now without Chapman's expertise in walking fire up against their own positions, would be wiped out. Two and a half men behind a lone rock, only marginally supported from below by a single two-man fire team without heavy weapons, were powerless to stop a rush.

"Are you hit in the chest?" he asked.

"No, I'm hit in the legs." That was good.

"Can you move?"

"Yeah."

They'd been on the mountain now for eight minutes, with two more casualties, a dwindling supply of ammo, and no better command of the terrain than when they'd landed. Slab had used up his entire supply of 40mm grenades and had discarded his M203 in the snow, leaving him only his sniper rifle. He made his decision: They were retreating. Now.

The three SEALs wasted no time moving off the summit and rapidly past Bunker 1. The first fire-team-one SEAL had also been shot during the firefight, with a grazing wound to the knee. In their rush to retreat, no one checked Chapman's condition, though only Slab knew at the time that Chappy had been shot.

A Predator pilot leaned back in the chair of his "cockpit" inside an air-conditioned trailer fifteen hundred miles and a time zone away, silently watching the SEALs' and Chapman's battle for life. On his next pass, while the SEALs withdrew, the nameless pilot dropped the Predator a thousand feet to get a better view of the action. Though he didn't know their names, he watched the SEALs passing below the bunker. On his screen, Chapman's still-warm body very clearly showed under the bonsai tree and, slightly cooler, Roberts's body lay along the SEALs' path.

The pilot watched the SEALs as they huddled below Bunker 1. In defilade below the bunker and ten feet from the stricken Controller, they continued to return fire. Downslope, fire team two did the same, but the route from the outcrop to their current location did not pass Chapman. The most likely event in the dark is that Slab passed Roberts's body, which was between Bunker 1 and the outcrop but not *above* the bunker. Chapman, in his last engagement before going down, was above Bunker 1, where he had engaged the flanking Al Qaeda.[20]

For the moment, believing Chapman dead, Slab was concerned only with their survival. They were still a divided force, and unless they consolidated and moved off the mountain, they'd all end up like Chapman, who had bought them initial relief and salvation in the early part of the battle. They spent the next four minutes taking stock of their condition, ammo count, and situation, discussing the matters while still engaging the enemy from below the bunker.

When it was time, Slab tossed a smoke grenade to mask their retreat, and they left the summit for the final time just after 0510. The 60 gunner, with his damaged legs, went first as the three began to scramble and slide toward the lower fire team. The last to leave the position, Slab was suddenly confronted with a donkey on the far side of Bunker 1. He pumped two rounds into it as it sat in the snow, believing it would help to mask their retreat.

The three stopped at the edge of a cliff and waited for fire team two to join them. The lower fire team was across an open saddle where it extended out onto a ridge, projecting out to a rock fin at the end. Throughout the engagement, two Al Qaeda fighters had traversed the ridge, encroaching and then withdrawing from the fire team, seemingly torn between closing with the enemy in the darkness and fearing the consequences if they did.

---

20   This scenario resolves several conflicting theories put forth in other accounts and after-action reports, and Slab's own statements. Slab remains confident he checked a body. However, Slab's own testimony in various interviews, historical recordings, and witness statements is not consistent on the matter, some versions contradicting others. Fifteen years later, in the course of the Air Force's Medal of Honor investigation, the five surviving SEALs would change their stories further, countering their original witness statements widely circulated and used in awarding Chapman's Air Force Cross and confounding the Air Force's efforts. Later, Slab would claim to have moved across the Controller's feet and wondered why he didn't react if he was alive. But he never stopped to check a pulse or otherwise inspect the fallen man, who in reality was almost certainly Roberts.

Fire team two made the move to consolidate with the others across the nearly fifty-meter open saddle. As they ran, pursued by the PKM from Bunker 2, one of the SEALs shouted out in pain and fell. He'd been hit in the right ankle, the round nearly severing the SEAL's foot from his leg. His teammate half supported, half dragged him the remaining distance. When they joined the other three survivors, one of the SEALs took a head count. Coming up one short, he asked, "Where's Chappy?"

"He's dead," Slab told him. Slab again took stock of his diminishing team. Two dead, three injured, two of them seriously. The fire-team-two SEAL who'd been shot was bleeding heavily and in great pain. They were off this rock. There was only one direction to go—down—but the terrain below was a nearly vertical snow-covered slope interrupted only by straight ledge drops of unknown height. If they could gain enough distance, Slab could perhaps get on the radio and have Grim-32 destroy the entire summit. He couldn't know with absolute certainty, but Roberts *had* to be dead. And as for Chappy, Slab believed him to be dead too. Blowing the mountaintop would not change that fact.[21]

In Bunker 2, the Chechens continued to engage. Despite the smoke, the SEALs were now more exposed to incoming fire and vulnerable in the morning twilight. For men without NVGs, the pre-dawn broadcast movement. And the American weapons were easily identified, if not by their muzzle flashes and disciplined fire rates,

---

21 Of Chapman's initial actions ahead of all the SEALs and in the face of an unknown and superior-positioned enemy, Slab would state unequivocally in his testimony, "I know if John hadn't engaged the first enemy position, it would have surely killed us all before we reached cover." Adding, "John died saving us from the enemy fire which was effective from three sides when he was killed," concluding with, "I feel privileged, honored to have known him and have called him my Friend. John deserves the highest medal we can get for him." These words, while expressing gratitude for the Combat Controller's bravery and audacity, would prove challenging to live by for some of Slab's higher-ups at SEAL Team Six in the years to come.

then by the report of their bullets leaving the barrel. US 7.62 and 5.56 ammunition, the only two rounds the SEALs were using, have a distinct sound all combat veterans know well. The same is true of the Eastern Bloc 7.62 coupled with the AK-47. There is no mistaking the weapon. Whether or not the Chechens and Uzbeks knew how much damage they had inflicted on their enemies, or the limited number of Americans they fought, will never be known. What *was* clear was their willingness to engage in a fight.

At this point in the battle, it was academic for the SEALs. They'd now huddled below Chapman for over five minutes and started down the cliff thirteen minutes after they'd stepped off the helicopter's ramp. The first to move created a snowslide down the vertical. The rest followed. The snow may have saved their lives as surely as Chapman had. The steepness allowed the two severely wounded SEALs to slide and drag themselves without having to stand erect. Even the Predator video showed the snowslides preceding the men down the mountain, gaining speed as they traveled.

When the Americans stopped firing at Bunker 2, it emboldened the now three Al Qaeda fighters on the fin above them. Barely a minute after the SEALs began their sliding retreat, two of the Muslim brothers began to move again. No longer taking fire, the two walked to overlook the Americans at the far end of the fin, where it terminated in a rocky outcrop and sheer fifty-foot drop. The Americans could be clearly seen sliding down the slope, presenting the perfect opportunity to kill them all.

Under the bonsai-shaped tree above Bunker 1, Chapman's body lay inert. To all appearances he was dead.

CHAPTER

20

———

4 March

APPROX. 0300 HOURS

WHILE THE GUNSHIPS AND CCT IN THE SHAHI KHOT WERE MAKING SHORT work of Al Qaeda,[22] Staff Sergeant Gabe Brown was sound asleep in his rack at Bagram Airfield, when he was shaken by the shoulder. From the depths of a sound sleep, Gabe couldn't comprehend who it was, merely a voice as though from far away, "They need you." Bleary eyed, he shook off the cobwebs, tumbled into a semblance of uniform, and stumbled to the JOC. Another false alarm, no doubt. He'd never had a combat search and rescue notification turn out to be anything other than false.

---

22   The following excerpt demonstrates the international composition of the enemy's forces: *With the first signs of night, [AC-130] planes arrived that carried machine guns similar in caliber to the DShK (12.7mm), although they were also able to fire missiles, and had night vision, which would allow vision for a distance of up to six kilometers away. We could do nothing but raise our hands and pray to Allah. Our brothers had dispersed, and were motionlessly positioned in trenches, for the enemy's weapons could detect any movement. Since the brothers had been engaged in battle until night, the planes found us to be easy night-targets and on that night, about twenty mujahideen were killed by their planes. Seven of them were Arabs, these being: Abul-Baraa Al-Maghribi (Morocco), Abul-Baraa Ash-Shami (Syria), Abu Bakr Al-Maghribi (Morocco), Abul-Hasan As-Somali (Somalia), Khalid Al-Islambooli Al-Ghamidi (Arabian Peninsula), Abu Bakr Azzam Al-Urduni (Jordan), and Abdus-Salam Ghazi Al-Misri (Egypt).*

The twenty-nine-year-old Combat Controller had been in Afghanistan for only a couple weeks and felt lucky to be in-country at all. To be on alert with TF-160 for CSAR along with two PJs—team leader Keary Miller and Jason Cunningham, who like Gabe was part of a "pickup" game of augmentees from other assignments for roles such as this—was good fortune indeed.

That's not to say that combat search and rescue duty provided real opportunities. It was known among the CCT that, while CSAR was potentially stimulating, the odds of a real crash in which you engaged the enemy and killed them with airstrikes while saving fellow Americans were slim. The last time Special Tactics had conducted a CSAR of any note was in Somalia in 1993, during the battle infamously known as Black Hawk Down. There, the 24 STS package of two PJs and a CCT saved the lives of multiple Rangers and Delta Force operators over the grueling and deadly eighteen-hour battle. Gabe had pulled CSAR enough to know these things.

The CSAR package and its associated Quick Reaction Force (QRF) of Rangers were pre-staged at Bagram Airfield for contingencies, on alert twenty-four hours a day. Comprising a Ranger platoon and a three-man Air Force Special Tactics team tailored to CSAR, it had one Combat Controller and two PJs. Their job was to fly into the worst fight or crash site and take control, providing relief, fire support, and recovery all in one package. The Rangers provided the relief, the CCT the fire support, and the PJs the recovery.

A quietly determined and confident man, Gabe is stocky at five foot nine, thick in every direction, with a full head of auburn hair and calm features. He smiles often, with or without a beer in hand. He's not built like the typical image of a Controller, but if told he needed to walk from the Yukon Territory to Hudson Bay unsupported and starting tomorrow morning, he would shrug his shoulders as if to say "yeah, okay," pack a rucksack, and set off without so much as a question, to reappear four months later on the other side of the continent, looking for a beer.

In the fall of 2001, seven years into his Combat Control career, he was midway through what he considered an administrative assignment: supporting the C-130 pilot school at Little Rock AFB in Arkansas. He'd taken the assignment to focus on his goal of finishing a degree, an endeavor he was diligently pursuing along with raising a young family. Unlike some of his contemporaries, he hadn't chosen to pursue an assignment at the 24. "I was never one of those guys that was setting myself up for the two-four: doing extra workouts at night, focusing on operational academic excellence. I'd rather drink a beer in the evening." But when the 9/11 terror strikes hit, he felt left out in the backwater eddy of Arkansas, so he volunteered to deploy with the 23rd STS out of Hurlburt Field, Florida.

His big break came when he joined Keary Miller's CSAR team in Afghanistan in February of 2002. He liked Keary—a giant of a man at six foot four, with a mop of brown hair—who had a down-to-earth personality and didn't mind bending a few rules. He was well respected throughout the Special Tactics community, and particularly at the 24, for his calm demeanor and expertise with trauma medicine.

The second PJ, Jason Cunningham, was a twenty-six-year-old golden boy on a thin, five-eleven frame—boyish smile and talkative personality. As a senior airman, he was the lowest ranking and least experienced of the three-man team. Like Gabe, he had a young family. Two little girls waited at home with his wife, Theresa: Kyla, age four, and Hannah, barely one. He and Gabe talked about family a lot together.

When Gabe arrived at the JOC, he was told, "There's a missing aircrew member down south, beginning self SAR." That was all the information they had. "Self SAR" indicated the individual was separated from the rest of his crew and friendly forces, but didn't add any details of value to the Combat Controller. It also didn't make a great deal of sense. "I didn't think much of it. Likely just another spin up for no reason, and I expected to go back to bed."

However, on the flight line where the helicopters were staged, Gabe, Keary, and Jason ran into a sister CSAR team from the 24—CCT Greg Pittman, PJ Scott Duffman, and another PJ. Greg's team was just coming off another mission. All highly experienced in their jobs, the two CCT and four PJs huddled to discuss which team would take the now very real mission. Of the six men standing on the ramp in Bagram on that frigid March morning, bristling with gear and weapons in the scant illumination, two would die in Afghanistan—one killed in the next few hours, the other less than four years later.

On the ramp, with the MH-47 blades spinning, things were developing fast. A Ranger QRF was also assigned to the mission. Consisting of a dozen young Rangers and led by Captain Nate Self, they were clearly going to launch. The question: Which package of CCT and PJ experts in trauma medicine, aircraft recovery, and close air support was going to take the mission?

"Greg Pittman and Scott Duffman were just coming off a mission. I think it was airborne support for the Anaconda insertions for AFO. Anyway, Keary, as a two-four member and our team leader, ended up having a bit of a debate with them but must have come out on top because he said [to Gabe and Jason], 'We're going,' and that was it. So I went and found the Rangers and their team leader, Captain Self, who I didn't know, to sort out fires," recalls Gabe.[23]

Furious activity swirled around the designated CSAR helicopter, another TF-160 MH-47E, call sign Razor-01, piloted by Chief Warrant Officer Greg Calvert, the pilot who'd flown down to swap out the helo

---

23   The young Ranger officer had an embedded Air Force Tactical Air Control Party, but when Gabe and Self talked, the Ranger told him, "You're fires," thus settling any confusion as to who would be controlling airstrikes once the team hit the ground.

with the runaway engine at Gardez just an hour before, and who was therefore somewhat familiar with the area. Furthermore, Calvert and the other pilots (the CSAR bird flew with three—one riding jump seat at the rear of the cockpit) had practiced rescue scenarios with the 24 teams and other forces in preparation for just such a crisis. Gabe, Jason, and Keary dashed for their nearby gear and returned to the spinning rotors of Razor-01, clambering aboard along with the Rangers.

Gabe recalls, "We launched without any additional information. On the hour flight toward [Shahi Khot], Self passed around a grease board with some coordinates on it, which didn't mean shit to me. Might as well put me in space and point at the earth for all the good it would do." He'd have to go in blind.

For Calvert, the situation was frustrating. He may not have known the details, but he certainly knew the men flying with him. In the cockpit, they discussed the grid coordinates they'd received with the sketchy information on the ground situation. "We could see on the moving map that the objective was the pinnacle of a tall mountain we had been flying around, twice I believe. There was some confusion as to whether this was 'the place.' We still had the idea the isolated person and Razor-03 may have been colocated (or close). [The other two pilots] and I did discuss that something just did not feel right, and the fact that we all had that 'hair on the back of my neck standing up' feeling. Don [the most senior pilot, riding in the jump seat], to lighten the mood, said that it was just his fingers on the back of my neck."

But the aircrew's instincts were telling them more than TF-11 could. Things were happening on Takur Ghar, and none of the pilots or QRF whirling their way to the mountain knew what the outcome was going to be.

CHAPTER

21

—

JOHN CHAPMAN MUST HAVE BECOME AWARE OF HIMSELF, GRADUALLY... and painfully. He was lying in the snow, crumpled on top of his own legs. He wasn't sure what had happened, not exactly. It was dark but his NVGs were still on. The night sky was clear and the air bitterly cold. Above him was a lone tree with a thick trunk extending perhaps ten feet toward the heavens before spreading out into a thick crown, like a supersize Japanese bonsai tree, though arboreal aesthetics were immaterial. He needed to figure out what had happened. And he couldn't ignore the pain. A cursory check would reveal two gunshot wounds in his torso. He ached, not only from the impact of the AK-47 bullets to his body, which had shocked the tissue around their points of entry, leaving already-dying flesh surrounding the holes, but also from the ungodly pain in his abdomen. One hole was just above his navel on the right side. The other bullet had entered just below the ribs on the same side. There was blood on his uniform, sticky and dark in the night, where the bullets had penetrated. The pain was intense. Was he bleeding internally? It would be difficult to say what damage lay beneath his uniform. Since none of the team had worn body armor, the rounds tore through his tissue like a hot knife stabbed into a pat of butter.

His cursory self-inspection complete, John needed to focus on his situation. A quick scan revealed his surroundings. Next to him was the trench from which the Al Qaeda fighters had attacked him as he'd charged uphill. Two bodies lay dark and lifeless in its recesses. Nearby was the body of another fighter, the man who'd shot him. At least *he* was dead. To his left was the large rock outcropping where he'd last seen Slab. Where the hell were Slab and the others? Were they dead? Or had they left *him* for dead? *Fuck.*

Gunfire from Bunker 2 above brought the situation into instant focus. The PKM was firing, but not at him. Answering fire from far behind and below, easily identifiable, answered his SEAL question. They were down there somewhere—not far, but a lifetime away for a wounded man. He couldn't see them, but maybe he could reach them on his MBITR.

He fought through the pain as his frozen fingers fumbled with the radio on his chest. He was no longer sweating; shock and the cold were attacking his capabilities, and the pain was intense. His watch read a bit past 0520; still dark, though morning twilight would illuminate the mountain to the unaided eye in another thirty minutes. He needed help immediately, or the Chechens and Uzbeks would surely overrun him in the daylight...if he lived that long.

Switching from the fire control frequency he'd preset for airstrikes before they left Gardez, he dialed it to a LOS UHF battlefield common frequency. Airstrikes were not what he needed at this moment. He didn't know where Slab and his team were or how many might still be alive, although clearly they weren't on the summit any longer. But there were other Combat Controllers in the vicinity, Jay and Andy in particular, and all CCT viewed battlefield common as their private comms freq, even if that wasn't expressly what the frequency was for.

"Any station, any station, this is Mako Three Zero Charlie." And he waited alone in the dark.

It's nearly impossible for the average human to understand the implications of true abandonment. The worst thing for a soldier is to be left on the battlefield, and that is exactly what happened to John. At this point, John Chapman was essentially a grunt, the basic individual battlefield element in combat. The distilled essence is kill or be killed, and his extensive specialized training, while not negated, was much marginalized. All the men on the mountain—Al Qaeda, SEALs, himself—were simply soldiers in the classical sense, fighting as soldiers have always done, in sweat, in cold, in fear, and in determination. The overriding imperative was their commitment to their comrades they lived and fought alongside.

And the one *absolute* of combat among soldiers is: *Never* leave a comrade behind or to the enemy. Heroics, courage, cowardice . . . These things can vary, even within an individual, depending on the circumstances and the day. It's a concept difficult for civilians to understand. To them, a soldier soldiers on, rising to an occasion to perform some act of heroism when called for. But the truth for men in combat is the opposite. Courage is nothing but the necessity of action when a comrade is in trouble. To *not* act is cowardice, the opposite of the requirement to save one's brothers. Invariably, those awarded medals for courageous acts on the battlefield view their actions as "Just doing my duty. They would have done the same for me." This is most acute in the face of a friend under fire and threat of capture by the enemy.

Yet now, the unbreakable rule had been broken. For men who are willing to fight and contend with the fear of capture by an enemy whose objective is to torture and *then* kill their captives, abandonment by their brothers is tantamount to a mother who abandons her child. It strains credulity. To the individual—child or soldier—this new reality comes crashing through the mind's barriers. "This can't be happening." One can only imagine the impact on Chapman when the realization of abandonment hit home.

———

Three kilometers away, Jay Hill also sat freezing on a 10,000-foot peak, with his friend and Delta team leader, Kris. Despite the cold, Jay was busy. Extremely busy. On his mountaintop OP, his radios were arrayed around him, each within grasp. Now entering their fourth nonstop day observing Al Qaeda positions, he'd been up for the last seventy-two hours straight. No sleep and the constant cold were a fierce combination in an endless struggle deep inside enemy territory.

Earlier in the night, they were shocked to watch as Mako-30 made its undeclared insertion attempt directly onto Takur Ghar. "From my position I had good vis [visibility] on their summit. We were surprised they went in there, we didn't know beforehand.

"It was busy at our location too. We were getting mortared, but I'd just laid down from being up for three days straight. When the mortars came in, the [Delta] guys picked up my radio and were talking to a flight of B-52s who were checking in. I woke up and heard them and told them, 'Hey guys, you gotta get off the radio. Let me do that, that's *my* job. You guys keep eyes on and provide security.' They were using the laser rangefinder to coordinate, but had the wrong coordinates for strikes, so I got up and worked it. But I don't want to give the wrong impression. It was a team effort. I needed to double-check coordinates for the calculus, then plot it on the map. We were using FalconView on a Toughbook at the time and a 1:24 map to cross-reference. It was all pretty dicey compared to how we do it now."

Two hours later, Juliet Team had been stunned to watch a second MH-47 fly onto Takur Ghar, a location Juliet had passed during their infil, choosing instead their current peak, nearly as high but unoccupied. "We'd pulled up to that spot and realized it was a great location to observe the valley. We were gonna use it, but it's got bad dudes all over it." That night on Takur Ghar, "you could see the helos going in and see flashes of gunfire. RPGs. I could see the bonsai tree, but not the base of it."

Jay was working on the net, talking to Andy and Hotaling, sharing information and air assets, when he heard Chapman call the first time. He didn't know where Chapman was calling from, but knew it was his fellow 24 STS teammate; he recognized Chappy's voice. And no one else used the Charlie suffix, so it wasn't the SEALs of Mako-30.

"Mako Three Zero Charlie, this is Yankee Uniform Three, go ahead." YU3 was Jay's call sign on J Team, one of the few CCT call signs not to use a *C* suffix. He was rewarded only with static. With no response from Chapman, Jay returned his attention to his own tasks.

Over the air a few minutes later, it came again: "Any station, Mako Three Zero Charlie."

"Go ahead Three Zero Charlie." Nothing but static. Jay checked his radio in the dark, something he could do by feel. It was configured correctly. Chapman was calling on a battlefield common UHF frequency, one used for non–fire control or emergencies to communicate among friendly US SOF.

Of the transmissions, Jay said, "His voice was . . . He was struggling to get words out. He was stressed, you could hear it in his voice. You knew it was him. Besides just his voice, only Controllers used the 'Charlie' suffix."

It's impossible to say what John felt on Takur Ghar in the moment of realization that he was completely alone. Fear surely, and pain and shock were already gripping his body. But determination must have compelled him. When he got no reply to his transmissions, he likely worked through the mechanics of his radio equipment one component at a time—the radio first, then his comm cord, connecting it to his headset, and finally the earpiece and mike. He tried calling multiple times but must never have heard Jay's responses, for reasons unknown. He gave up on his radio for the moment. He was getting colder from blood loss. All he had worn for warmth was a thin layer of black Capilene liners for his legs, a lightweight green fleece top, and his desert camo pants and blouse. His feet were warm in wool socks and leather heavy-duty Asolo hiking boots, and he had gray, loosely-weaved fingerless gloves on his hands, but without body armor or a helmet, his torso and head were suffering from exposure. His PVS-15 NVGs were mounted on a padded bracket, universally referred to by the guys as the "fucked-up head harness," which allowed the goggles to be worn without a helmet but was uncomfortable and awkward with its pads and straps.

His MBITR was connected to a single-ear headset with a boom-type mike for speaking. To transmit, he merely needed to push a button with his index finger and the programmed frequency would send the signal. Only now, he was receiving no response.

At least his M4 was working. That was critical. It had a reflex-style sight as well as an AN/PEQ-2 laser—the same pointer Slab had seen moving just before the SEALs retreated—and a suppressor, not that suppression mattered. It would provide no masking of his location at this range, which raised a question: Did the Chechens and Uzbeks know he was here?

As Chapman took stock of his situation, two Al Qaeda fighters were moving upslope in his direction along the ridge below, but their sights were set on the SEALs sliding down the cliff face. They slowly encroached, attempting to gain a view of the Americans. If they could get over the top, they'd be able to strike at them.

Slab and the other SEALs were still only fifty meters from Chapman, but he had been cast from their thoughts. Their focus was survival. Without the Combat Controller, Slab was forced to break out his MBITR and work through the presets to find the fire direction net frequency.

Turner, overhead in his gunship, had been watching the calamity unfold, powerless to help and not able to reach Chapman or the team as the "firefight in a phone booth" unfolded five thousand feet below. In the back of the AC-130, Staff Sergeant Chris Walker sat in the "sensor booth"—essentially a room built into the right side of the fuselage opposite the 25mm GAU-12 Gatling cannon, 40mm Bofors, and M102 105mm howitzer. As the low-light-level TV operator (LLLTV), he was responsible for illuminating targets covertly in the dark. The images could be amplified to produce a clear battlefield picture even without moonlight. He was joined by three others, the infrared (IR) system operator, an electronic warfare officer, and an observer. They sat in a claustrophobic row. Together, with both pilots and a fire control officer on the flight deck, they saw everything that happened on the ground below.

When Slab raised Grim-32 on the radio, the aircrew was relieved to find someone, anyone, to talk to. Now they could get down to business, doing what no other fire support platform in the world could—orbit a friendly force surrounded by hostiles and turn back the tide.

The first thing Slab called for was the Quick Reaction Force. With his request relayed, Slab turned his attention to the gunship's weapons, telling Turner, "We're kind of hiding on the edge of a little precipice. I know how to call for fire and I know I'm danger close, but I'm telling you I need the fire now." He went on to describe the peak.

"There's no friendlies up top?" asked the leery pilot. Only two days earlier, Turner's gunship had been involved in the friendly-fire incident with Blaber and Haas's convoy. He was not about to repeat history. The SEALs had by now turned on an IR strobe, which Walker clearly identified on his screen. Walker could also see the SEALs.

"No," replied Slab. Neither he nor the gunship had any idea Chapman was now moving under the tree just below the summit. And Chapman, no longer on the fire direction frequency, had no idea he was now in greater peril from his compatriots than from Al Qaeda.

"I want guns on two big clusters of trees up there. Only two are up there near a big rock. You got the strobe?" Meaning his own location.

"Yeah, I got the strobe." Thirty seconds later, the gunship put several rounds down on the summit and asked the SEAL for corrections, but Slab had no means of observing where the rounds were impacting. With the SEALs unable to adjust their fire, the gunship was shooting blindly. Chapman, sheltering below the bonsai tree, remained crouched in the bunker as the mountain exploded around him.

On the ridge above and just south of the SEALs, the two Al Qaeda fighters continued stalking the Americans. Another fighter remained on the point of the rock fin, watching the two "brothers." He was safer in his rock position, observing the events unfold.

In the gunship, the copilot asked Slab, "Do you have anybody to your south?"

"No. I have all my guys."

"I have two or three guys moving to the south."

"They are not mine."

"Roger."

A 105mm howitzer round exploded on the rocky fin's farther-most point, destroying the rock outcropping and vaporizing the observer.

"They aren't moving anymore," came the gunship's simple as-sessment.

The two stalkers, a mere 150 feet from the detonation, changed their minds, withdrew from the ridgeline, and moved into a small collection of rocks just below Razor-04's landing site. One of them, an Uzbek, had on Roberts's desert camo Gore-Tex pants, which he'd rifled out of the dead SEAL's rucksack. The two were soon joined by another, who came up the draw by himself. There they discussed what should be done. The Americans may have retreated but they still possessed immense firepower in the form of the AC-130 that could be heard droning relentlessly overhead. The summit was taking a pounding beyond Bunkers 1 and 2, and the jihadists could do little during the onslaught but wait and pray to Allah.

A few kilometers in the opposite direction, Combat Control-ler Ben Miller and Mako-21 were observing the chaos. With the obvious fight unfolding a scant distance away, they were anxious to get into it. Ben made repeated requests on their behalf, stating Mako-21 "is about seven klicks west of current situation" and able to assist if only headquarters "can send a helo their way." Pete Blaber, now mobile in the valley below, monitoring a number of troops in contact, and with a clear view of the mountain, listened patiently. Eventually he told the team, "Hold what you got." Al, the team leader, had to quell a near mutiny by the other SEALs, who felt their place was in the battle. "Blaber wouldn't let us leave our mountain." But Blaber knew the CSAR helicopter would be on its way, and it was impossible to generate another to move the men, who weren't equipped for a sustained gunfight the way Gabe, Keary, Jason, and the Rangers were, with multiple heavy machine guns, ammunition, and grenades. Mako-21 was also not even close to its own objective and was struggling in the frozen terrain. They'd already passed J Team's resupply to the 101st for delivery instead of taking it themselves. With their own mission a long way off, they needed to focus.[24]

———

A distressed Chapman repeatedly called out on his radio, each time heard four klicks away by Jay, who responded immediately every time. Chapman either never received the replies or couldn't hear them under the fire of the gunship. However, John must not have been monitoring the AC-130's fires net or he would have made himself known to the aircraft. Jay was increasingly concerned for his friend; the gunship was churning up the mountain. "On our OP we were talking [about what was happening on Takur Ghar]. Everyone agreed there were two elements on the mountain. You could hear Slab on the FDO [fire direction frequency] talking to Grim. And Chapman was on either LOS or another freq."

In his bunker, John continued to bleed. The pounding by the AC-130 was terrifying, and he knew, better than others, that if a 105 round hit his position, he'd be obliterated. Intermittently, he reached out to raise someone, anyone, on UHF without success. His attention was diverted by the enemy, who now knew he was there. Their intentions were announced by an RPG exploding against Bunker 1's upper berm a few feet above his head, showering him

---

24 As with Mako-30, SEAL Team Six leadership rushed Mako-21 into the field, ill-prepared for their mission and leaving critical gear behind. Unbeknownst to AFO personnel in Gardez, they also established a separate line of communication with the TF-Blue TOC in Bagram, asking to be pulled from the mission. Ultimately they were extracted early without putting eyes on their objective or calling any airstrikes.

with dirt. With a blast kill radius of several meters, he survived only because most of the detonation was deflected over his head, yet it still damaged his ears and left them ringing. Okay. They knew he was here. Ironically, it was likely the unwitting gunship and its rounds ravaging the summit that had prevented a rush by the Chechens and Uzbeks. To allay any doubt about their under-standing of the situation, a grenade tossed from Bunker 2 exploded between the combatants. Using his PEQ-2, John fired his weapon over the top of the berm and hunkered down lower, while the Al Qaeda in Bunker 2 continued to pound his position repeatedly with AK-47 and PKM fire.

Despite the gunship, the mountain was now populated across its upper slopes by additional fighters converging on the Americans. Here and there, pairs and singles of Al Qaeda searched for targets. One of the fighters, the Uzbek who'd taken Roberts's Gore-Tex pants, made a decision. It was obvious an American was in Bunker 1, a fortified position he himself had helped to build and occupy in preparation for the glorious battle he hoped to wage against the Americans. And now, one of the infidels had the audacity to occupy "his" mountain. He began to snake his way upslope at an oblique angle to Chapman's position, using the fire from Bunker 2 as a mask.

Other Al Qaeda knew the Americans were now split, with one group falling down the cliff face the jihadists had avoided, and at least one more in Bunker 1, where the only true firefight was raging on. It drew most of their attention to the beleaguered Combat Controller. As a consequence, it also drew most of the fire, alleviating the pressure on the wounded and retreating SEALs, who continued to slide down the mountain in order to gain distance from the enemy. On the Predator's camera, the unfolding violence was captured silently by its unblinking eye.

John's world became an interminable one-man stand as he fired sparingly, trying to pace his ammo depletion. He was either already too weak from blood loss or thought better of exposing himself to throw any hand grenades. Whatever his reasons, he used none of them. Mortars now rocked his position as well, as the jihadists on the lower slopes lobbed rounds onto the mountain, apparently unmoved by the potential fratricide this might produce. More alone than ever and shaking from the cold and shock, John fought on. He had no choice. Either the SEALs would come back, a rescue force would arrive, or they would not, and he would fire until he was out of ammunition or killed. The SEALs were no longer firing, so they were either dead or had left the summit. Either way, he was alone in this battle.

As he lay there in an enemy trench, the sun slowly crept toward the horizon, chasing the darkness from the mountain. Its deadly illumination was already snatching John's few remaining advantages by laying the predawn twilight at Al Qaeda's feet. He snapped his NVGs, now useless, up onto his "fucking head harness." His watch read 0553, twenty minutes before true sunrise, but that hardly mattered. This high on the mountain it was already light enough to see, for *everyone* to see.

Overhead, Chris Walker continued to watch the events unfold. Next to him Gordon Bower, as the infrared sensor operator, was working Grim-32's IR system to target the enemy for the pilots. The AC-130H IR system did not pick up infrared strobes like the one John had now activated. Rather, the plane's IR system registered heat signatures only, so that anything warmer than the surrounding terrain appeared as a black outline. The two sensor operators frequently compared inputs to events on the ground, allowing them to form a comprehensive picture. As Walker recalled in his witness statement, "Indications of friendly engagement from within Bunker 1 against the enemy were frequent and consistent. I continued to observe glint tape, strobe lights, muzzle flashes, and IZLID laser movement after

0042Z [the GMT time at which the SEALs retreated from the summit]
from Bunker 1."

Those innocuous and sanitized observations failed to convey the
carnage on the ground. John Chapman was fighting for his life
and losing the battle. He was now marred by shrapnel in his arms
and body, his misery compounded by growing weakness as the
bleeding in his abdomen continued. "Any station, any station, this
is Mako Three Zero Charlie," he tried again in vain. Jay Hill heard
the call and responded for the dozenth time, but his transmission
never reached John's ear.

A fusillade from Bunker 2, including yet another RPG, seized
John's attention. This was followed by an Al Qaeda flanker from
his right, across the slope and from below Bunker 2. John quickly
dispatched the threat with a few well-aimed shots.

There was no time to regroup in his isolated bunker. Without
warning, the Uzbek in Roberts's desert Gore-Tex pants, dyed henna
beard, and green Russian camo charged him from the boulder above
Bunker 1, firing as he rushed over Roberts's dead body. Fortunately,
Gore-Tex Pants was struggling to make ground on John as quickly
as he hoped. He was wearing slip-on shoes with no tread, and his
progress was slowed by the lack of traction. Still, he was only feet
away and firing point-blank at the American. John swung his M4,
and from a distance of a mere ten feet, felled the Uzbek with several
precious rounds to the chest. The Uzbek dropped like a rock onto
his back into a twisted final pose, never to rise again, his lifeless eyes
staring skyward. The time was exactly 0600.

John was breathing heavily now, the pain pushed back by true
fight-or-flight adrenaline but by no means eliminated. Two rushers
attacked in as many minutes. He was now going through ammunition
at an alarming pace. Of the seven thirty-round magazines he started
with, he was down to only a couple. And unlike the SEALs, he had
no pistol secondary.

A lull arrived like a double-edged blessing. True, no one was shooting at him for the moment. But huddled in the bottom of the dirty narrow trench, surrounded by frozen bloody snow and dead bodies, John was now more alone than ever. Seconds felt like minutes. Time stretched, the pain dragging it out. An eternity. With no options, he waited.

Four minutes passed. He tried another unsuccessful radio call. How many did that make? He'd lost count.

The threats all seemed to come from above and his left and right, certainly the heavy machine-gun fire. What John didn't realize was, while the first flanker charged from the right and Gore-Tex Pants had been approaching from the left in preparation for his own assault, another lone gunman was making his way upslope.

Silently the stalker advanced. Seeing his two "brothers" fall to the man in the bunker, he decided another rush assault was inadvisable. Clearly the American, armed with an M4 by the sound of its report, was deadly with his weapon. Stealth was called for. Sporadic fire from Bunker 2 directed at Bunker 1 assisted in masking his approach and keeping the American's attention, and so the man pushed forward.

At 0606, the lone gunman arrived below Bunker 1, in precisely the location the SEALs had occupied just before leaving Chapman behind. Who struck first will remain forever unknown, but John engaged the gunman in fierce hand-to-hand combat, his already shrapnel-ridden and bleeding body drastically diminished. The gunman connected with the Controller at least a few times, leaving "blunt-force injuries of the head, neck and extremities," "a contused forehead," and "abrasions of the lips, nose, and cheeks," as noted in the official forensic pathology report.

Somehow, the severely injured Chapman overwhelmed his attacker and killed him, leaving the body at the mouth of the bunker. Exhausted and hyped-up on another rush of adrenaline, he had no time to recover. Bunker 2 launched an even more ferocious attack, firing one more RPG into Chapman's redoubt.[25]

Chapman heard the MH-47's heavy rotors beating the cold clear air in the early morning twilight. He may have even seen the helicopter's approach, though whether he did or not was immaterial. There was only one place the rotor sound of a laden MH-47 laboring up the mountain slopes would be headed: Takur Ghar. A wave of relief surely washed over him as he realized that either Slab, their insertion helo, or headquarters must have initiated the QRF. They were coming back for him. Another reality: With no one else to defend the HLZ, this MH-47 would meet the same fate as the previous two. Though he couldn't have known, this helo was stuffed with Rangers, two Air Force PJs, and fellow Combat Controller Gabe Brown. All totaled, eighteen men. The loss of life, should it fall victim to a fully alerted and prepared enemy with multiple RPG firing positions and heavy weapons, would be catastrophic, the worst in the war to date.

Chapman knew what the enemy wanted. His fighting position, Bunker 1, had a clear view of the helicopter's approach and a direct line of fire where it would set down. As things stood, from their positions higher on the mountain, the enemy couldn't engage the rescue team; they needed his position to place their RPGs. If the Rangers made it to the hilltop intact, the roles would reverse, and Al Qaeda would be the ones in danger of being overrun, not Chapman.

His options were nil. To save the lives of the rescue force sent to

---

25   Attempts to claim that Bunker 1 is not occupied by the live Chapman are refuted by the fact that only those in Bunker 2 could have occupied Bunker 1. Only Gore-Tex Pants and the lone stalker from below came from elsewhere. Also, Bunker 2 had been attacking Bunker 1 repeatedly. Since that is the case, even if Gore-Tex Pants charging to hand-to-hand distance is a mistake, and then six minutes later the lone gunman does the same, the follow-on firefight that ensues (again) between the two bunkers is otherwise inexplicable. They'd know if it was fellow Al Qaeda at this point, having seen them and because they originally sent the forces to take the bunker in the form of the first flanker. Finally, it is now daylight.

save his own, he needed to negate the threat—just as he had done an hour before, saving the lives of his entire SEAL team. If he was to survive, he'd need to somehow climb out of the bunker, battered, bleeding, and severely wounded, and take the fight to the enemy, challenging the jaws of death once more. Remaining static would surely be his demise. He had one weapon and little ammo, but the course of action was clear.

John's commitment to his comrades was clearly evident that morning, and it necessitated rising from the bunker to save the men he didn't know on Razor-01. His actions can best be summed up in a word: brotherhood. And to men in combat, brotherhood is love. There's no difference between the two words. While it's impossible to say if the thought crossed his mind, or even if he recognized it at all in that short moment, his decision to act at this point was surely the embodiment of those two interchangeable words.

At 0611, with a glorious sunrise striking his east-facing bunker, John Chapman, face battered and bloodied, his body wracked with pain, made the bravest decision of his life. He mounted the shrapnel-spattered berm onto the dirty and bloodstained snow, blinking against the blinding rays of the morning sun. If the Chechens and Uzbeks had any questions as to whether the lone American was still alive, he answered them with his first volley, a multi-round burst aimed directly at their PKM, his ejected casings glinting in the morning sunlight as they launched skyward. He emptied the magazine in his M4, then switched mags before dropping prone in the snow in the face of the PKM's response.

A barrage was unleashed on Bunker 1 as Al Qaeda fighters saw the loaded MH-47 making its final approach, seconds from landing. On the far side of the summit, a lone RPG gunner moved into position, while a second RPG warhead was mounted on a launcher inside Bunker 2. Elsewhere across the slopes, fighters continued to converge. Another flank attempt was made from the east.

John slid down the slope on his side with his legs in front of him, stopping just below his bunker and the bonsai tree. With a fresh magazine, he engaged and killed the eastern flanker. But there was absolutely no time to stay in the relative safety of defilade below the tree. Struggling up the rocky snow-covered bank, he turned his adrenaline on the PKM again, firing as he moved, until more AK-47 rounds assaulted him from the east. Staring into the blazing sunlight, he searched for targets, firing rounds in desperation to protect the helicopter now throwing snow from its rotor wash and drowning out the noise of enemy gunfire with the thumping of its mighty turbine engines. John leaned his haggard body against the giant bonsai, using it for protection, methodically engaging any movement on the mountain. There were just too many targets for one man.

More fighters appeared to the south along the ridge like ants from an anthill. The unmistakable sound of an exploding RPG warhead stopped time. Behind John, the giant MH-47 reeled under the impact of a direct hit as the grenade exploded against its right engine, destroying it instantly. The left engine immediately compensated for the loss of power by revving. It was no use. Overloaded and at high altitude, its fate was sealed. The copilot had already been shot in the leg and helmet. Calvert, the pilot, considered making a single-engine descent from the summit but realized he'd never clear the ridge in front of him. He immediately dropped the helo down expertly with a thump.

As the Chinook settled onto the slope, John resumed engaging the Al Qaeda fighters. Dropping prone again, he fired at the most immediate threat to the devastated helicopter, which had yet to disgorge any soldiers or airmen. The fighters along the ridge enjoyed a broadside view of the bird and immediately set about raking it with heavy fire, including more RPGs, killing several Rangers and a crewman instantly. As John fired along the ridgeline, his back was exposed to the concentration of fighters from Bunker 2 and the DShK position.

As the Rangers, PJs, and Gabe Brown began to pour out onto the snow from the helo's ramp, John was raked with fire from behind, several rounds connecting with his legs. Two entered his lower left leg, lacerating his left calf, and another embedded in his heel. His right leg was devastated. One round entered above the kneecap, exiting out the other side a few inches away. Two rounds slammed into his thigh, the first shattering his femur. His body jerked involuntarily with the impact.

Though his body was mangled by small-arms fire and shrapnel, John Chapman battled on, changing out to his last good magazine. The only other he had on him had been shot through on his Rhodesian vest, rendering it useless. He fired at any target he could see along the ridge, unaware of the many enemies converging behind him, focused intently on his back.

One of them, Chechen or Uzbek, took aim at the prone American now in the open and on the ground, an easy target at a handful of steps, and fired two rounds from his AK-47.

John, quite literally firing the last of his ammunition at the enemy immediately in front of him, would have felt the bullets strike home. The tight two-round shot group entered his upper torso close together on their trajectory until connecting with his aorta, exploding the organ and dropping his blood pressure to zero. His ammunition and life expended, John Chapman died. The last images before his eyes closed forever were of blood-spattered rock and snow on a desolate mountain peak, while other men raged around him, fighting for their own lives.

CHAPTER

22

---

4 March

0613 HOURS

ON HIS FIRST APPROACH TO TAKUR GHAR, GREG CALVERT WAS CONCERNED about what they were going to find on landing. Both pilots decided to make a pass to assess the situation before committing themselves and the men in back. "During the high-speed pass over the pinnacle, I saw out the right window that there seemed to be several black spots that I said looked like explosive impacts. I also saw flashes from what I assumed was small-arms fire coming from a large rock outcropping and tree at the very pinnacle. That passed off the right side and we dove down over the cliff to regain speed. I did some jinking to make sure that we weren't too easy of a target."

Razor-01, carrying the QRF, may or may not have been an easy target, but one thing was certain: Their landing was not going to be easy. "We came up a draw on the backside of the mountain to stay as invisible as possible to the pinnacle. I picked out a landing area with the big rock and tree at the two o'clock position. Everything from here on out seemed to move in slow motion. On short final, at about 100 feet, I remember thinking, 'Well, this is it, make it a good one,' and put the aircraft in a decelerative attitude." As he looked out the cockpit, trying to judge his final approach, "the whole cockpit seemed to erupt. Although I only heard the aircraft noises, holes started popping through the windscreen and side windows, but I continued the approach. I called out, 'Taking fire from two o'clock' and heard Sergeant Phil Svitak's gun open up on the right side. I felt the 'breeze' of rounds whizzing by me, and my head was 'nudged' several times to the left. Also felt several hits to my chest [body armor]."

Then the situation turned, in the worst possible way for a helicopter pilot. The first RPG slammed into the right side of Razor-01, destroying the engine and sending burning shrapnel slicing through the rear of the fuselage. Calvert "felt the aircraft shudder and nose pitch up and knew by the sound and feel that we lost an engine, although I didn't know which one."

The aircraft was coming down; there was no longer any doubt. Calvert, drawing on over a decade of flying MH-47s, still managed a "near zero airspeed landing." Despite the steep angle of the mountain and lack of control, "[I] felt we made a good, but firm, landing under the circumstances, but the aircraft did not feel stable so I held the controls, knowing that the customers in the back would be offloading while Chuck [the copilot] reached up and pulled back the [power control levers]. That was my first realization that we would not take off again. Chuck reached over, slapped my arm, yelled, 'I'm outta here,' and disappeared out the left emergency exit."

The cockpit was filling with smoke. Flames came out of the instrument and power distribution panels in front of Calvert. Outside, he could see three people firing at them from a large rock outcropping.[26] The pilot grabbed his M4, charged the weapon, and began shooting through the window, while still holding the helicopter stable with

---

26 The outcropping seen by Calvert was the same rock that the 60 gunner SEAL tumbled off when he got shot in the leg, just next to Bunker 1, which Chapman no doubt had just vacated.

his left hand on the cyclic. It was a remarkable display of calm and courage, especially given he was the only one left in the cockpit.

When the helo seemed to finally settle and stabilize, he took his left hand off the cyclic, reached up, and tried to open the emergency exit, thinking, *I've never done this before.* He managed to get it open, kicking the panel free, and it fell to the snow four feet below. Still firing his weapon one-handed, his left arm up in the air, "I felt it slam away from me to the left. I don't know how long I sat there, but I can remember just sitting there staring at my hand. The glove had popped off, inside out, hanging on by just the tips of my fingers. It didn't hurt, and I can remember thinking that [my hand] looked like a lava lamp. Blood was squirting out of it, it had fallen over the side of my wrist, and it glowed." What Calvert didn't realize in his shock: The glowing object was actually a 7.62 tracer round, burning inside his hand.

In the rear of the aircraft, Gabe was sitting in his seat, close to the cockpit and right behind Phil Svitak, the right-door minigun gunner. He felt the aircraft shudder and, even over the whine of the engines and rotors, heard the RPG's detonation. He and Keary made eye contact, "both of us thinking the same thing, 'Here we go!'" The entire troop compartment rocked back and forth just as Svitak opened up at six thousand rounds per minute, projecting a liquid stream of bullets that connected him to the enemy. The M134 made a loud *vrrrrt!* sound for a second, then abruptly stopped. Gabe watched the aerial gunner slump over his weapon, shot dead from a machine-gun burst that struck him in the chest.

The carnage grew inside the helicopter as the stricken bird settled to the ground. Inside, a Ranger, Specialist Marc Anderson, leader of a two-man M240 machine-gun crew, shouted to his assistant gunner, "Today I feel like a Ranger!" amid the cacophony. His words had no sooner left his lips than he fell dead from rounds fired by unseen assailants, striking him through the paper-thin aircraft skin. As men ran off the back, two others, Sergeant Brad Crose and Corporal Matt Commons, fared no better. The two platoon mates dropped dead only steps from the open ramp, cut down by more machine-gun fire.

Gabe, now on his feet, was waiting his turn to get the hell out of the death trap. Things *must* be better outside. When Svitak absorbed the full blast of the machine gun, he probably saved the Combat Controller's life, at the cost of his own. There wasn't time to reflect on luck. Gabe hadn't even stepped off the helicopter and he had already seen three men fall. At that rate, all of them would be dead in the next five minutes, and he still had no idea where exactly he was. None of them had maps of the mountain or area, another CSAR curse (there were never maps of the target area, simply because the location was never known until after a crisis occurred). He waited to die or escape the helicopter as the men in front of him attempted to "un-ass" the destroyed helicopter. The time was 0615.

As soon as he stepped off the back, he saw Jason and Keary working on casualties. "They were doing PJ things, treating guys." As the Controller stumbled into the snow, he found himself asking, "What do I need to do? How can I positively affect this?" He took cover at a rock as fire erupted all around him, snow dancing and dirt pitching into the air as rounds struck. Behind him, the helicopter took another RPG round, this time to the nose, but the blast and its concussive force carried all the way to the rear and to Gabe. He looked at his rock, which was only calf height, and took a knee. There was nothing else but snow. He shouted to the closest Rangers, "Who's the team leader?" It sounds odd, "but you have to remember, I'd never met the guy and everybody's wearing the same damn helmet. And it's chaos. I don't know who's dead."

Gabe and Self shared a brief exchange amid the deafening fire as the Rangers were lighting up the hilltop. Above them, the enemy reoccupied Bunker 1. With John Chapman dead, the position opened up new opportunities to plunge fire down on the latest group of infidels to land on their mountain. Even with their own casualties mounting, it was hard to believe their good fortune of a *third* helicopter, no doubt delivered into their hands, all praise to Allah. And while this one had a larger fighting force, they had the numbers, the high ground, and superior firepower.

With no place to hide and needing to orient himself, take stock of the terrain, and gain control of all the air assets that were surely coming his way, Gabe Brown single-handedly set about changing the enemy's advantages. His immediate call was on the gunship common frequency to the AC-130s he could still hear overhead. "I got hold of Mike Bushe and also [CCT] Joel Hicks, each on different gunships, but both of them told me, 'We have to go,' and they left." So much for gunship support, but it wasn't their fault.[27]

This mission was not going to be easy. "So now I'm trying to coordinate and figure out what's going on. You have to deal with what you've got. Or not got, depending..." One thing seemed obvious: He was not likely to survive in the open. He made a quick scan for better cover, looking to his left at the smoking wreckage of the helicopter, hit by yet another RPG, this one skipping across the tail ramp and down the mountain, confirming *that* was definitely not the place to go. In front of him, looking uphill, were Rangers and open space, where he saw bodies strewn on the ground. To his right, two more Rangers were fighting furiously. He elected to stay put.

The next crucial call, to get air support, would need to take

---

27   The gunships above Operation Anaconda have sometimes received criticism for their failure to deliver results or remain on station. This is best refuted by D. J. Turner and his Grim-32 crew who remained on station overhead as the dawn broke, completely against AC-130 protocol and despite direct orders to return to base. As they flew north toward K2 airfield, headed for a severe "ass chewing" from Colonel Mulholland, the Task Force Dagger commander, the entire crew agreed it was the right thing to remain into daylight until fuel forced them from the battle. Gabe and the QRF had arrived at a coincidentally unfortunate time.

place via satellite. He set about getting his SATCOM running, calmly erecting his satellite antenna, connecting it to his PRC-117 radio, and immediately making comms with Champ-20, the TF-11 fire support call sign, whose job it was to obtain and push aircraft to the Combat Controller. Gabe's call sign was Slick-01, and Slick had just become the number-one priority of America's entire war effort, holding the lives of everyone on the mountain in his handset.

Aircraft were already being diverted to him by Champ. The first to arrive were F-15 Strike Eagles. Their presence wasn't going to be enough. Before he (or any CCT) called in airstrikes in a dynamic and chaotic crisis, he needed to ensure his air support did not hit any friendlies. It took precious minutes to determine there were SEALs nearby (the remainder of Mako-30) but not on top of the mountain. Satisfied striking the rock and bonsai tree above his position posed no threat to the closest friendlies, he started the lengthy process of "talking on" the pilots to his location. With Gabe and the Rangers so close, they weren't willing to drop bombs...not yet. However, anything to keep the enemy suppressed would help and, possibly, save lives immediately. But "the F-15s had never done gun runs like this. Their cannons were designed for air-to-air engagements, and they had to start their runs from 20,000 feet, using a much steeper than acceptable angle. They did it anyway. The pilots really stepped up their game. During my entire day and night of calling CAS, I only had to call two 'Knock it off's' [aborts]. It was amazing, really."

———

Back inside the helicopter, Calvert was looking out the side of his cockpit to the snow below and suddenly decided that it didn't seem like such a good idea to drop onto the ground below on the same side as the enemy fire. He pushed into the rear after his flight gear got hung up on his seat. He hollered at the closest medic, the helicopter's own Cory Lamoreaux, "I'm hit!" just as the RPG round Gabe had seen struck the nose. The medic's garbled response didn't make any sense until he very clearly heard him shout, "Take your fucking helmet off!" He tumbled into a heap near several others as he took off his helmet, and Cory began to work on him, applying a tourniquet to stem the blood loss. "I remember thinking how big and purple my hand looked. And I was pissed because they had shot off the new watch my wife had sent me." Calvert looked at the spent tracer round protruding from his hand. "I don't know why, but I pulled it out and put it in my sleeve pocket." He then watched Cory put an IV in his arm, followed by Jason trying to put an oximeter on his finger to measure the oxygen levels in his blood, only to find it wouldn't work. Frustrated, Jason discovered one of the wire leads had been severed by a bullet. The PJ tried to put a pressure sleeve on the IV bag to increase the fluid's flow rate but discovered it, too, had been shot. Calvert remembers seeing Svitak and wondering why the two medics weren't working on him. He looked up at them and recalls, "We were still taking rounds through the aircraft, but Cory and Jason were still up and moving around. I told them to 'Get the hell down, we can't afford to lose you guys.'"

They eventually moved the pilot out of the aircraft, placing him alongside other wounded crewmen. "Cory, Don [the third pilot], and Jason would alternatively work on us and fire back at the enemy that were now firing from the six o'clock of the aircraft, behind a large rock and what looked like a large bonsai tree. I wanted my M4 back, but somebody had already taken that."

Meanwhile, Gabe was getting multiple aircraft support. "I had [F-]15s, 16s, you name it. Then Jay comes up on the radio, which was helpful." The two Controllers began shaping the battle together. From Gabe's position on the side of the hill, he couldn't get a good sense of the Al Qaeda defenses above him, their numbers, or locations of fighters. J Team had a clear view looking at it from the north, and from their repeated exchanges, Gabe's challenges slowly came into sharper focus.

As he gained confidence, he began to "walk" bombs onto the mountain. Bunker 1 continued to pour fire down on the QRF. One Ranger had his SAW machine gun shot to pieces in his hands as others were struck down around him.

The SEALs of Mako-30, while not on top of the mountain, remained missing for Gabe. Pinning down their location was critical because more enemy forces would most assuredly converge. Hotaling, 3,200 meters to the south, finally put eyes on the beleaguered remnants of Mako-30. Champ-20 also keyed in on this information and asked him to contact the SEALs. At 0745 Hotaling reported, "Negative contact with Mako. Jaguar [Hotaling] is south of their location. Bombs getting ready to drop [in vicinity] of helo in approx. 30 seconds. Helo on top of hill. Fighter was talking to Slick [Gabe]." From Hotaling's position, he and the Aussies continued trying to find the survivors of Mako-30. Finally, he spotted them and called Champ. "Jaguar reports they are south of the [helo's] location looking up the valley onto the western side of the ridge."

With all friendly positions accounted for, the three Combat Controllers—Gabe, Jay, and Hotaling—began managing all the airstrikes and dominating airspace above the battle raging around Razor-01. To those unfamiliar with exchanges like those between the Controllers, Champ-20, and the strike aircraft, they can appear confusing. Like air traffic controllers, each party uses abbreviated speech, acronyms, and sequencing to convey precise information. The following transmissions come from the battle's official logs and take place over the span of four minutes. These are the only ones that were captured in the record. During the event, the volume of radio traffic was extreme and challenging for even an expert ear to decipher:

AFO [Blaber]: Aussie commander intends to push an element to the 16 88 grid square. Watch the valley to the east, south of Marzak. They will be dropping bombs there.

Champ: Trying to get Mako [-31, Andy Martin] down south to control the fire. [J Team] said they have eyes on the location. [AFO] is going to push the bomber to [J Team].

Jay: Roger. Be advised, friendlies are danger, danger close!

Hotaling: Aussies on channel [frequency] internal freq while moving.

AFO: Need [J Team] to work anything on the whale that comes up.

Jay: Roger.

Champ to Gabe: Slick 01, you got a Wild Fire above you that is armed. You've got 13 Rangers at the base of the mountain. They are working there [sic] way up the hill. Have you linked up yet?[28]

Gabe to Champ: Negative. [Have] 4 dead, numerous wounded. Slick 01 going back to work the fighters. [In order to alternate between fire direction frequencies and SATCOM, Gabe recalls: "I was playing the antenna game, switching between SATCOM and UHF line of sight because I only had the one PRC-117 (radio). Every time I did, they thought I'd died because I kept going off the air."]

---

28   This was a second MH-47 with nothing but Rangers and the second part of the QRF. Diverted to Gardez until the situation stabilized or crystallized, it eventually landed at the base of Takur Ghar and disgorged thirteen more Rangers. Also aboard was Vic, the SEAL who left the safe house and hopped on the helicopter to get to Mako-30 without informing Blaber or anyone else. This would have far-reaching implications as the battle wore on.

Hotaling to Champ and Gabe: Slick 01 was working F-15s. Now out of bullets. Two by F-16s now in area. Is Slick good with comms with AC [aircraft]?
Gabe: Yes, F-15s are dead on with their bullets. Bullet runs only.

From Jay's OP, where he was simultaneously dropping bombs on the Whale and keeping an eye on his friend's precarious position, he saw Al Qaeda fighters at the bonsai tree and told Gabe, "Hey, they're still alive. I can see them moving behind that tree. I can see them. One guy, two."

Gabe reported, "Anybody up there. You've got a guy with the high ground. All he has to do is roll over, and pin any one of us trying to run uphill."

Enter Wildfire, the CIA drone mentioned in the transmissions above. Gabe recalls, "Wildfire showed up and he's selling me on this shot on [Bunker 1]." Realizing this shot is going to be no more than fifty meters from the closest Rangers, Gabe discussed it with the team leader, trying to convince him that the bonsai tree was a good point of reference and was a known position, and the Wildfire pilot who, unlike the fighters, had been circling and observing the battle for some time knew what he was doing. "Self [the Ranger team leader] is not about this shot. Didn't want me to take it. But the Wildfire guy is insisting he can take it." A tense minute of consideration and calculation passes for the young Combat Controller who is embroiled in his first gunfight with life-and-death airstrikes. "Finally I tell him 'kill the fucking tree' but I'm thinking, *Holy shit, I hope this works out.* Because of the danger close, back then we were waaaay inside the danger range, I had to give him my initials to authorize it, 'Cleared hot Golf Bravo,' and crossed my fingers. And he hit right in the bunker.

"And that's when we began our transition up the hill."

———

At the rear of Razor-01, Jason was rotating among his growing number of patients. Calvert remembers, "Jason was trying to start an IV in my neck but was unsuccessful." Cory, who was working another patient, said, "We'll take care of that later."

Calvert was beginning to feel the accumulated damage to his body. In addition to his arm and the excruciating pain, he'd also absorbed several pieces of shrapnel from one of the RPG impacts. Lying in the snow, strapped to a litter, he faced his body armor toward the enemy and was anything but sure of the day's outcome. "Dirt and snow continued to be kicked up on us from rounds." He passed out several times. When Cory bent over to check him once, "I asked him that if I didn't make it, please tell my family we did a good job that day, and that I love them very much."

"Cut that shit out, we're gonna be off this mountain before you know it," replied the medic, who was glad the pilot continued to engage and remain aware. The time was 1030 and Calvert remembered "hearing and seeing the Predator overhead. [I] could also hear fast movers, but never saw them. It was strangely comforting to hear and feel them strafe close to us."

By then, Gabe was getting saturated by air support, which was a double-edged sword. In order to keep those higher in the command chain informed and reduce the number of times he was switching antennas, he resorted to using Jay Hill and Hotaling as his relays. He also wanted to get the worst of the casualties off the mountain and told Jay he believed he could get a medevac in safely—probably an MH-60 would be best, since their approaches and departures were accomplished significantly faster than the lumbering MH-47s'.

Jay to Blaber: Slick 01 has taken the hill but is [taking] ineffective mortar fire 200 meters east of his position. He feels it is safe to bring in a MEDEVAC at this time.

Blaber: Advise him that ATF is firing mortars [in other words, it is friendly fire].

Jay: Roger. Slick has linked up with the QRF [the thirteen Rangers from the second helo]. Believes personnel 800 meters to the east are enemy. Once he gets MEDEVAC he will direct [strike aircraft] onto location. Slick feels he can secure the HLZ and requests ETA of MEDEVAC.

AFO (backing the man on the ground) to Champ: [AFO] copied transmission. Hill secure, ineffective mortar fire to the east. [Slick] feels safe to bring in MEDEVAC. Linked up with Chalk 2 pax [the second group of Rangers].

Jay: [J Team] advises Slick wants MEDEVAC to come in on top of hill beside crash site. Slick will vector [aircraft] in.

In Bagram and Masirah, where all the "rank" resided, they remained unsure of the ground situation, and compounded their fundamental misunderstanding by relying on the Predator feeds being pumped onto computer monitors through the two TF-11 JOCs. Trebon and his staff were not willing to commit another helicopter and crew to attempt the evacuation. This exchange—Gabe and Self asking for a medevac and TF-11 denying or delaying the request—continued throughout the entire mission.

As the day wore on, Gabe continued his onslaught while using Jay to relay information, occasionally handing planes off to or receiving them from Hotaling, who was bombing Al Qaeda positions to the south.

To Calvert, this very personal firsthand experience of close air support was new. As a helicopter pilot he'd never been on the ground with troops before, and what he was experiencing for the first time was similar to everyone else on the hill. The "danger close" aspects of Gabe's airstrikes were unlike anything seen by the men on the mountain, including the Controller. Imagine standing on a point, then throwing a Frisbee the distance an average adult can manage. Frisbee distance does not produce the standoff measurement one hopes to be from a 500-pound bomb when it explodes. Consider, still, that this lethal delivery is provided courtesy of a twenty-eight-year-old pilot flying a fighter jet at 500 mph using a joystick. These considerations do not make being on the mountaintop, mere feet away from detonation, desirable, unless one has supreme faith in the pilot and the Combat Controller.

"We would hear [Gabe] yell 'thirty seconds to impact,' not knowing what that meant at first, but realized it when the first bomb hit. The whole world seemed to shake. It was like the earthquakes at Bagram [the city experienced a 7.4-magnitude quake the day before, killing 150 people across the torn country], but more violent. It seemed to me at the time that I could see the bombs coming in, screaming across the sky. I can remember saying to Chuck that I hoped these guys were good, because the bombs seemed to go right across my vision and hitting close."

He had no idea just how close the skilled CCT was cutting it until "I remember watching the rock and bonsai tree. When the bombs hit, I saw bodies flying, and dirt and shrapnel fell around us. That felt good to me. After the noise subsided, I could hear screaming from behind the rocks." But Calvert and the men around him were not free from danger. Their hilltop redoubt was being assaulted from multiple directions. The summit had merely been *one* of the enemy pockets. Even with the addition of more Rangers, the possibility of being overrun remained a threat as the casualties continued to mount.

Rounds were impacting all around Calvert and the others who

lay prone at what had become the casualty collection point. There was no safe place to put the injured. "We could actually see them firing at us. I yelled to Cory and Jason, who were up on their knees working on us still, to 'get down or get the hell out of there.'" The two trained lifesavers ignored him...and their constant exposure to enemy fire finally caught up with them a moment after Calvert shouted his warning. Both men were hit by the same burst of fire. "I watched them both fall over, and when they didn't move, I thought they were dead." Eventually Cory stirred and managed to check his own injuries. He'd been shot in the belly, twice. "It felt like someone hit me as hard as they could with a sledgehammer," recalled the father of two who, as he came around, felt it was manifestly unfair to his children that he was going to die on this mountain. Jason lay still, his injuries grave. As Cory checked him, he realized his fellow trauma expert was bleeding heavily internally; his pelvis was in pieces from the round that shattered it. It was now 1130.

The airstrikes continued throughout the day. From his new perch on the top of the mountain, Gabe found some company in the form of a dead Chechen. "He was this little brown dude in a Rastafarian hat, clutching his weapon, crumpled up next to me, up to his knees in snow. I tilted his hat back and, holy shit, a perfect head shot from one of the Rangers. And so I spent the day with that guy. It was the best vantage spot I had."

> 1217: **Gabe to Champ:** Currently working Scarface 11 [two F-16s], but he is unable to drop JDAMs. He has to go refuel.
>
> **Champ:** Champ will go to Bossman [AWACS circling overhead] and get more CAS.
>
> 1310: **Champ to Gabe:** Do you have comms with any CAS [strike aircraft]?
>
> **Gabe:** Roger. Talking to Stone 31 at this time.

Champp: Be prepared to receive Snake 41 [carrier-launched F-14s] after this.

1330: **Champ to Jaguar 12:** [J Team] just completed bombing run with B-1. [Now] observing eastern ridge. Need Jaguar to continue to push suppression on the south.

Hotaling: Jaguar 12 copies all and will standby this freq.

1420: **Gabe to Champ:** Slick 01 advises total pax to exfil is 33 and that the 2 casualties that were on the HLZ prior [Roberts and Chapman] may be booby trapped. 6 total patients: 5 litter, of those two urgent surgical, 3 priority, 1 routine. 6 KIA, includes 2 found on LZ.

Champ: Champ will pass info to hospital and medical so they will be ready. Let the boys know we are going to take care of them. We will pass this off to the [exfil rescue] commander. They still haven't had authority to launch.

Gabe: Slick would like to keep CAS coming to keep enemy off [our] backs.

1440: **Hotaling to Champ:** Jaguar observed no scattering of troops. [Will] continue to work southern targets and to the west.

Champ: When we get to H-hour [the extraction of Gabe, the Rangers, and casualties], we want you to go to Bossman and get CAS and split it between you and Slick. [To] help prep the area before the Apaches come in from the north and west. Suppress the ridgeline and valley on their way in.

Hotaling: Jaguar copies all.

1456: **Champ to Gabe:** You are having a two ship of fighters being pushed to you. Right now [J Team] has them because they are receiving mortar fire.

Gabe: Roger.

1607: **Hotaling to Champ:** Jaguar will take care of C2 [command and control] tent and truck location. Slick is too busy with troops in contact. Don't know if Slick has enemy contact, just that he is busy with CAS overhead. Need to confirm no friendly [positions] within 1.5 km of target.

Champ: Roger.

1758: **Jay to Champ:** [J Team] wants a 400 by 1000 meter box of bombs to be dropped vicinity WB177914 to get rid of some pesky mortars.

Champ: Champ verifying no friendly pax in the box.

As the day wore on, Gabe continued his attempts to convince TF-11 to send them a medevac to get the critically wounded out. By 1800, Captain Self also called Champ, stating: "KA16R [Self's call sign] requesting through Champ to bump up exfil time. If not, [am] sure two critical will die." Champ's consistent response: They are working it.

Unfortunately, the "golden hour," so called because if a casualty is treated within the first sixty minutes, his chances of survival are more than doubled, had long since passed. Matt LaFrenz, the Ranger medic, was now treating Jason as best he could since Cory had lapsed into incapacitation. Calvert, himself in severe shock and shivering in the cold darkness that had enveloped them, watched and recalled, "I can remember them working on Jason, and then announcing he was dead. Heard the anger in Matt's voice, telling Captain Self that we had lost another man. I can remember saying a prayer for Jason and his family."

At 1814, Self got on the radio to Champ and confirmed all sensitive items (communications equipment) were zeroed on Razor-01, meaning it was now clean to be abandoned when the QRF and casualties were extracted, adding flatly at the end of his transmission, "KIA numbers to seven." Jason Cunningham, the young PJ so focused on learning all he could to treat and save others, became the last man to die on Takur Ghar.

When the extraction helicopters finally began to arrive, the first landed at 2016, two hours after Cunningham had passed away. That first helo, another TF-160 MH-47, bore the wounded for their long flight to Germany and then home.[29]

The second, and last, exfil helicopter arrived at 2027. Gabe handed CAS control over to Dave Smith, another CCT from the 24, who had flown in on the helicopter. "I did a handshake with the two-four operator. I briefed him on 'Here's where we're taking fires.' He asked me if I had any spare batteries. I just laughed. 'No.'"

The second MH-47 carried the dead who'd been staged on the top of the mountain to await transportation, including Chapman and Roberts. Remembers Keary Miller, "We were concerned that the bodies might be booby-trapped so the Rangers initially moved them with ropes." It took the PJ some time to discover one of the bodies was his 24 Green Team teammate, a shock to the veteran operator because "we were told there was only one American on the mountain going in, and when we finally got on top, in addition to John the enemy were also wearing some of Roberts's [American] clothing." With the dead went the remainder of the original Rangers and Gabe. As he trudged up the ramp, exhausted, emotionally drained yet still amped up, he remembers vividly, "We had to climb over the dead bodies, stacked like wood, in a weird way, which have a certain smell, and it's combined with the fuel smell of helicopters. I was sitting farthest to the rear." His brain was still on. "I was mentally preparing

---

29 Cory Lamoreaux survived to see his children. Greg Calvert kept his hand and, more remarkably, returned to full flight status and continued his career as a pilot.

myself. 'If we go down, I'm going to have to start this again.' Preparing my equipment, ready to execute if we get shot down again. In my mind, it was a bit like being back at Combat Control School, 'Are we done yet?'"

———

Ten time zones away, in Fayetteville, North Carolina, it's a mild and sunny March morning. The East Coast grass is already coming to life, introducing patches of green to its winter brown. Valerie Chapman has just dropped off five-year-old Madison at kindergarten, having deposited her younger sister, Brianna, at preschool. She stops at the office where she works as a nurse doing in-home care. At her desk, she dials the 24 and gets an admin person. They exchange pleasantries and Val asks for John's new mailing address, because she has a package to mail him. With address in hand, she hops in her green family minivan and heads to her first appointment.

By lunch, she's headed to a simple case, short-term wound care. Much easier than some of her other housebound patients, this one is the father of her supervisor. Val was assigned him because her boss knows she will do a good job. She sits on the couch and looks over the wound; nothing serious. In the background, he has his TV tuned to Fox News. They both see the ever-present BREAKING NEWS banner at the bottom. This particular one announces SIX TO SEVEN SPECIAL FORCES SOLDIERS WERE KILLED TODAY IN COMBAT OPERATIONS IN AFGHANISTAN'S HEAVIEST FIGHTING TO DATE.

Valerie and her patient, a veteran, read the banner, but no other information comes from the talking head. She thinks, *Gosh, I feel bad for those Army families.* A sad thing, they both agree. Her duties complete, she reverses the process, retrieving the girls from school, and heads home to make dinner.

CHAPTER

23

—

4 March

LATE AFTERNOON

COMBAT CONTROLLER JEFF GEORGE HAD JUST ARRIVED IN BAGRAM AT the TF-Blue JOC. He and his SEAL troop had finished conducting blocking point operations and were standing by as additional QRF in support of other operations underway in Kandahar, several hundred miles to the south. The missions weren't particularly fruitful, and the men had returned to base looking for more work.

As he rolled into the SEAL operations center on 4 March, it was clear something big was going down. Outside, Captain Kernan, the SEAL Team Six commander, was on an Iridium satellite phone talking with Vic, who was by then on the lower slopes of Takur Ghar with Slab and the other surviving members of Mako-30. "You could see the stress he was under in his face and posture. He was clearly out of his element but trying to make sound decisions. The guy was maxed out," Jeff recalls.

Inside was charged pandemonium. Brigadier General Trebon was technically in charge, but the TF-Blue TOC was wholly a SEAL Team Six affair. It was the general's presence that made it a higher headquarters—TF-11, but the SEALs were running the show.

Jeff and his teammates were put on notice for the possibility of being the QRF to the QRF on Takur Ghar. He recalls, "We're waiting for word that we're going to go or for the situation to sort itself out. As the day went on, information began to trickle in. Then word comes that there's casualties and some KIAs, but we're not going anywhere."

He wandered in and out of the TF-Blue TOC as day turned to dusk and then into evening. "Meanwhile, we're waiting for helos to bring the guys back." Finally, word came that the first helo was inbound. Jeff was helping with the transloading of wounded when the second helicopter landed carrying Gabe and the bodies of those killed in action. The deceased were collected by some of the 24 and 23rd STS PJs in Bagram for forward movement to Germany and then Dover Air Force Base, Delaware, where all KIA US service members are received and prepped before being released to their families.

Ross, one of the SEALs and a friend of Jeff's from mobility troop, approached the twenty-seven-year-old Controller and cut right to the heart of the matter. "Sorry, man. Chappy's one of the guys."

"I was the first Air Force guy to learn," he recalls of hearing about his friend and fellow 24 CCT. Shortly afterward, the Rangers were looking for someone from the 24. Jeff was the only one nearby when one asked him, "Who's taking care of this?" The Ranger was holding a green aviator's kit bag, the ubiquitous military two-foot-square canvas carryall, which held all of Chapman's gear. Everything had been stripped from his body by medical personnel, with the exception of his uniform. Jeff took the kit bag and headed toward the 24 "hooch" area, where John's cot and personal items remained, just as he'd left them forty-eight hours before. Unlike most operators' living areas, Chapman's—a cot with a low row of unfinished wood shelves and a small card table for a nightstand/desk—was neatly arranged. On the stand were several pictures of Madison and Brianna.

Inside the bag, Jeff looked at the final artifacts of the Controller's life. His weapon, which had absorbed multiple rounds, was junked.

His Rhodesian vest was shredded, clear signs of struggle, and was covered in blood. Inside the vest was a full magazine, useless. It had been shot through by one of the AK rounds that killed or wounded his friend. He set the bag down with the rest of his friend's belongings and, with nothing more to do, left the muddied and bloodied vestiges of John Chapman, the photos of his daughters standing sentinel over them.

———

At home in North Carolina, Valerie and John's tiny sentinels are settling in for the evening on 5 March. Outside, she checks her mailbox and encounters her neighbors, Laverne and Roger. "They were this older couple, a sort of mom and pop we were very close to, and Laverne said, 'You have this different aura about you,' and I'm thinking, *Okay, not sure what that means.* But I didn't feel anything was 'different.'" Infinitely practical and not prone to superstition, she bids farewell and sets about her evening. The nearly complete family has an ordinary dinner, and by 9:00 p.m. the girls are in bed, when the doorbell rings. Both of them, excited by the distraction and the possibility of putting sleep off a bit, rush to the door, shouting, "Who's that?"

"Daddy's friends," calls their mother, stepping in from another room. But Valerie can see blue uniforms through the sidelight window, and she knows what's coming. "Go back to bed, girls," she tells them, and the two scamper off in knee-length nightgowns, trailing blond and brown curls.

At the door, she braces herself, opens it, and steps outside so the girls won't hear. On the doorstep stood Lieutenant Colonel Ken Rodriguez, the 24 commander, Master Sergeant Kenny Longfritz, the unit's first sergeant (whose job is the welfare of and assistance to unit members and their families), and an Air Force chaplain.

"Please tell me he's just hurt badly," she implores. But Rodriguez shakes his head and asks if they can come inside. Valerie tells them to wait on the porch while she calls the neighbor to have them collect the girls first. They stand uncomfortably over the prolonging of their grim task.

When the girls had been spirited away, the three men step inside and everyone sits down. Without preamble, Rodriguez speaks the words every wife dreads: "Valerie, I'm sorry, John's been killed in combat." This is not the Air Force–approved script, which is explicit in its delivery and simplicity, but on the way to the house, Rodriguez had been hit by a realization that directed how he would proceed. "This news was going to change the lives of all three girls irrevocably, and the process, starting with the news, was about helping Val and the girls as best I can . . . if at all. The last thing I was going to do was deliver some bureaucratic bullshit."

Sitting on her couch, leaning toward Rodriguez and looking directly at him, she asks, "What happened? I want to know." She knows his answer will avow that life as she knows it is over . . . forever.

Rodriguez, a deeply religious and emotional man, said, "I'll tell you everything I know, including classified information. What I know so far is John's actions were very selfless and likely saved the lives of members of his team," and went on to recount what he knew at the time, which wasn't everything—not yet.

Valerie, alone in her own home with three messengers of death, absorbs the information and asks a few more questions as they wait for another member of the 24 to arrive. Alex Johns was John's friend and fellow Controller, and would serve as Valerie's family liaison officer, whose job was to see to the widow's needs throughout the repatriation, funeral, and subsequent memorials. Alex would virtually live with Valerie and the girls for the next few weeks, only going home for the occasional shower and change of clothes.

Before Rodriguez and Longfritz depart, the commander asks, "Is it okay if we pray together?" The compassionate gesture is completely outside notification protocol, but in that moment and without reservation, Rodriguez felt it was exactly what to do. His instincts proved correct when the two of them, one burdened with immense loss, the other with the obligation to deliver the message, dropped to their knees in prayer. In that moment, Valerie and Rodriguez, two people, relative strangers bonded by death, began an unlikely and lifelong friendship.

———

Back in Bagram, Gabe Brown arrived at the 23rd STS area on a different part of the former Soviet airbase from the 24 and TF-Blue forces. His first thought was to place a call to his wife, Gloria. "It was a quick call. I told her I was in a series of bad situations that were significant events for me, but that I was okay," he recalls with understatement. His deployed commander, Lieutenant Colonel Patrick Pihana, managed to produce a bottle of whiskey and waited to have shots with Gabe and Keary. Gabe did a single shot and went to bed, exhausted. The next day, he recalled a conversation he'd had with Jason Cunningham in the week leading up to Takur Ghar. "We were walking, bored one day, throwing rocks toward this minefield and joking about how maybe we could set one off," when the PJ mentioned, almost in passing, "My daughter [four-year-old Kyla] had a dream and told me, 'Daddy, Daddy, you're going to get shot and die.'" Even as Cunningham lay bleeding out and dying, Gabe recalls, "I still believed he'd pull through. I'm a hopelessly optimistic guy." The entire experience—the mission, Jason's death, and his little girl's dream—left Gabe feeling "ready to go home and see my family. I'd had a part to play; did it well. Could have done better. But feel I was the right guy at the right time. I was glad I was there. It all goes back to how I grew up and became a part of this thing [CCT]."

Operation Anaconda was considered to be a failure by most

measures. No fleeing masses of Al Qaeda fighters were smashed by the hammer of Commander Zia's ATF against the 10th Mountain and 101st Airborne anvil. For the men of AFO, though, it was a solid success. In the end, they were responsible for the majority of the killing. The Pentagon estimated the number of enemy killed was upwards of 800. This figure is almost certainly spurious. Based on captured documents, enemy intercepts, and physical evidence, a more likely figure is between 150 and 300. In General Trebon's estimation, the thirteen men of Blaber's AFO were responsible for 60 percent of enemy casualties, but the TF-11 commander's estimation leaves out an important calculus: The vast majority of those enemy numbers can be attributed to five men—Jay Hill, Andy Martin, and, once the battle for the summit of Takur Ghar is included, Jim Hotaling, Gabe Brown, and John Chapman.

The travesty at the end of the operation is the loss of the seven men on Takur Ghar. Those deaths—SEAL Neil Roberts, CCT John Chapman, PJ Jason Cunningham, air crewman Phil Svitak, and the three Rangers, Marc Anderson, Bradley Crose, and Matthew Commons—do not lie at the feet of Delta's Pete Blaber and AFO, but the leaders of SEAL Team Six, specifically Joe Kernan and Tim Szymanski, and their rush to push men into the battle and take over operations from Blaber. But to Blaber, Vic (the SEAL officer in Gardez) abandoning the safe house without coordinating was tantamount to dereliction, and the confusion it caused on the mountain directly resulted in Jason Cunningham's death.

But the losses to Al Qaeda were also significant. There is strong evidence that al-Zawahiri, the number-two AQ leader, was present in the valley, perhaps even wounded with a head injury, but escaped. Tohir Yuldashev, leader of the Islamic Movement of Uzbekistan, also escaped. One other was not so lucky: Saif-ur-Rahman Mansoor, the symbolic guidon–wielding fighter who led his men bravely from the front, was killed. Their failed last effort to stand ground and combat the allied troops en masse did cause an exodus, though the allied victory may have been pyrrhic. Many would return in future battles in both Afghanistan and Iraq.

———

From the enemy:

We begged our commander, Saif-ur-Rahman Mansoor, to allow the brothers to leave the valley. This was the way of the Mujahideen, move away from an enemy that outnumbers and possesses superior weapons. We had no water, my mouth was bleeding, and the sores prevented me from eating my bread. All the Uzbeks were now martyred; the Afghans were all gone.

Then I received word that our commander was martyred and I began to cry. We tried to get to his body to carry him away but the bombs were too many and the enemy were now everywhere.

I asked all our brothers to retreat, except the ones manning the PK machine gun and RPG-7 rocket launcher. Brother Abu Talib As-Saudi insisted upon staying and said to me, "I feel ashamed in front of Allah to retreat from the Americans." Due to the heavy bombardment, a large portion of his head was missing, but he joined us as we began our retreat.

The brothers all dispersed in different directions. I traveled with ten Arab brothers. Due to the increased numbers of Coalition forces blocking the area, as well as the aerial channels the enemy had, we were forced to travel for three days and nights in conditions that were extremely harsh. We had nothing to eat with us, except a case of green tea and a pot in which to boil snow. After this long journey, enduring the cold and the snow, and traveling over mountain peaks and through valleys, we finally reached a village where we received a great welcome, such that it made us forget all that we had suffered and endured, and All Praise belongs to Allah Alone.

Mansoor was killed by Jay Hill in a B-1 bomb strike. J Team had watched the leader through their optics. Recalls Kris, "He was short (5′4″–5′8″), stocky-strong, wore a medium length beard, black hair, carried the banner/flag when it was taken down, and gave hand and arm signals. [Jay] was finally handed a B-1 and ordered a bomb box with 6 JDAMs set on airburst. The bombs scored one direct hit, one near direct hit." They watched the site for signs of follow-up activity, and the next day, "seven enemy in white turbans moved to the destroyed fighting positions and attempted to remove the leader from the wreckage."

AFO had accomplished its mission better than anyone could have expected. For Blaber, it was validation of his method, his men, and their mission. Andy Martin and Mako-31 had slipped out, passing through friendly 10th Mountain force lines and back to Gardez at the very time Chapman was fighting for his life. They woke the next morning to the news of Chapman's and Roberts's deaths.

Two days later, J Team crept off the mountain to end its mission. Jay had called in his last airstrike only an hour or so before they mounted their trusty ATVs and started down the mountainside, now purged of Al Qaeda. Along the way the team paused to examine the cave complex they'd bombed the first morning, from which the Al Qaeda fighters nearly ambushed them. They found two Soviet D-30 artillery pieces, a destroyed 37mm antiaircraft gun, and fire pits inside the surrounding buildings, which were accented with planted trees and rock curbs along the road—signs of a senior AQ leader. In the buildings, they found discarded sleeping bags, fruit juice boxes with Arabic writing, and well-established fighting positions surrounding the compound. Tire tracks led away from the complex, heading east . . . toward Pakistan.

Having witnessed some of the near-fratricide incidents firsthand, they left in daylight so as to pass through the 101st lines before dark.

Jay had secured a P-3 escort, just in case. After dark and their safe passage through friendly lines, they were met by two MH-47s. The exhausted men sat silently on their ATVs, watching the helicopters as they made their way across the valley toward their extraction HLZ. The team loaded onto the helicopters, blades spinning, and were carried above the devastation they'd wrought throughout the valley. They could see the destruction on the features below as they passed on their way back to Gardez, the last of the original AFO teams. All of J Team faced the risks and challenges of Blaber's AFO missions, but only one carried the burden of precision and "no fail" aspects of the destruction of the enemy they faced—Jay Hill, the lone Combat Controller.

For Combat Control, Anaconda exemplified the maturation of a nearly forty-year evolution beginning in the jungles of Laos. Without direction or pre-planning, individual Controllers, some of whom didn't even know one another, established a self-organizing and -directing network that destroyed the most organized and effective force Al Qaeda and the Taliban would ever muster on a field of battle. In all, there were fourteen CCT involved in the operation.

Of the role of CCT in Anaconda and elsewhere, Jay Hill states, "We [Combat Controllers] were the most technically savvy guys out there. We pull our experience from the best in the world: Aussie SAS, British SBS, Delta, ST6, all of them. Nobody else, *nobody* [emphasis added], has that exposure and experience. None of the units we work with work with each other like that, aside from an occasional bilateral op [operation]. Sometimes, when you raise your hand [during operational briefings], younger SEALs or Delta operators roll their eyes, 'What's the Air Force guy got to say?' But older guys know."

PART III

—

AFTERMATH

CHAPTER

24

—

5 March

IN WINDSOR LOCKS, CONNECTICUT, TERRY WAS IN HER KITCHEN PULLING meat off a chicken carcass to make chicken soup. At 10:30 p.m., she heard a knock at the front door. No one *ever* went to the front door. Terry says, "If they knew us, they came to the back door. I went into the living room, flipped on the light, and opened the door. All I could say was, 'No, not my Johnny. Not my Johnny!' I let them in and yelled for my husband Nicholas as I sat on the couch, crying uncontrollably while they read their statement."

Around 10:45, Nick called John's sister Lori. Waking from a dead sleep, she immediately knew something was wrong; *no one* called her that late. She could hear Terry wailing in the background, and all Nick could muster was, "It's your brother." Lori slammed the phone down, woke her daughter, Rachel, and piled her into the car for the five-minute drive, all the while begging, "*Please* let him just be injured!" A dark vehicle was pulling away from the front of the house, and she knew. Lori bounded up the back steps, where she was met by her mother. Terry fell into her arms as she managed to shriek through halted speech and a torrent of tears, "Johnny's gone! My Johnny's gone!"

After hugs and tears, Terry said, "We need to tell Kevin and Tammy. I can't. I just can't do it." Lori called her sister, Tammy, in Vermont first because it was late; Kevin was two hours behind. When Tammy answered, Lori asked, "Is David right there with you?" She didn't have to say anything else; Tammy knew. She had seen the news but waited for Lori to continue. "We lost John today." Tammy fell to the floor, where David found her curled into the fetal position.

Rattled, Lori hung up to call Kevin. It was 9:30 Colorado time. When Kevin answered, Lori wasn't as composed as she tried to be and blurted, "I have bad news. We lost John today." She gave him time to absorb her words, but he had collapsed onto the floor, unable to speak. Kevin's wife, Connie, came on the line and, when she heard the news, said, "I have to go. Kevin needs me," and hung up.

The tidal wave of raw pain coursed toward Michigan to an unsuspecting Gene and his wife, Tess. The Air Force notification team had trouble finding their house, so by the time they arrived, Gene and Tess already knew. Gene passed away in January of 2004, but Tess remembers that night vividly. "We were waiting. I don't know exactly why they couldn't find our address, so by the time they came to us, it was already late. They came to the door and they knew we already knew, but they had to tell us anyway. Gene was standing in front of me, and he about ... Even though we knew, he still about dropped to the floor."

Starting the next day, and for more than a week following, while the world continued to spin, time moved in slow motion for the Chapman family as they converged on Fayetteville, North Carolina. The 24 held a memorial service in a giant hangar on Pope AFB. The cavernous building was standing room only, filled with a sea of red berets and blue uniforms as Colonel Rodriguez took the podium to speak of John and his bravery in facing "the jaws of death." The audience was spellbound. As the family began meeting many of John's comrades, they started to truly understand the caliber of men John worked alongside; they were cut from the same cloth as he.

Two of those men, Technical Sergeant David Gendron and Staff Sergeant Scott Toner, volunteered to escort John's body from Dover AFB in Delaware to his final resting place in Windber, Pennsylvania. They were honored to flank John on his final mission.

Valerie thought she would move back to Windber to raise her girls near her parents, so she chose to have John buried there instead of in the country's heroes' resting place, Arlington National Cemetery. After the memorial service at Pope, everyone traveled en masse to the small Pennsylvania town. Many of John's childhood friends made the seven-hour drive from Connecticut to say their final "Goodbye." Three of them—Brian Topor, David Wrabel, and Michael Toce— traveled together, laughing, crying, and reminiscing about their time with John. By the time they reached Windber, they had decided that the funeral "*can't* be it; this *can't* be forever for John."

Windber, with a population of 4,000, was even smaller than John's hometown, but it had the same "circle the wagons" mentality as Windsor Locks. Word spread quickly that John would be laid to rest there, and townsfolk rallied to welcome his family and friends. As mourners, quite literally, flooded the town, they were greeted by friendly townspeople and American flags lining the streets.

One thousand people passed by John's open casket at William Kisiel Funeral Home while Gendron and Toner took turns standing rigid and solemn next to him. In the outer rooms of the funeral home, and later in the confines of a hotel bar, childhood friends were meeting John's 24 brothers for the first time, and they bonded over memories of Chappy. Countless CCT, family, and friends gathered at the hotel's bar, sharing stories of John, raising a glass, and toasting the nation's newest hero, eventually running the bar dry. Brian Topor was one of the throng, and he remembers, "The night before the funeral, we went to a hotel and a bunch of the guys [from the 24] were there, and that was our introduction to Combat Control, to John's other brotherhood. It was overwhelming for me because these guys were...They're the cream of the crop and they treated us great. The neat part is that these guys are your friends, somebody else's brother, and even though they may be ordinary people, they are *extraordinary* in what they do. They're a different breed, and I saw in them what I saw in John—he had no fear, he was bright...He was *very* smart...confident. He wasn't arrogant, he wasn't reckless. Yeah, he took risks, but there's a difference between risky and reckless. He didn't fail." David Wrabel's takeaway from meeting John's 24 team-mates was, "It became obvious by listening that he was the exact same Chappy that we knew and loved in childhood."

The next morning, over four hundred people pressed into St. Elizabeth Ann Seton Church for John's funeral service, including another sea of red berets. John's younger sister, Tammy, spoke to the congregation about her brother, ending with, "John has always been my hero. Now he's your hero too." There weren't enough tissues to go around as Kevin also spoke about growing up with John, how proud he was of him, and how much he'd miss him. Topor and Wrabel gave the eulogy. "As young kids, we often played Army (or Air Force) and dreamed of one day being Green Berets (or Combat Controllers) and becoming heroes. After we found out John was a member of the 24, we were able to, once again, relive our dreams through him." At the pulpit, Brian recalled, "I remember a conversation I had with him when he spoke of going to Texas for some training. He was always vague when talking about CCT, so when I asked him, 'What kind of training?' he responded, 'Military training.' I always hoped that, after retirement, we'd sit back with a few beers and I could coax more stories from John."

As the miles-long procession serpentined to Saint Mary Byzantine Catholic Church Cemetery, Wrabel recalls, the military's "sense of their community was forever burned in our minds. We saw an elderly man, obviously a veteran, standing in his front yard by his American flag, saluting John as he traveled to his final resting place." People came out to wave flags and show their respect all along the route to the cemetery. As mourners watched the Air Force Honor Guard slowly bring John's casket graveside, a missing-man formation flyover by Air Force A-10 Thunderbolts roared overhead. Valerie sat solemnly in the front row, flanked by Madison and Brianna, as Colonel Rodriguez presented her, in honor of John's sacrifice, with the tightly folded flag that had covered her husband's casket. Gene and Terry sat sobbing as they each accepted the flags he presented, listening to him thank them for their sacrifice. They were officially part of a club no one wants to join and from which there is no escape.

As family and friends passed John's casket for their final farewell, some placed flowers, some placed coins. Terry kissed the casket before turning away. Gene held his hand on top as he silently said goodbye. A handful of John's CCT brothers lingered at his side one last time, not wanting to leave. Those tough, hardened warriors hugged and cried before leaving coins and a beret pin on the casket lid, leaning on each other as they turned away.

John is buried only twenty miles from Shanksville, Pennsylvania. Shanksville is the tragic resting place of United Flight 93, the fourth and "missing" plane on 9/11, the day that brought the call for John and his brothers to fight terror in Afghanistan, the beginning of the end for John. Before leaving Windber, Gene spoke with Valerie's father, Jim, about John's gravesite. Jim, who loved John like his own, lives a short walk down the hill from Saint Mary's Cemetery, and he promised Gene that he would take care of John's plot. To this day, he takes his daily walk to the cemetery where he tends John's grave. Anyone searching for it need only look for the greenest and best-kept site, thanks to Jim Novak and a promise between two dads.

The trip back to Connecticut proved therapeutic and productive for John's three friends, Brian, David, and Michael. Since they had decided on the way to Windber that the funeral couldn't be the end of it for John, they used the trip home to brainstorm about what to do. Determined to keep John's memory from fading into yesterday's news, David recalls, "We tossed around so many ideas—renaming the airport or a street or a stretch of highway—we were all over the place. Then we finally settled on *where* John's memorial should be, and that led us in the direction of *what* it should be. It was most fitting to be at Windsor Locks High School, by the soccer field where we had all played." Brian adds, "We thought that keeping the memorial in town was the most meaningful, but we also thought, since Chappy wasn't buried in Windsor Locks, or even close by, we wanted a place for people to go and remember him. And we did it for his mom too."

In the end, they accomplished in only seven balls-to-the-wall months what seasoned organizers couldn't do in a year. David remembers with pride, "For a bunch of unorganized guys, it impressed me what we *could* do, what a group of people can do—grass roots—when we put the effort together." Brian added, "When you have people that have a common bond, such strong feelings for John, you get it done no matter what. I put more work into that, at that time, than I did at my job!" David agreed: "Yup, me too. And I was new to my job!" Michael nodded in agreement as Brian said, "If we weren't working our jobs, we were working on the memorial." Michael quipped, "It almost cost us our jobs *and* our marriages!" though the latter part was just to emphasize how much time the men put into the memorial. In reality, their wives were totally supportive, because they knew what this project meant—what John meant—to their husbands.

John's memorial was dedicated on 19 October 2002—ironically, the same date as the first ground deployments of Operation Enduring Freedom the previous year. It sits at the corner of the soccer field at Windsor Locks High, beside a grove of hardwood trees. The design is simple—a thirty-foot-tall flagpole topped with a golden eagle that roosts high above a large boulder. On the boulder is a bronze plaque that reads:

IN MEMORY OF
John A. Chapman
"Chappy"
WLHS Class of 1983
You Will Never Be Forgotten
Fellow Student, Dedicated Athlete, Loyal Friend, Committed
Family Man, True Patriot

Members of the 24 came, including Kenny Longfritz and another support teammate, Master Sergeant Mike Rizzuto. Kicking off the ceremony, Rizzuto slowly raised the American flag as Longfritz unfurled it from its triangle. Standing next to the flagpole, hands over their hearts, were John's childhood friends, their upward gaze locked on the flag as it rose over their heads. Their dream, their blood, sweat, and tears, their tribute to John, had come to glorious fruition. As the flag met the golden eagle and the last notes of "The Star-Spangled Banner" faded, Brian Topor stepped to the podium to dedicate the memorial. "Those who never met John will only know him as an American hero. But in school, he was 'Chappy,' a fellow classmate, a student, a teammate, and a friend. He had a wonderful zest for life and a firm commitment to teamwork." In dedicating the memorial, Brian stated, "Having this here is fitting, so people can come to talk, laugh, or cry out loud. Without individuals like John, we would not be able to sleep peacefully at night."

In a moving tribute, childhood and high school friend Bill Brooks credited John for changing the course of his life with unconditional friendship and encouragement. "I was a painfully shy kid, even throughout most of high school. I couldn't talk to *anyone*." Over time, John coaxed Bill into believing in himself, so much so that he went on to be a chef who travels the world, speaking to large groups. "I don't know if he even knew he was helping me all those years ago, but he helped me get to where I am now. After high school, we kind of went in and out of each other's lives, but the times that he came back into my life are the times that I needed him there. I can't imagine how my life would have been without John in it."

Colonel Ken Rodriguez then took the podium to offer his tribute to John, closing with, "*This* is what it's all about, this great American town. This is what John was fighting for." The ceremony ended with a lone bagpiper, Pipe Major Patrick Whelan of the Connecticut State Police Pipes and Drums Unit, standing behind the memorial, his pipes echoing "Amazing Grace" over the fields.

At that point in 2002, the Chapman family didn't know the truth of what happened on Takur Ghar, but each one of them had a sixth sense that there was much more to the story than they had been told. The Navy had immediately added John's name, the only non-SEAL, to their Wall of Honor in Virginia Beach. Why, the family wondered, would they do that if he'd merely played a minor role on the mission? And why were there debates within the Air Force as to the level of medal they would award him? Air Force Cross? Medal of Honor? Ultimately, he was posthumously awarded the Air Force Cross on 10 January 2003, but the debate over the award level created more questions for the family.

———

Time passed, and though John's family continued to mull over trickles of new information, life pushed them forward. In early 2005, they received word that the Navy was going to rename a ship after John. The MV *Merlin*, a 670-foot cargo container and roll-on/roll-off ship, owned by Sealift Inc. and leased by the Navy's Military Sealift

Command, was renamed MV *TSgt John A. Chapman* in a sunny ceremony on 8 April 2005 at the Military Ocean Terminal, Sunny Point,
North Carolina. It was fitting that the ship—a munitions vessel—
would be named for John, a Combat Controller whose profession,
among all the elite of special operations, relied on those munitions to
change the course of battles and lives.

The publication of this book will be the latest in a long line of
honors bestowed upon John and his legacy. On 14 June 2006, during
the sixtieth anniversary celebration at Lackland AFB honoring enlisted heroes, Terry attended the unveiling of the Chapman Training
Complex, home of the 326th Training Squadron. Many more honors
have come, including a nephew namesake (John Chapman Longfritz),
multiple renamings of streets, an FOB (forward operating base), and
a score of tattoos. John's three childhood friends were right...The
funeral *wasn't* "it" for him, his name, and his legacy.

CHAPTER

25

—

JOHN'S ORIGINAL AIR FORCE CROSS WOULD HAVE REMAINED JUST THAT, the nation's second-highest award for selfless action and heroism, had it not been for chance. Secretary of the Air Force Deborah Lee James strolled across her office, enjoying a few free moments in an otherwise busy daily schedule that was blocked out in ten-minute increments, controlled more by her handlers than herself. The fifteenth of May 2015 was a beautiful spring morning, and the windows of her office on the fourth floor of the Pentagon's desirable E wing afforded million-dollar views of the nation's capital and monuments. She liked to joke that the Air Force sat above the secretary of defense's office, directly below on the third floor.

Dressed in a vibrant red business suit (she felt a bit of color added to the muted tones of most Pentagon staffers), she chanced to pick up a copy of the *Air Force Times*, the service's weekly newspaper, and sat down to check the voice of "her people." "The press is a great source of information and gauge of what people are thinking," she reminded those who viewed journalists as the enemy. Savoring the momentary respite, she leafed through the pages, and an article caught her eye. Titled "He saved 80 lives: Why not the Medal of Honor?" it recounted the story of two Combat Controllers. The first was Senior Airman Dustin Temple, who delivered eighty Americans and Afghans from death the previous September while exposing himself repeatedly to direct enemy fire as he killed eighteen enemy combatants. The other was Staff Sergeant Robert Gutierrez, who saved the life of his wounded Green Beret team leader during an ambush, only to be shot in the chest himself. His lungs collapsed, yet he refused to get off the radio and stop calling airstrikes, some within thirty feet of his location, thereby saving his entire Special Forces team. Instead, a Green Beret medic jammed a syringe into his chest to reinflate his lungs...twice. The article asked a valid but pointed question: What does it take for an airman to get the Medal of Honor?

Looking up from the article, Secretary James was struck by the sentiment. *That's a damn good point*, she thought. As her next meeting swept into her office, she tore out the page, scribbled in the margin "What does it take?" and gave the paper to her aide, an Air Force colonel, instructing him to have her staff look into the matter. Thus began the three-year journey of the most thoroughly investigated and documented Medal of Honor in history.

When the secretary of the Air Force asks a question, an army of staffers activates immediately. With a bit more guidance from the SECAF, the task morphed into a review of all Air Force Silver Stars and Air Force Crosses awarded since 9/11 to see if any might be worthy of upgrade based on new information. After months of investigation across the entire force, her query was answered. Late that summer she received a call from Lieutenant General Brad Heithold, commander of Air Force Special Operations Command (AFSOC). He had one case, the only one in the Air Force that met her criteria for reinvestigation. "There may be some injustice here," he told the

Air Force's most senior civilian leader. "He was alive and we have technical proof that he was."

"Great," she told him. "Let's do this."

At Heithold's direction, AFSOC's 24th Special Operations Wing (responsible for all Special Tactics squadrons and Combat Control) established a dedicated team to investigate the Air Force's first potential Medal of Honor since Vietnam. The team consulted Air Force targeting (including the Air Force's chief targeter on duty during the battle) and intelligence analysts and submitted their video assessment to the National Geospatial-Intelligence Agency, the nation's foremost imagery experts, who validated the team's findings. They also pulled from Anaconda after-action reports, JSOC's official investigation into the events of 3–4 March 2002, witness statements, John's autopsy (consulting the doctor who conducted the original autopsy in addition to a forensic pathologist), and new interviews with surviving AFO members. It provided Lieutenant General Heithold an airtight case—John had earned the nation's highest award. Concurrently, JSOC held a special awards board and also endorsed an upgrade for John's medal, starting a separate but equally important chain of decisions within the special operations community that would end with US Special Operations Command's endorsement of his upgrade. Throughout the year that followed her tasking, "I kept asking about progress on John." When AFSOC's recommendation finally arrived on Secretary James's desk on 9 June 2016, she signed it and forwarded her recommendation to the secretary of defense the same day.

Still, for the next two years, AFSOC and the Air Force continued investigating and validating their findings while simultaneously fighting with certain leaders from SEAL Team Six, who could not abide the fact they'd left a man for dead. The contestation rose to senior levels of the Navy and represented the first time in the history of the medal that one service attempted to obstruct the submission of another, according to experts on the Medal of Honor.[30] For two men, the need to protect the unit's image overrode the facts of John's having survived after the SEALs retreated. Two officers drove the Navy's contestation, the (at the time) current commander of ST6, a man known by the initials JW, and Admiral Tim Szymanski, now head of all naval special warfare. Szymanski was the man both Pete Blaber and Jimmy Reese contend was the root source of the mission's botched planning and execution.

In the course of time and politics, Air Force Secretary James was replaced when the new administration swept into office in January 2017. Her pledge to see John's medal come to fruition was taken up by others, among them and notably Deputy Secretary of Defense Bob Work. By summer 2017, it was clear that Chapman's medal was headed for the White House. In one of his final emails as the DepSecDef, Bob Work wrote to new Secretary of the Air Force Heather Wilson and Chief of Staff General David Goldfein. Dated 12 July 2017 and titled "White Smoke," it stated:

Team Air Force,

I'm happy to inform you that the Secretary has approved the upgrade of TechSgt Chapman's AF Cross to the Medal of Honor, citing both material finding one and two. As previously agreed, material finding two will be discussed only in the classified portion of the award; the citation will make mention that Chappie fought on until he succumbed to his wounds.

---

30   According to the Pentagon's foremost Medal of Honor staffing expert, John Chapman earned not one but two Medals of Honor that morning. The first by charging and destroying the machine-gun bunker ahead of the SEALs and saving their lives and the second when he protected the CSAR helicopter. Each action rose to the level of the nation's highest honor, but the Air Force chose to pursue only a single medal, preferring (one presumes) to combine his actions into one irrefutable package.

After extensive analysis, the FBI concluded that a firefight continued on the top of the hill for an hour after the Team ex-filed down the mountain. Although they could not conclusively determine whether it was blue on red or a red on red engagement, the Secretary concluded it was blue on red based on the following factors:

1. The team (SEALs) never conclusively determined Chappie was dead.
2. TechSgt Chapman's body was found in a different location than indicated by the team.
3. He was wounded seven times and had expended almost all of his ammo, indicating an extended fight.
4. The last part of the engagement occurred in daylight, and close ranges. The Secretary noted the reports of an M4 and AK47 are distinctly different, and therefore does not find the explanation of an extended red-on-red fire-fight plausible.

We are working the package now. Thanks for your patience and perseverance. May TechSgt Chapman and his family rest more peacefully once they are told. Aim High!

Best, Bob

He retired two days later, a stalwart for John's full actions to the end.

On 24 October 2017, the Office of the Secretary of Defense informed the chief of staff and secretary of the Air Force that John's Medal of Honor had been forwarded to the president of the United States. Finally, on 26 March 2018, President Trump called Valerie with the news. It was her birthday.

CHAPTER

26

—

22–24 August 2018
THE WHITE HOUSE, PENTAGON HALL OF HEROES,
AND AIR FORCE MEMORIAL—THROUGH LORI'S EYES

SIXTEEN YEARS AGO, I KNEW. I KNEW THAT MY BROTHER JOHN'S ACTIONS were greater than we were told. I knew he didn't die right away. My intuition was finally validated when John was awarded the Medal of Honor at the White House. It's been a long and emotional roller coaster, these last sixteen years, but to witness my brother being awarded our nation's highest military honor left me speechless. To think it all began when then Secretary of the Air Force Deborah Lee James asked a simple question, "What *does* it take for an airman to receive the Medal of Honor?" The answer took more than two frustrating years of intense investigation, culminating in a week of extraordinary celebrations of John's life, the first of which was the 22 August 2018 White House ceremony.

I was struck by the elegance of the East Room. The white walls, golden curtains, and crystal chandeliers made it regal, the perfect room for a special honor. Soft light filling the room through the front windows of the White House lent a timeless air. Row after row of gold chairs curved around the stage, each one with a beautifully crafted program laid upon its white cushioned seat. The silence of the room was solemn, but not sad. The small stage was equally fitting, with another golden curtain serving as the backdrop for three flags: our American flag, the congressional flag, and that of our United States Air Force.

As our family gathered, the mood became more celebratory when the realization set in that we were finally going to see John honored appropriately. We talked and laughed, nervous excitement pouring from us. Tears filled my eyes as I stole a moment to take in the entire space. Dozens of media cameras stood silently on tripods at the back, poised to capture this historic event. White House staff and Air Force protocol were buzzing around, making sure everything was perfect. And as the guests started filing in, I could feel the energy in the room rise as each person found a seat and chatted excitedly with those around them. The room was filled with people John loved; people who loved him back. So many of his childhood friends came to watch him be honored, marveling that the little boy they grew up with, the young man they shared laughter, tears, and secrets with, was an American hero. His Special Tactics brothers were there en masse. Men in blue dress uniforms—the Controllers obvious in their parachute wings and rows of medals—and former CCT in crisp dark suits sat shoulder to shoulder, just as they had when they served with John at one time, a lifetime ago. They, more than many, understood the magnitude of what was about to happen.

I sat between my son, John, and husband, Kenny, in the front row to the left of center stage and kept checking my watch, excited for the ceremony to begin. I looked back at my brother, Kevin. He and his wife, Connie, were beaming with anticipation while my nephew and niece, Jake and Sierra, smiled with moistened eyes, eager to be witness to their uncle's honor.

As I turned toward the front, my mom, Brianna, Madison, and Val were escorted to their seats. They had just met with President Trump and their smiles spoke volumes. (Mom later told Kenny she was ecstatic that the president had signed the medal certificate and the citation in front of them, and after Val presented him with the photo of John and the Afghan girl, he looked at the photo, then at Mom, and said, "He looks like you." Those four little words meant the world to her.) The first notes of "Hail to the Chief" signaled for all to rise as the president's arrival was announced. My heartbeat quickened as I rose. It wasn't the president who spurred my heart, but the knowledge that his presence beckoned John's medal ever closer. When he stepped onstage and turned to the audience, I was in awe, being only feet away from him, the man who signed John's Medal of Honor package and who was about to present what I knew John earned. President Trump stood at the podium and spoke in soft, soothing tones. I dropped my gaze. I knew the story he would tell; I knew how John's citation would read; and I didn't want to hear it again . . . not then. My mind drifted off to happy times with John; fun times that I hold dear in my heart; times when the four of us got silly; times when I thought we would all grow old together and reminisce. It was a quick interlude, but one that filled me with happiness and peace. I felt John with us in that room. As the reading of the citation came to an end, I released those memories to the Heavens so I could be present in the moment of the presentation.

Watching Valerie accept John's Medal of Honor did not make me any prouder of him than I already was, but it was a moment that filled me with immense delight and satisfaction after sixteen years of wanting it to happen. It felt surreal. There we were . . . in the White House . . . witnessing my brother being honored by the president, his actions fully acknowledged. What I'd wanted and fought for was finally happening! At times, I couldn't focus on what was being said; it was somewhat a blur, but I watched with a jubilant heart. Val was gracious as she accepted John's medal and thanked the president, who motioned for Madison, Brianna, and my mom to join them on the stage. Every guest rose for a standing ovation, but they weren't standing for those onstage; they were standing for John, for what *he* earned...and they were standing because he couldn't. The applause, the standing ovation, and the gratitude were all for John and what he meant to each one of us.

I was joyous at having witnessed my brother being awarded our nation's highest military honor. As his sister, I wanted his actions acknowledged; I wanted people to know that he died how he lived...selflessly. John was a hero to countless unnamed people throughout his life, but it was his actions on 4 March 2002 that propelled him into American hero status. I've always been his proud big sister, but 22 August 2018 wasn't about pride in him, it was about being grateful that his selfless actions on that fateful day had finally and forever been recognized. He wouldn't have cared about recognition, but *I* do. I care because of my mom; I care because it's right; and I care because of truth.

Witnessing John being awarded the Medal of Honor gave me the greatest satisfaction, but it was the ceremonies at the Pentagon's Hall of Heroes and the Air Force Memorial that deeply touched me emotionally, because they were to *celebrate* John, not just acknowledge his actions. At John's induction ceremony into the Hall of Heroes on 23 August, I saw countless men who trained and worked with John, men who were there because they wanted to see him being honored the way they have honored him all these years. I was thrilled to finally be able to talk about John—about my brother—and when my mom and I spoke, I saw how our words affected them all. As my husband said afterward, many of them must have been passing around an onion, because there were quite a few tears filling the eyes of those tough men, and it touched my heart that they care so deeply about John.

The 24 August ceremony at the Air Force Memorial was even more incredible. As our motorcade made its way to the memorial, I saw countless people, many in uniform, hurrying to get there on time.

One officer stopped and saluted as we passed...an *officer*! It made me cry to see such respect and honor. The Air Force had expected seven hundred airmen and other military personnel to attend the ceremony, and I later found out there were over 1,200 in attendance. As I turned to look behind me, the sea of red berets, blue uniforms, and excited faces extended past my line of sight. And when John's name was unveiled on the memorial wall—the *sole* name listed for Afghanistan—my heart burst with pride and I couldn't hold back the tears. What I wouldn't give to have *him* there instead of his name, but I am so proud.

As if the previous honors weren't enough, after John's name was unveiled, the ceremony continued as he was posthumously promoted to the rank of Master Sergeant. He would be humbled. And as the ceremony concluded, the throng of John's military brothers and sisters made their way to the foot of the Air Force Memorial to perform not only the very first memorial push-ups at that location but also probably the largest contingent. The mass of brave men and women were, quite literally, side by side side as they rose and fell to the called cadence. Who would have thought the boy I grew up with would someday be honored in so many ways?

If John were alive today, he would quietly say, "I was just doing my job, what had to be done." Well, my dear brother, you went above and beyond "just doing your job." You deserve this honor. You *earned* it. It makes me sad that we won't be able to sit around when we're old and gray, beers in hand, talking about things you couldn't tell us, but I am honored to have grown up with you, one of the Chapman Four. Echoing Tammy's words at your funeral: You have always been my hero; now you're America's hero too. And though I'm in no hurry, I look forward to seeing you again so we can finally have that talk. My heart aches as I miss you every single day. I love you forever.

EPILOGUE

———

JOHN CHAPMAN'S QUEST FOR CHALLENGE LIT UPON ONE OF THE MOST selective, and certainly most unique, special operations forces in the world. And like most young men entering an SOF discipline, he was not fully aware of how unique his chosen field was until after he was a full-fledged member. When he cross-trained in 1989 there were fewer than three hundred Combat Controllers in the world. Over the course of America's longest-running war, CCT has grown to nearly six hundred operators, still only a fraction of sister-service SOFs such as the Green Berets, Rangers, and SEALs, who number in the thousands, yet the ratios are appropriate. Controllers continue to operate as lone warriors among the teams of men they join and protect in war.

For those aspiring to become a Combat Controller, the pipeline has evolved as well, just as twenty-first-century warfare itself has advanced. What was essentially a year plus of hell and trial by fire from day one for John Chapman and the others of his day has morphed into a two-and-a-half-year journey, including an entire year of advanced skills training after graduation from Combat Control School. The sophistication of instruction and the preparation of candidates for the challenges ahead of them are some of the improvements, yet attrition remains 75 percent due to the punishing nature of the training and exacting standards demanded.

———

Despite its name and combat focus, there is a second and arguably more valuable role Combat Control fulfills—that of humanitarian. With this secondary mission, CCT is the only deliberately dual-role SOF force. In 1978, three Panama-based CCT were given a no-notice task to hop a plane for Guyana in late November, only to find themselves amid the evil and senseless carnage of the Jonestown massacre. As the only men capable of single-handedly spearheading the body recovery and providing situational awareness to the highest levels of government back in the US, they spent their Thanksgiving among the hundreds of dead in order to return the 918 victims to their loved ones on American soil.

CCT has gone on to reprise this role as the world's first-of-the-first responders time and again. For Americans, this was most evident during Hurricane Katrina in 2005, when CCT from both Air National Guard Special Tactics squadrons led the rescue, staging, and recovery effort for thousands of homeless and desperate Louisianans, turning Interstate 10 into a major heliport and surging small Zodiac boats to isolated victims. CCT then repeated the feat during hurricanes Rita and Ike in 2005 and 2008, respectively.

In the Indian Ocean shortly after Christmas turned to Boxing Day in 2004, the third largest earthquake ever recorded unleashed a tsunami that devastated multiple countries. John Chapman's former unit, the 320th Special Tactics Squadron, responded to the worst-affected and most remote Indonesian province of Aceh to deliver aid and assist with rescues where the massive quake-generated wave crested a hundred feet and washed away entire villages.

The most significant humanitarian Combat Control operation, however, took place closer to home and earned a distinction no other US military enlisted person has ever received. Tony Travis, a career CCT master sergeant at Hurlburt's 23rd Special Tactics Squadron, was called into work on the evening of 12 January 2010 after a 7.0 earthquake rocked and devastated the impoverished island nation of Haiti. Two million people were affected in the capital of Port-au-Prince alone.

Packed and ready to go within hours, Tony led the first forces on the ground, arriving at 1536 the next day. Their mission: Secure, open, and control Toussaint Louverture International Airport. Eight Combat Controllers, equipped with only their portable radios and two ATVs, cleared and established control within twenty-eight minutes, meeting the self-imposed CCT standard and launching their first plane with two minutes to spare (Tony started his stopwatch the instant he stepped onto Haitian soil). From their ATVs and a scavenged folding table, the men ran the airport amid international chaos for the next thirteen days (when they were relieved by Air Force air traffic controllers). Armed with a personal letter from President René Garcia Préval granting Tony personal control of all Haitian airspace, CCT landed the more than 250 aircraft converging daily from fifty-plus nations, exceeding the expected capacity of the airfield by 1,400 percent. The expert austere airfield operators managed to shoehorn planes and helicopters onto every inch of the airport with zero incidents. Additionally, when more CCT arrived, they surveyed, established, and controlled thirty remote landing and drop zones for aerial delivery of 150,000 pounds of humanitarian supplies. A man with extensive combat experience, including an unfortunate knife kill ("I fucked up clearing a building and was forced to go to my knife when I couldn't get to my secondary pistol"), he was profoundly impacted by his experiences in Haiti. "You do a lot of things in combat but never see the results. In Haiti the positive feedback was immediate." For him, delivering global first responders, sending out the injured, and bringing order to the chaotic airfield was the essence of Combat Control. "It's what we do. Go in, set up, and control airspace. I don't believe any other organization in the world can do that without advance notice." For leading the effort to establish a beachhead amid the anarchy of a global response converging on a single ill-equipped and devastated runway in one of the most impoverished nations in the world, Tony Travis was recognized as one of *Time* magazine's 100 most influential people of the year.

Like Tony Travis, John Chapman was already one of the most elite warriors in the world, but chose to take another, ultimate step toward being *the* best, placing himself in the top 10 percent of all CCT. And as with the select handful of Green Berets and Rangers who try out for Delta Force, or their counterparts in the Navy, drawn from the ranks of the "vanilla" SEAL teams, who volunteer to join Team Six, John successfully ascended to the most elite unit in the Air Force—by some measures, the world—and joined "the 24."

Throughout its history, CCT has accomplished unique "firsts" in and out of combat, particularly using parachutes, their favored means of insertion. In 1955 and '56, America was building a presence in Antarctica and used Air Force aircraft to airdrop and land on the continent. During this expansion, the first site to be built up was situated on the precise South Pole. Staging from Christchurch, New Zealand, USAF C-124 Globemasters ferried equipment and supplies to the austere environment. When the uncontrolled cargo parachute drops began failing and missing their target drop zones (DZs), damaging significant portions of critical and specialized equipment, the call went out for someone with expertise in precision airdrops. In stepped Technical Sergeant Richard J. Patton, an airman with merely thirty-one parachute jumps. At exactly 0154 hours, Greenwich Mean Time, Sunday, 25 November 1956, at an altitude of 2,000 feet, he jumped from a C-124 christened the *State of New Jersey*. One minute later, he drifted to the ice to become the first person to make or even attempt a jump at the South Pole. Within hours, he established and operated a DZ and delivered near 100 percent accuracy. For his actions, Dick Patton earned a Distinguished Flying Cross and presidential citation.

Five years later, another Combat Controller, James A. "Jim" Howell, successfully became the first "human subject" to eject live while testing the upward rotational supersonic "B" ejection seat. From an F-106B slicing through the air at 560 knots and 22,060 feet over Holloman Air Force Base, New Mexico, he was fired into the atmosphere, giving new meaning to the term "test dummy." The intrepid Combat Controller stayed with the rocket-powered seat for forty-three seconds until he passed through 14,000 feet, then separated and opened his parachute without incident, successfully capping a nearly five-year test program.

Forty years later and a world away, a much younger Combat Controller set a different kind of record on 14 November 2001. It was a frozen night over Afghanistan, the temperature at altitude was in excess of minus 80 degrees Fahrenheit, and Staff Sergeant Mike Bain, a member of the 24, conducted the first-ever combat HALO tandem cargo bundle parachute drop. Also executing this historic first were Delta Force sergeants major Kris and Bill (the same two operators who would accompany Jay Hill on Anaconda and witness John Chapman's one-man stand), each with their own bundles. Mike was pushed off the ramp of an MC-130 Combat Talon at 18,500 feet, strapped on top of a three-foot-diameter, eight-foot-long, 528-pound tube crammed with his Delta team's rucksacks. Bill carried the team's food and water, and Kris more equipment. No surprise, their mission was to call airstrikes on a Taliban-controlled pass. It was a daring feat of courage. As audacious as it was, what Mike did after his parachute opened 6,500 feet above the enemy could be drawn from the pages of James Bond. Under canopy on his radio, Mike received his first strike aircraft, a flight of two F-15s, and managed to work up his first three targets by writing with a grease pen on the compass navigation board mounted on his chest. Also talking with his ISR platform, a Navy P-3, he was ready to destroy targets passed to him from the P-3 before he even hit the ground. Mike had the imagination, foresight, and expertise to plan for the possibility, an unprecedented innovation and application of airpower. To many fellow "black" operators, it was the most impressive combat parachute jump in history. To a layman it simply sounds unbelievable.

The men landed in an isolated high-elevation mountain valley, with Mike hitting the intended impact point dead center. Mike and his Delta team then spent the next twenty-four hours climbing across two mountain summits with their hundred-pound rucks. The enemy, knowing the mountainous terrain was inaccessible, assumed their passage was safe from American eyes and bombs. They were wrong. The team, with Mike on the radio (naturally), destroyed ammunition and fuel trucks on the first day of operations. That night, Mike had an AC-130 crater the road to slow traffic so the team could ensure they struck only Taliban forces. For three days, the Delta team and Mike denied all Taliban reinforcements between Kandahar and Kabul along their key supply route.

Sixty-six years into its history, CCT is just beginning to reach full potential. It's come a long way from Jim Stanford standing on the wing of a puddle jumper in the middle of enemy territory, pumping his own gas, to John Chapman fighting to save the lives of his five remaining SEAL teammates and another eighteen men he'd never met. Yet they share a common brotherhood: an Air Force no one knew or even suspected existed.

John's life and this book both end on the battlefields of Afghanistan in 2002. In the seventeen years since those events, the three to six hundred Combat Controllers that have comprised the force have earned hundreds of Bronze Stars with Valor, thirty-five of the Air

Force's seventy-five Silver Stars, six of its nine Air Force Crosses, and its only Medal of Honor. From a uniformed force of approximately 500,000, Combat Control comprises 0.1 percent of the Air Force yet accounts for nearly half of its Silver Stars and two-thirds of its highest award, the Air Force Cross. Those heroics are for chronicling in another volume of Combat Control's history. What is significant at the conclusion of this book is the impact this deadly shadow force has had on the Air Force and the nation. The future promises more of the same.

In discussing that future, Brigadier General Mike Martin, the former commander of the 24th Special Operations Wing, the most decorated wing in the modern Air Force,[31] explained why it's critical for CCT to continue to push into new frontiers:

> No one is tasked or organized to exploit and manage space into the battlefield. We are. You'd expect SEALs to own the maritime domain, but they don't. Same with [Army] Special Forces. I don't think anyone exploits those multiple domains more so than CCT.
>
> The contested nature of future environments will likely change what we do. Combat Control's abilities in denied and degraded environments allow us maneuverability unavailable to others. This in turn allows us to inform and shape the air and even space kinetic strike missions that will be required. Going forward, if I can put a [Special Tactics team] in suborbital low earth orbit, I can infiltrate it within forty-five minutes globally. Using Operation Anaconda as an example, the forces supporting CCT in conducting those strikes, the kinetics, hypersonics

---

31   For the first time in the history of air forces—any air force—the most decorated organization of a nation is not a flying unit. There are no pilots in the 24 SOW.

and the like, must be able to keep up with our "First There" forces. B-52s, a weapon Combat Control used extensively, can't keep up with that kind of rapidity.

Regardless of future advances, today's Combat Controllers remain the deadliest individuals to walk a battlefield in the history of warfare, with the power and expertise to orchestrate the destruction of key strategic targets or hundreds of enemy at a time on any battleground onto which they step, as exemplified by Joe O'Keefe's stunning 688,000 pounds of bomb tonnage at Tora Bora. At the same time and using their unique expertise—blending the world's mightiest air force with unequalled battlefield acumen and three-dimensional awareness—they are the first to deliver hope and salvation to suffering masses anywhere in the world, at a moment's notice.

———

Regarding the fight for Takur Ghar, it is proportionally the most valorous battle in the history of the United States military. Of the twenty-five men on the mountain at sunrise, thirteen would receive Silver Stars, one a Navy Cross, and two the Air Force Cross. And finally, two ultimately received Medals of Honor. But a battle sometimes referred to as Roberts Ridge (for the SEAL who inadvertently fell from a helicopter) more accurately centered on John Chapman, the man abandoned for dead and who became the fulcrum by which the two opposing forces levered the larger fight.

During his final hour, John was the deadliest man on the mountain summit battlefield on which he found himself—the lone Combat Controller—not because of airpower but by virtue of his spirit in the tradition of the American fighting man: a solitary warrior, one of his nation's finest, fighting as CCT have always done even when integrated into a team, as a man with the burden of the lives of many others in his hands. After saving the lives of his five SEAL team-mates at the cost of two mortal wounds, he held two dozen enemy fighters at bay for more than an hour, until in his final moments, in excruciating pain, his body ravaged by sixteen gunshot and shrapnel wounds and battered from hand-to-hand combat, he chose self-sacrifice over self-preservation and with his last breath delivered eighteen comrades he'd never met into salvation.

ACKNOWLEDGMENTS

——

Dan Schilling

I did not want to write this book. Having retired from the military in September 2016, I was interested in spending time with my wife, writing fiction, and skiing and climbing mountains, roughly in that order. So when my friend and fellow CCT Kyle Stanbro approached me a week into retirement about helping Lori write John's story I turned him down, agreeing only to help her shape a proposal and connect her with my agent. However, thirty years of military service taught me that missions often come our way whether we feel prepared for them or not. Over the next two weeks I realized I was in the unique position not only to write John's story but also to share the remarkable stories of his Combat Control brothers, of whom I am fortunate to count myself among their ranks. So I called Lori back and told her I'd commit myself fully to the project, which turned out to be two full years of effort. The result is this book.

To Lori: Thank you for trusting me with John's legacy and working together over those two years. It was a momentous occasion to witness John's Medal of Honor ceremony in the White House, and as I looked across his many friends and family in attendance, I was happiest for you. I extend my thanks to John's entire family for their faith in me to help Lori bring John's life to the public. To Valerie Novak Chapman Nessel, who survived the loss not only of John but also her next husband, and whom I think of as a dear friend, thank you for your trust and openness. You inspire so many with your indomitable spirit.

I'd like to thank the following CCT whom I interviewed while writing this book. I apologize that so many amazing stories of your prowess and courage failed to make it onto the pages; there simply was not enough room in this particular volume. Some are my mentors, others fellow veterans of combat operations, and a few I feel privileged to have instructed at the Combat Control School, but all are brothers. Any mistakes that may appear in these pages are my fault alone. In no particular order: Jay Hill, Andy Martin, Gabe Brown, Mike Stockdale, Mike Lamonica, Jeff George, Joe O'Keefe, Calvin Markham, Ben Miller, Dink Dalton, David Netterville, Mike Lampe, Wayne Norrad (who, along with his lovely wife, Tracy, has always provided a home away from home, exceptional wine, and cigars at Hurlburt), Jim Hotaling, Bob Bieber, Jack Teague, Gene Adcock, Bob Azeltine, Chris Baradat, Bart Decker, Ron Mann, Alan Yoshida, Don Stevens, Bruce Dixon, Ed Priest, Dave Gendron, Greg Pittman, Mike Snyder, Joe Maynor, Bruce Barry, Pat Elko, John Wylie, Phil Freeman, Scott Light, Kyle Stanbro, John Koren, Tony Travis, Mike Bain. The following STOs were also interviewed and/or contributed: John Carney, Ken Rodriguez, Mike Martin, Spence Cocanour, Mike Fazio. Thanks to the STOs and CCT who wished to remain anonymous and anyone I've failed to list. Thanks also to PJ Keary Miller and Mike Rizzuto (who single-handedly runs the 724th STG).

There were many who were involved in Operation Anaconda and/or the investigation of John's actions who assisted me. Pete Blaber, friend, former Delta commander, and leader of AFO in Anaconda, thanks for your insight and honest input. The same goes for Delta officers Jimmy Reese and Tom DiTomasso (fellow veteran of Operation Gothic Serpent); Delta operator "Ironhead," one of the great operators I've known; AC-130 pilot D. J. Turner; and sensor operator Chris

Walker. Greg Daly, friend and former commander of the Australian Special Air Service Regiment, thanks for the Aussie perspective.

To STO Mike Wendelken, who dedicated nearly two years to the investigation of John's actions and who knows more about that time than anyone else, special thanks for your commitment to the truth and constant willingness to be interrupted with last-minute questions as I researched the events for myself. Also thanks to STO Kyle Whittier and public affairs officers Katrina Cheesman and Jackie Pienkowski at the 24th Special Operations Wing, and AFSOC public affairs officer Pete Hughes for critical assistance in gaining official USAF approval to conduct research. To Tim Brown at the historian's office and Dr. Forrest Marion at the Air Force Historical Research Agency. Dan Chykirda at DoD Prepublication and Security Review marshaled the manuscript through the review process needed for a book of this nature. Thanks to former JAG Mike Smidt for his expertise on esoteric classification matters.

At Grand Central: Ben Sevier, publisher of Grand Central, who personally acquired and then edited our book, thanks for immediately recognizing the value of this story and your no-nonsense approach in shaping it. I'm very grateful for your commitment despite many demands on your time. Jonathan Valuckas and Elizabeth Kulhanek in Ben's office for coordinating efforts. Brian McLendon, Joseph Benincase, Karen Torres, and Amanda Pritzker for their expertise in marketing and sales, the backbone of a book's success. Matthew Ballast, Jimmy Franco, Brittany Lowe, and Alli Rosenthal in publicity for promoting the book across America. Our senior production editor, Mari Okuda, copy editor, Rick Ball, and proofreaders Kristin Roth Nappier and Kristin Vorce Duran corrected much and smoothed all. Thanks to Elece Green and Ghenet Harvey for the audio version production, and to Jeffrey L. Ward for creating the maps.

Exceptional author Jim DeFelice, on whom I originally attempted to foist this project and who told me unequivocally, "No. You need to write this," thanks for your mentorship, feedback, and steadfast belief (also cigars). To the honorable Debbie James, former secretary of the Air Force, thank you for starting John's medal on its journey and facing down all opposition.

My agents Larry Weissman and Sascha Alper, thanks for all your career management, encouragement, and expertise, especially Larry's demand that I stop all else and write this book. You are both more friends than agents.

Finally, my wife, Julie, who served as my first editor, believes in my writing, and always said yes when I'd announce, "Well, they're asking me to do this one more thing..." You are the center of my existence and words cannot express my love and admiration.

Lori Chapman Longfritz

Above all, I want to thank my husband, Kenny Longfritz, for your patience, support, and encouragement. Without you, I may not have had the confidence to finally take the first step after years of hesitation. You have been my untiring sounding board and confidant. When I had doubts, you were there to push me onward, and when we learned more of the truth, you shared my pain, wiped my tears, and soothed my anger. You knew John as his First Sergeant and know him better now as family. He brought us together, and now, *because of you*, I can share John's heroism and legacy with the world. I love you!

Thanks to my son, John Chapman Longfritz, for understanding in your adolescent brain that I needed to spend time behind closed doors. My hope is that this book will help you understand more about your uncle and why it is such an honor for you to be his namesake. I love you to infinity and beyond! Rachel McQueeney Smith, my smart daughter, thank you for your support and for reminding me that it's okay to say "No" to my littles when they wanted to see me. It's hard to deny them anything! I love you all to the moon and back!

Thank you, Ben Goettler and Kyle Stanbro, for stepping forward to help as only CCT can. Though none of us knew what the hell we were doing, you were willing to muddle through figuring out how to write and publish a book with me. We were essentially the blind leading the blind, until Kyle's lunch with Dan "to catch up" turned into something bigger than any of us could have foreseen! Were it not for you two, *Alone at Dawn* would never have been written.

What can I say, Dan Schilling?! When you offered to help, I immediately trusted the pairing because in addition to being a published author, you were Combat Control. My original book idea morphed into a masterpiece because of your vision to include Combat Control; you understand what it takes to become the most lethal human weapon in our military arsenal, and you therefore brought a more dynamic military narrative to the book. You tirelessly gathered information I didn't even know existed and your guidance and encouragement were selfless: Though you penned our military narrative, you also encouraged my newfound joy of editing. Thank you for putting your retired life with Julie on hold to commit two years and counting to this book! I am happy to call you my friend and wish you nothing but continued success in your future writing projects! Julie Schilling, thank you for graciously postponing your life plans with Dan. Your support and interest in John's story means so very much. Dan owes you a really long vacation!

Mike Wendelken: You are an amazing man and humble hero whose brain works on a level way above my comprehension. For two years you painstakingly stitched together two videos of the battle on Takur Ghar. The end result uncovered the facts of the battle, and revealed John's heroism to his last breath. Without you, your team, and your collective determination, the absolute truth may never have become known. I thank you from the bottom of my heart, along with Wolfe Davidson, Mike Martin, Bruce Dixon, and so many others who helped prove John's actions.

Many thanks to our literary agents, Larry Weissman and Sascha

ACKNOWLEDGMENTS

Alper of Larry Weissman Literary LLC. Your dedication in helping us create a powerful and dynamic book proposal, coupled with your invaluable creative ideas and absolute enthusiasm for John's story, resulted in our book being picked up by the best publisher we could hope to have. Thank you for believing in us and for all you've done in the representation and promotion of us and our book.

Heartfelt thanks to Ben Sevier, publisher at Grand Central Publishing, for your expertise and belief in Dan and me! You immediately understood the importance of telling this story, took on our project, and offered sage insight into the direction and composition of *Alone at Dawn*. That guidance helped us focus more narrowly, resulting in the page-turning truth of what really happened on Takur Ghar, while offering a fine-tuned glimpse into Combat Control.

I have so much appreciation for Grand Central Publishing and those who were part of this journey. Elizabeth Kulhanek, as Ben's assistant, you were always available to help me. Senior director of publicity, Jimmy Franco, you calmed my nerves and helped me focus on how to represent myself and our book. Matthew Ballast, publicity director, and publicity assistants Brittany Lowe and Alli Rosenthal were instrumental in coordinating how our book was promoted. Dear editors and proofreaders, especially Rick Ball and Mari Okuda, thank you for your expertise and your research to confirm every detail. I know there are many others I've not met who have helped *Alone at Dawn* be the best book possible, including Flag, Kristen Lemire, Tom Louie, Sean Ford, Dan Lynch, and Laura Eisenhard, and I thank you all!

Kevin Chapman and Connie Russo, Tammy and David Klein: Your encouragement was priceless to me. Tess Chapman (my stepmom), through your recollections and Dad's letter to the 24 STS after John died, I was able to shed light on some very important stories. Thank you for being willing to relive those memories! I wish Dad were here to read the truth, but he already knows now, doesn't he? Valerie

Nessel, you were open to sharing your precious memories of your time with John—even the difficult ones—and I am grateful for that. And Madison, though you were so very young when your dad gave his life, what you *did* remember was valuable! I love you all!

There are many members of the Special Tactics family who were gracious enough to spend time sharing memories and laughs about Chappy. Special thanks to: Tony Baldwin, Randy Blythe, Kurt Buller, Ron and Ann Childress, Steve Coronato, Bruce Dixon, Rob Donlan, Pat Elko, Bob Holmes, Mike Lamonica, Kenny Longfritz, Wayne Norrad, Ken Rodriguez, Billy Sasser, Jeremy Shoop, Summa Stelly, Mike West, and Travis Woodworth. Every word, every memory helps, whether in this book, in another, or in my heart. I am happy to share John with you and grateful that you are willing to share your memories with me. To you and every member of our military, past, present, and future, thank you for your service!

John's hometown friends: You gave me your precious time and memories, and I hung on your every word. You are testament that John chose his friends well: Tom and Diane Allen, Brian Topor and David Wrabel (John's "brothers from other mothers"), Stanley Topor (John's second dad), Mike Toce, Michael DuPont, Dan Walsh, Bill Brooks, Dan Tracey, Kelly Cray Savery, Kathy Toce, Lynn Noyes Klein (high school friend John adored), Suzy Lindberg Brinegar, Mark Nolan, and Suzanne Giaccone Roberts and Karen Starr Giannelli (special friends who opened their homes to me when I visited Windsor Locks). Thank you all for your time and memories!

Lastly, I personally want to dedicate this book to my mom, Terry Chapman. You supported my efforts and were willing to open the floodgates of tears and laughter to help me remember stories about John. Emotions be damned, Mom, you came through for me, endured countless calls asking you to relive memories big and small, and never swayed from helping me get it right. This is for *you* . . . because you deserve to finally know the truth. I love you lots!

SELECTED BIBLIOGRAPHY

BOOKS

Beckwith, Charlie A., and Donald Knox. *Delta Force: The Army's Elite Counterterrorist Unit*. New York: Avon Books, 2000.

Berntsen, Gary, and Ralph Pezzullo. *Jawbreaker: The Attack on Bin Laden and Al-Qaeda; A Personal Account by the CIA's Key Field Commander*. Reprint ed. New York: Three Rivers Press, 2006.

Blaber, Pete. *The Mission, the Men, and Me: Lessons from a Former Delta Force Commander*. Reprint ed. New York: Dutton Caliber, 2010.

Carney, John T., Jr., and Benjamin F. Schemmer. *No Room for Error: The Covert Operations of America's Special Tactics Units from Iran to Afghanistan*. New York: Ballantine, 2002.

Churchill, Jan. *Classified Secret: Controlling Airstrikes in the Clandestine War in Laos*. Manhattan, KS: Sunflower University Press, 2000.

Coll, Steve. *Ghost Wars: The Secret History of the CIA, Afghanistan, and bin Laden, from the Soviet Invasion to September 10, 2001*. New York: Penguin, 2004.

Fury, Dalton. *Kill Bin Laden: A Delta Force Commander's Account of the Hunt for the World's Most Wanted Man*. New York: St. Martin's Griffin, 2009.

Haney, Eric L. *Inside Delta Force: The Story of America's Elite Counterterrorist Unit*. New York: Dell, 2003.

MacPherson, Malcolm. *Roberts Ridge: A Story of Courage and Sacrifice on Takur Ghar Mountain, Afghanistan*. New York: Bantam Dell, 2006.

Marion, Forrest L. *Brothers in Berets: The Evolution of Air Force Special Tactics, 1953–2003*. Maxwell Air Force Base, AL: Air University Press, Curtis E. LeMay Center for Doctrine Development and Education, 2018.

Naylor, Sean. *Not a Good Day to Die: The Untold Story of Operation Anaconda*. New York: Berkley Caliber, 2005.

Naylor, Sean. *Relentless Strike: The Secret History of Joint Special Operations Command*. New York: St. Martin's, 2015.

Rasimus, Ed. *When Thunder Rolled: An F-105 Pilot over North Vietnam*. Washington, DC: Smithsonian Books, 2003.

Robbins, Christopher. *The Ravens: The Men Who Flew in America's Secret War in Laos*. New York: Pocket Books, 1989.

Stanton, Doug. *Horse Soldiers: The Extraordinary Story of a Band of U.S. Soldiers Who Rode to Victory in Afghanistan*. New York: Scribner, 2009.

SELECTED BIBLIOGRAPHY

GOVERNMENT DOCUMENTS

———

"Executive Summary of the Battle of Takur Ghar." Released through the Department of Defense, 24 May 2002.

Fleri, Major Edgar, Colonel Ernest Howard, Jeffrey Hukill, and Thomas R. Searle. *Operation Anaconda Case Study*. Maxwell Air Force Base, AL: College of Aerospace Doctrine, Research and Education, 2003.

Milani, Colonel Andrew N. "Pitfalls of Technology: A Case Study of the Battle on Takur Ghar Mountain, Afghanistan." Carlisle Barracks, PA: US Army War College, 2003.

INTERNET SITES

———

Cole, Matthew. "The Crimes of SEAL Team 6." *The Intercept*, 10 January 2017. theintercept.com/2017/01/10/the-crimes-of-seal-team-6/.

Cole, Matthew. "With Medal of Honor, SEAL Team 6 Rewards a Culture of War Crimes." *The Intercept*, 22 May 2018. theintercept.com/2018/05/22/medal-of-honor-navy -seal-team-6-britt-slabinski/.

Naylor, Sean D. "The Navy SEALs Allegedly Left Behind a Man in Afghanistan. Did They Also Try to Block His Medal of Honor?" *Newsweek*, 7 May 2018. http://www.newsweek.com/2018/05/18/navy-seals-seal-team-6-left -behind-die-operation-anaconda-slabinski-chapman-912343.html.

Naylor, Sean D., and Christopher Drew. "SEAL Team 6 and a Man Left for Dead: A Grainy Picture of Valor." *New York Times*, 27 August 2016. https://www.nytimes.com /2016/08/28/world/asia/seal-team-6-afghanistan-man-left-for-dead.html.

"Operation Anaconda or Operation Giant Mongoose?" Bangladesh.com Discussion Forum. *Bangladesh.com Bangladesh Channel*, 27 August 2002. www.bangladesh.com /forums/religion/10948-operation-anaconda-operation-giant-mongoose.html.

MAGAZINES AND JOURNALS

———

Ehrlich, Richard S. "Afghanistan: An American Graveyard?" *Laissez Faire City Times*, 29 October 2001.

ABOUT THE AUTHORS

———

A thirty-year special operations and Combat Control veteran, DAN SCHILLING has had numerous combat and clandestine deployments around the world, including the operation popularly known as Black Hawk Down, where he is credited with saving the lives of a Ranger and SEAL under fire. He later founded and then served as the first commander of two special operations squadrons. An adrenaline enthusiast, he holds the Guinness World Record for most BASE jumps in twenty-four hours and is a mountain speed wing flyer and ski instructor at Wasatch Adaptive Sports. He and his wife live in the alpine town of Alta, Utah. Visit him at DanSchillingBooks.com.

* * *

LORI CHAPMAN LONGFRITZ is the second of four children born to Gene and Terry Chapman and shares the "middle child" slot with John. She was a longtime advocate for his Medal of Honor and is proud to share the story of her brother, who stood out from the ordinary long before he ever put on a uniform. Lori lives with her husband and their son, John, in the "Forever West" town of Cheyenne, Wyoming.